BO

Maury Allen

BO

Pitching and Wooing

with the uncensored cooperation of
Bo Belinsky

The Dial Press   *New York 1973*

Library of Congress Cataloging in Publication Data

Allen, Maury, 1932–
  Bo: pitching and wooing.

    1. Belinsky, Bo, 1936–   I. Title.
GV865.B34A79   796.357'092'4 [B]   73-3047

Manufactured in the United States of America

First printing, 1973

For Jennifer, Teddy and Stevie

With lotions of love

Contents

Photographs

BO

He's out in Malibu Beach now. That ain't Coney Island, you know.

—*MRS. ANNA BELINSKY*

Little Boy Bo

His name is Robert Belinsky. He is a retired baseball player, a former left-handed pitcher who won twenty-eight games in his major league career and never earned more than eighteen thousand dollars in any one season. He did it all, really—the penthouse apartment, the Hollywood scene, the millionaire hangers-on, the stars and the starlets—on the strength of one game, a no-hit, no-run game on May 5, 1962, the first in history by a big league California player, before Sandy Koufax did it, before Juan Marichal, before Gaylord Perry, before Bill Singer, before any of them. Hollywood made him an instant hero.

Today his hair is long, almost shoulder length, and falls down his neck in waves. At six-two and 185, his body is lean and his stomach is flat. There is an angry, ugly scar over the left cheek and just under the eye, exactly where the Hollywood set would want it. There is some gray showing at the edges of his hair and his face is lined with the memories of a thousand battles. His eyes are wide and brown and sensitive.

He thinks life is a kick. He never took any of it seriously. He knows why he never became a great pitcher.

"The night before my no-hitter," he says, "I banged into this secretary out on the Strip. She was tall and thin and black haired. We had a couple of drinks and I wound up making it with her at her pad. She turned out to be not too b.a.d. I got home at four A.M. That night I pitched my no-hitter. After the game I went back to look for her. I couldn't find her. I never did again. She was my good luck charm. When I lost her I lost all my pitching luck."

His mother, Mrs. Anna Belinsky, never could quite understand the appeal her boy Bo seemed to have for a thousand women across a dozen states and a half dozen countries.

"When he was a boy," she says, "he wouldn't even dress up to take out a girl. I never knew he was interested in girls. He never talked about it. He never brought any of them home."

Anna Belinsky is a cherubic fifty-seven-year-old woman from the Bronx. She comes from Russian Jewish background. She finished high school in 1933 and went to work for Gotham Gold Stripe Hosiery Company as an inspector on ladies stockings. Early that year she went to a dance at St. Nicholas Arena in Manhattan with some girl friends. Edward Belinsky, a tall, lean, fairly handsome man from Trenton, New Jersey, was on leave from his Coast Guard duties at the port of New York. They were introduced by friends.

"The way I heard it," says Bo Belinsky, "was that he picked her up in the subway."

"Ed was a very nice fellow, quiet, a gentleman in every way," says Anna Belinsky. "He asked to take me home on the subway and we started dating."

The Polish Catholic and the Russian Jew announced to their families later that year that they had decided to be married. It was not happy news.

"We weren't religious people," Anna Belinsky says, "but my mother didn't like it. 'What's the matter, there aren't any Jewish boys around?' She didn't like the idea of me marrying out of my religion. Even more than that she didn't like the idea of me being married at all. I was only eighteen years old. But we went ahead with it anyway. Everybody accepted Ed after that. He's a very likable fellow. We never bothered with religion. I never liked the idea that Bo would tell people he was Catholic when he got into baseball. Catholic? What kind of Catholic? We had him circumcised, didn't we?"

Ed and Anna Belinsky moved in with her parents at 1000 Simpson Street in the Bronx. It was the depth of the depression and Ed left the Coast Guard to try for a job that would pay more money. They paid part of the rent in the Simpson Street apartment and needed greater income. Ed worked as a day laborer, came home at night to sleep and went out early the next morning to start all over again. On December 7, 1936, at 4:05 in the afternoon at Beth Israel Hospital on Delancey Street on the Lower East Side of Manhattan, a Jewish ghetto, Robert Belinsky was born to Edward and Anna Belinsky. He was a natural-born hustler: he weighed seven-eleven at birth. Seven years later a girl, named Lorraine, was born to the Belinskys.

Edward Belinsky, at sixty, is white-haired and thin. He has his own small television repair business. He and Anna live at 244 Hewitt Street in Trenton, a small attached home on a dingy street in an ugly town. "No one," says Bo Belinsky, "should have to come from Trenton." Ed and Anna sit in the small living room of their home. They share it with fourteen cats, one fox terrier named Midgie, and a parrot from Venezuela, a gift from Bo. There is a huge picture of Bo on the wall behind the sofa. It was painted and given to him when he pitched in nearby Philadelphia and was honored with a day. On the opposite wall there is a cover of a *Sports Illustrated* magazine dated March 1, 1965. It shows Bo in his Philadelphia uniform with pitcher Jim Bunning. It advertises a new era in Philadelphia pitching history.

"Bo doesn't like the painting," Anna says. "He thinks the eyes are slightly crossed."

It is as if Bo was pitching in the game but looking into the stands.

"He was an adorable baby," Mrs. Belinsky says, "round-faced and full of fun. He was always laughing and was always making us laugh."

"You know, I'm hard of hearing," she says. "I finally got around to wearing a hearing aid that works. Wait, I'll turn up the volume a little so I can hear better. Bo used to kid me about it when he was little. He would walk around the house with a Coke bottle against his ear, and he would be going, 'Eh, eh, can you hear me, eh?' He was some comedian.

"Well, you want to know about Bo as a little boy. When he was small we called him Robert or Bobby. My mother called him *bubbaleh*, you know, that's Jewish for little boy or little Bobby or something like that. I'll tell you the truth, I don't even know where the Bo came from. We called him Bobby. I think his boyfriends at school called him Bo. I think it had something to do with some fighter, Bobo Olson, who was always getting knocked down, just like Bo in school."

Anna Belinsky still has the ring of the Bronx in her voice and pours out words in a steady stream. Her husband sits quietly at her side and listens.

"We lived with my mother at that Simpson Street apartment until after Bo was born. Then we had to move, it was just too crowded. We moved to 1683 Amsterdam Avenue in the Bronx and my mother immediately moved nearby. In those days you could do that. We paid forty-five dollars a month for our place. My mother helped me out with Bo and I helped her out. Bo was a happy child. We always had fun with him. One day I took him down to this park on Southern Boulevard, one of those parks where the old Jewish men and women sat around all day. If it was a nice day they would sun themselves, if not they would sit there all bundled up playing checkers.

"All of a sudden he gets out of his stroller and he starts following this old man who was walking through the park. The man was very old with a beard and bent over. He had his hands behind his back and he was walking with his head down, you know very deep in thought. All of a sudden Bo is following right behind him with his hands behind his back, his head down, making believe he was thinking deeply just like the old man. I'll tell you he was a funny devil. He had all the people in that park laughing. Every day after that when we would go for a walk there they would ask Bo to take a walk like an old man. He loved the fussing by everybody. Still does."

In 1940, when Bo was a little more than three years old, Ed and Anna Belinsky decided to move back to Trenton, Ed's hometown.

"The war was coming on, we could see that, and with Ed having been in the Coast Guard we figured he would be called back again, he was only thirty-six, thirty-seven years old then and healthy, so he decided to go into war work. First he worked for Roebling's and then he went over to General Motors and made parts for airplanes during the war. When Bo was four years old we put him in kindergarten at the Franklin School. We lived on Cummings Avenue then, just around the corner from where we live now. We've been in this place, oh, twenty-five years or so. I don't think Bo remembers much about the Cummings Avenue place. He liked it here. We always had enough room. It is a good house."

Ed Belinsky had played some baseball in the Coast Guard, and Bo began showing signs of interest in the game when he was about seven or eight.

"Oh, that caused me trouble," Anna Belinsky said. "Just after Lorraine was born he started staying late in the playgrounds. He never would come home for supper. I didn't want to let him stay out until it got dark. He didn't care about eating. He would just play ball all day and night. One time I had to leave Lorraine with neighbors and go after him. She must have been two or three months old only. I finally found Bo in the park, all by himself, swinging at some stones with a wooden stick. I'll tell you I grabbed him by the ears and marched him all the way home like that and he got a good wacking. But I couldn't stay mad at him very long. I'd be yelling and he'd say something funny and all of a sudden I'd be laughing. He was really a quippy kid."

Bo wasn't much of a student at the Franklin School in Trenton. He was too busy having fun.

"I've saved all his report cards," Mrs. Belinsky says, "and I could show them to you. He was always an ornery kid in school, would do anything for a laugh. I'd be called up to school all the time and the teachers would tell me he could do better but he didn't seem to want to. One time the teacher was really mad at him. A boy was making a speech in school on the stage of the auditorium. Bo was sitting halfway back and hit the boy right square in the head with a spitball, not once but twice. No other kid in school had an aim like that. I knew he was going to be a pitcher then. He's the only one that's left-handed in the family. Ed and Lorraine and me are all right-handed. My mother's left-handed, that's where he probably got it from."

There were a half dozen trophies in the living room and Mrs. Belinsky reached for one.

"See this thing, he got it for playing basketball about the time he was ten or eleven. He was real good, skinny but strong, just like his father. He played with neighborhood teams and he always won everything. He won a marbles tournament one time in school and brought home the decal for me to sew on his pea jacket. And then another time he brought home some trophy he got for being the best in his school with the yo-yo. He was always getting his name in the papers for some sport or other. One time he joined the Boy Scouts and won some badges. I had to go down to Gimbel's to buy him a uniform. Then he would walk down the street with it on and he didn't want me to walk near him. He wanted to be a big shot. He wanted to be on his own, even then.

"Boys you can't hold back. Girls are different. They'll stay close to you. That's why he never played ball for his high school team. It was too regimented. He didn't like practices and all that. He played in the sandlots. He could come and go as he pleased. I don't think he was that interested in ball to tell you the truth. I think what he really wanted then was a car. That was his whole life. He comes home one day and says, 'Ma, you gotta buy me a car.' I tell him I don't have to buy him no car. I told him he should have been born rich. Let me tell you something about Bo. He had high ideas and low pocketbooks."

Belinsky wanted that car badly. He started hustling for it in the local pool halls of Trenton.

"We'd drive him down there and pick him up five, six hours later. He didn't care about eating, he just liked to shoot pool. Sometimes I'd give him a dollar and he'd come back later and give me the dollar back. Can you imagine playing pool for five, six hours on the same dollar?"

Belinsky graduated from Trenton High School and spent most of the summer in Joe Russo's pool hall on West Front Street. He played some sandlot baseball, slept late at home and hung out downtown.

"Rex Bowen was a scout for the Pittsburgh club and he had seen Bo play in some of the sandlot games. He came around the house one day and he told Bo he wanted to sign him for the Pirates farm club in Brunswick, Georgia. They didn't give him any money. Nothing. Just a bus ticket. They don't ever tell you things like that. They just tell you about all the big bonus money they give out and how well they treat the boys. Let me tell you, it's a lie. They sent him to class D in 1956 without a nickel in his pocket. He starved all his way down on that bus. No money to buy a sandwich with. Not even a new pair of baseball shoes. I don't know why he signed. He just didn't have anything else to do and he wanted that car.

"He came back after that season and went to work in a pottery factory. He used to come home for lunch, and one day he walked in the door and he was really dirty with that dust and everything. He shook it all off in the house and then he says, 'I'm not going to work in any factory anymore. I'm through with this. I'm going to make money, I don't know how but I will. I'm going to make it big in baseball, I'm going to make it real big. . . .' "

When Bo was with the Los Angeles Angels in 1962, Ed and Anna Belinsky were listening to the radio on a Baltimore station. Belinsky was pitching against the Orioles. It was May 5.

"About the sixth inning I knew he had a no-hitter going," said Ed Belinsky. "I just couldn't stand listening to it. I was too nervous. I walked out of the house, went up to Pep's Steak House and had a couple of cups of coffee. Then I came back and the game was in the eighth or ninth inning. I listened to the last couple of outs. When he got it I just let out a large whoop. An hour or so later he called us from California. He must have had some phone bill. We really talked a long time."

"The baseball thing started off so nice," said Mrs. Belinsky. "He could have really been something, but they didn't want him to be. They would dwell on the fact that he liked to go out with girls. That's all we would read in the papers, nothing about his pitching, just that he was going out with Hollywood girls, Mamie Van Doren and all of them. What was so wrong? He was a single boy then. He wasn't hurting anybody. But baseball likes to beat down the kids. If he was a big bonus player they would have given him more chances, but you know they just didn't want to see him make it.

"I'll tell you one thing, they were jealous of him, all of them, all the attention he got, and the Hollywood stars and everything, they were jealous. We're simple people and one time Mamie pulls up here in front of our house to visit us in a chauffeured limousine. That was something for the neighbors to see. Now how many of them ever had boys who went out with Hollywood stars and came to visit the moms in chauffeured cars. I don't mind saying it. I enjoyed it. That was something nice to remember."

The celebrated front-page romance of Mamie Van Doren and Bo Belinsky echoed from Hollywood, California, to 244 Hewitt Street, Trenton, New Jersey.

"One day after they broke up," Mrs. Belinsky said, "I get this call from New York. I was just sitting around the house. I had broken my leg in a fall and I was resting in bed. All of a sudden Mamie's on the phone. She was playing in the Persian Room in New York and wanted to come over and say hello. She had been here before with Bo when he was playing in Philadelphia. She was a beautiful little thing, very friendly, very nice. Well, this one time she calls me and says she wanted to come over. What am I gonna say, *no?* So she comes over. She drives up in this chauffeured limousine and gets out and knocks on the door. She said she had heard all about the Belinsky steaks and was joining us for dinner. All she really wanted to do was cry on my shoulder. She wanted to talk about Bo and was wondering why she didn't see him any more, why he never called, what he was doing, who was he going with and all that kind of stuff.

"Well, I didn't get too involved in his doings like that, so I just told her that I didn't know and hadn't seen him for a while myself. I think she was just lonely for him and she thought maybe I could do something about it for her. I couldn't do anything. Bo never tells me nothing about his girl friends. He just says, 'Ma, it's nothing. I'll let you know when it's something.' It was a long time after he married someone else that I found out. He just called me one day and said he was coming over with his wife and baby.

"Well, anyway, you want to know about Mamie. She stayed for dinner and she cried a lot. Then somehow a reporter heard she was in my house and the next thing you know he is knocking on the door. She sat on the couch here where I'm sitting and he went across the room to take pictures. She started wiggling her eyes and moving her legs and all that. It was very glamorous to watch her, and that reporter took a long time with that camera before he got finished. It was all over the Trenton papers the next day: 'Mamie visits Bo's mother.' "

Mrs. Belinsky has her own theory on why the Los Angeles Angels officially frowned on Bo's relationship with Miss Van Doren.

"They were jealous," she said. "That's right, I think the Angels brass, Rigney and Haney and Autry and all of them, were jealous of Bo having such a glamorous movie actress for a girl friend. That's what I think."

Mrs. Belinsky managed to get in the middle of several of her son's romantic episodes. She remembers the visits of a girl named Penny best of all.

"One day when Bo was playing in Pensacola there's a knock on the door. The season was just over and Bo was upstairs sleeping in the bedroom. I go to the door and this cute little girl was there. She looks just like Keely Smith, big brown eyes and all. She was so sad-looking and she asks me if Bo is home. I said he wasn't. Bo always told me to say that. He didn't want people just dropping in on him. So I always told everybody he wasn't home.

"She starts out by saying, 'Mother, I'm an heiress and I'm taking Bo off your hands.' Imagine that. I'm doing the ironing and she tells me she is an heiress. Then she grabs the iron and starts doing all the clothes. I could tell by the way she handled that iron she wasn't no heiress. You ain't never seen no heiress handle an iron and you ain't likely to see one. I couldn't really get angry with the girl, she was a pretty thing and all that, and I didn't want to hurt her. Well, all of a sudden, here comes Bo parading downstairs in his bathrobe. When he saw her he was fit to be tied. They started yelling and I got out of there. I didn't want any part of that. Finally, everything calmed down and I made some coffee and they finally went out.

"She was trying to buy Bo's love. She would take him out to the best spots and drive him around in her car. He didn't care. He didn't have anything else to do that winter. He was just hanging around getting ready for spring training. She was a nice girl, though, that

Penny. When she got into trouble later, she never even brought
Bo's name into it.''

Ever since Belinsky became a ballplayer he knew his hometown
of Trenton was good for a gag line.

"You know that huge sign over the Bridge in Trenton?" Bo says.
"The thing reads, 'Trenton Makes, the World Takes.' The only
thing Trenton makes is dirt.''

"Ahh, he doesn't mean anything by that," Mrs. Belinsky said. "I
think he's proud of his hometown, but he just has gotten away from
it. He just says things like that for a joke. That's Bo. He'll say
anything if he thinks people will laugh about it. Why, one time he
was interviewed in the paper about his career and they asked him
why he didn't play for the high school team, being good enough for
the big leagues, and he said that he just didn't go for all that rah-rah
stuff in high school; playing on the high school team is all politics
anyway. Well, when that appeared in the papers, the phones really
began to ring. A bunch of them teachers at Trenton High called me
and they really let me have it. 'Why is Bo making fun of the school
and making fun of Trenton?' I had to tell them he didn't mean any
harm, he wasn't ashamed of Trenton, he just wanted to have a
laugh. They shouldn't be so senstitive and get so excited. If we
didn't like it here, we wouldn't be living here all these years. It's still
a free country.

"It's just that Bo likes other places better. You can't blame a boy
for that. What's there in Trenton for him, the pool halls? He can do
that any place. He likes Hollywood and Chicago and New York and
the big cities; that's just the way he is, just the way he always was.
I wouldn't stop him. You can't tell a boy where to live. I just want
to hear from him once in a while. There are times I don't hear from
him, and then I have to get on the phone and chase him down and
spend all kinds of money talking to him on the phone. We're just
plain working people. We don't have money for phone calls all over
America. But you know how boys are nowadays."

Belinsky would show up every winter during his baseball career
for a week or two with his parents, spend much of time with his pal,
Mike Petro, a beer truck driver, and be gone again for Florida for
spring training.

"Do you think he could still get back into baseball?" asked Ed Belinsky. "I think he could pitch if somebody would give him a job. He did good in Hawaii when he was out there, you know. Chuck Tanner, who is now the manager of the White Sox, gave him a big plug, and recommended him to the big leagues. Maybe he'll take him on again. He could build his arm back up again to where he could go nine. I think they ruined him when they made a relief pitcher out of him in Philadelphia. Bo was always a starter, in the major leagues, in the minors, in winter ball, everywhere. Why should they make a relief pitcher out of him? That's the way they do things in baseball sometimes. They don't think about the boy. They just think about themselves."

"You know," said Mrs. Belinsky, "I think the people in baseball tried to break his spirit. They never really wanted to see him happy. But they couldn't do it. Bo isn't like that. He just goes along and gets ready for the next day. He never looks back. He'll never say a bad thing about anybody. He'll never blame anybody. He's a happy boy but a lot of that is all on the outside. Inside, he's burning up and he has a right to it, the way they treated him in ball. Sometimes he would come home and his stomach would be all upset and he would have to take those pills to settle his stomach. I still got the bottle right upstairs in his room. There were times he just couldn't eat anything, his stomach was churning over so. Nobody ever tells you about that in baseball, nobody ever tells you how they take a boy and pay him nothing and ship him away from home and expect him to be able to do everything on his own. The ball clubs just don't watch out enough for the boys."

The doorbell rang and it was a man collecting for the Salvation Army. Mrs. Belinsky urged him away.

"I bet he takes the money, walks down the street and goes into the nearest gin mill with it," she said.

She talked some more and the bell rang again. It was a man delivering soda. She invited him in.

"Can we have an extra case of the Sprite?" she said. "We used it all up."

The soda man said he was all out of the Sprite, but would bring some the next time he delivered in this neighborhood.

"They're writing about Bo again," she said.

The soda man nodded. He picked up the empty cartons, collected his bill, and left. Mrs. Belinsky continued.

"The reporters used to call me up all the time here and ask about Bo. What could I tell them? They were always telling me things I didn't know. Half of them I didn't believe anyway, especially all that stuff about the girls and Hollywood and everything. Most of the time they were trying to make a fight or a scandal. One time Bo pitched against Al Downing in Yankee Stadium. Downing's from here, too. They said Bo wouldn't shake his hand. They were trying to make something of it because Downing was black. Newspapermen are always trying to make something of it. Why when Bo was with the Phillies, his best friend was Richie Allen. One time Allen was in the dugout and wiped himself off with the towel. Bo picked it right up and wiped his face and made believe he was looking at the towel to see if the black rubbed off on it. Bo would do anything to make people laugh. He's a lot like Richie Allen. He likes to go his own way and do what he wants."

The conversation with Bo's parents ended and darkness was falling. There would be one place left in Trenton to see.

"How do I get to Joe Russo's pool hall?"

Mr. Belinsky gave me directions and I drove down Broad Street to Front Street, past the ugly stores and the smell of burning wood. The only clean and attractive sights in the town seemed to be the office buildings of the State of New Jersey here in its capital city. There were several shabby stores on Front Street. Near the center of the block was a building with a small sign outside. Above the door it said "Russo's." The door was locked. The pool tables inside were covered with canvas. Russo's had gone out of business.

It was just as well. Bo Belinsky didn't belong here anymore.

Never try to snow a snowman.

—*BO BELINSKY*

Chalk Talk

United Airlines 747 flight number five flew out of the friendly skies over Kennedy Airport at noon and arrived in the smog over Los Angeles five hours and fifty-five minutes later. Below lay the Hollywood Hills and Beverly Hills, Sunset Strip, and a street intersection known across the country to every movie dreamer as fabulous Hollywood and Vine. Down there, somewhere, in this land of make believe nonsense, was the improbable retired baseball player Bo Belinsky.

It had been almost two years since I had last seen Belinsky. He had been in the spring training camp of the Cincinnati Reds, a fringe member of a club that was to excite all baseball that summer with a powerful attack led by Johnny Bench. He was hanging on then, hoping for one last chance, one more shot at that big money. Most of the swagger was gone.

"Damn, I thought I was going to be Sandy Koufax," he said of the days eight years before. "I'd stand out there throwing baseballs and I'd feel nobody could touch me. Sandy Koufax. And when I wasn't,

I started brooding and fooling around more. It didn't mean anything to me."

On this very afternoon, three thousand miles away, Sandy Koufax was accepting congratulations in the Monte Carlo suite of New York's Hotel Americana after his election to the Hall of Fame by the Baseball Writers of America.

"Listen," Bo had said that day in Tampa two years earlier, "I'm not trying to politician you or anything like that, but I know, man, I know if I ever get a shot, I can do good. You know, I want a break so bad, and it hurts, really hurts, not getting one."

Out of the airport and across the freeway, up on to the Pacific Coast Highway and past the large sign that said "Malibu." Rows of wooden beach houses. The landmark was a liquor store, Bo had said, and just beyond was the palatial residence of Burt Lancaster and down the next ravine was Rod Steiger's place.

"Bo said to give you the key," said the desk clerk. "He isn't home now. Make yourself comfortable. He'll call you later."

The motel apartment was huge and comfortable. There was a note on a coffee table from Bo's roommate, Helen, who had unexpectedly been called away. It read, "Make yourself at home. Bo is out of town. I'll call you later." After the long plane ride the chance to relax alone before tackling Bo was a welcome respite. Helen called fifteen minutes later.

"Bo had to go to Chicago," she said. "His baby is ill and his wife called him about it. He is supposed to get back tonight."

Bo and Jo had been living apart for seven months, she in Chicago as *Playboy* public relations girl, he in Malibu with Helen. Bo always had to have a roommate.

Helen arrived about midnight, a red-haired, attractive, pleasant girl with a soft, gentle voice. She had a smashing figure and wore pants the way pretty girls do, just a half-size too small.

"Hi, I'm Helen," she said. "Has Bo called?"

"No, he hasn't. Can we call him?"

"He'll call. He always calls when he says he will."

She walked into the kitchen and started boiling some water for instant coffee.

"Let's go out and have a sandwich. I'd like to ask you about Bo."

"Fine. I'll change my blouse."

She sat in a coffee shop down the road with her eyes looking off toward the window and the beach.

"He's talked about going back to Hawaii," she said. "I think he is just trying to find himself. He misses baseball. He isn't quite sure he knows yet what he wants to do."

It was apparent, whatever he did, Helen wanted to be included. She didn't push.

"I want him to be happy. I'll do anything he wants," she said.

She sounded like Bo's kind of girl.

It was two o'clock in the morning before Bo finally got around to calling.

"Hey, man," he said over the phone from Chicago, "it's snowing like hell out here. I'm trying to get out in the morning. I don't know if I can make it. How's Helen? She taking good care of you? She's a good kid. Make yourself comfortable with her. Look, I'm sorry for this hangup. Here, say hello to Jo."

Jo was sweet and apologetic as hell. "Bo really tried to get out. The weather here is just lousy. I'll see that he gets out tomorrow."

The snow continued for two days in Chicago. It was a week before he could get out. Bo said he would come to New York instead.

He arrived early one Tuesday evening, tall and thin as I had remembered him, his face lined and much older, his eyes tired, his hair hippie length. He wore a camel's hair coat and carried a small plaid suitcase.

"You look great, Bo."

"Tired as hell. And hungry. No food on that damn flight."

It took a meal and a night's rest and Belinsky was his old self again, laughing, needling, bouncing lines off waitresses and hotel clerks, looking suddenly younger again, talking in a strange combination of the Trenton streets, the New York gutters, the Hollywood jive.

"You saw my mother and father, right? How they doing? I haven't been around for a while. Just don't have the time. Too busy trying to get myself together," he said.

Trenton seemed so far away from Belinsky now as he lay on a motel bed in slacks and a T-shirt, a bottle of vodka on the small table beside him, his face relaxed and incredibly handsome in an animal sort of way, an explainable passkey to the pleasures of the past, present, and future.

"Christ, when I think of Trenton, I can't imagine how I lived there as long as I did. Things were tough when I was a kid. My father worked as a laborer and money was tight. The situation wasn't that good. They had their beefs but I didn't get into the middle of it. I was a Sagittarian at heart. I knew I would always follow the sun," he said.

As a small boy, thin and not overly aggressive, Belinsky was the victim of neighborhood brawls, some because he was small, some because he was a kid with a big mouth, some because he was Jewish and Polish in a neighborhood that was Jewish, Irish, Polish, Italian, and Swedish.

"We were really mixed up around Cummings Avenue there. Some of those kids would come over and whack me around for the fun of it. I didn't think anything of it. I figured that's the way it was with all kids. One of them used to beat up on me regularly. I think his name was Jimmy. He had been mashing me around pretty good. This one time I was about ten and I saw him coming. He was about twenty-two. I got a coke bottle and snuck up behind him and laid him out with it. I didn't have any more trouble with him."

"I kept myself loose," he said. "No gangs, no cliques, just me, ready to move wherever I wanted. I could fly the way the crow flies. Looking back I didn't want it any other way. What the hell for, for a lot of rah-rah, gee-whiz bullshit? That's why I never played on the high school baseball team. Too much gee-whiz bullshit and girls jumping up in their skirts with no panties on just to drive you wacky."

Belinsky survived in school. It was a lot of gee-whiz bullshit so he never was thrilled with the learning process.

"What I learned," he said, "I learned on the street. Everything. When I was ten I used to go to the movies a lot. One day I was watching this Clark Gable movie. He was loving some broad up on the screen and I wasn't interested in that so I went to the bathroom. A bunch of kids are in there smoking. One of them gives me a cigarette. I take it and smoke it, no coughing, nothing, just like a big man. I've been smoking ever since."

A major attraction in his young life was the regular visits to the Bronx to see his grandmother, Mrs. Millie Polnoff, in her apartment on Jerome Avenue. There was good food and happy conversation and a lot of fussing over young Bobby and his baby sister Lorraine.

"We used to go up there, and my parents would let me stay for two or three days in the summer. I would hang around with the kids in the building. I was visiting my grandmother once and I went downstairs to play. There's this girl about thirteen, big tits and everything already. I was about twelve and I was wearing a sweater tied around my waist, you know how kids do and I see her and I get a hard-on, bing, just like that; and I pull that sweater down right over it to hide it. Now the sweater stands up like a tent. How the hell am I going to hide it. The next thing I know she's moving over to me, giving me one of those back-of-the-neck jobs, blowing on my ears and all that shit.

"Now she tells me she wants to do it with me and all we gotta do is find a place. She suggests the fire escape. So we rush up the elevator, get to the roof, start climbing down the fire escape. It's the summertime and everybody is sitting on the fire escape steps drinking iced tea. Now I'm still carrying this goddamn tent, right? So we go down to the basement looking for the janitor's room. He's down there sweeping the crap into the garbage cans. Now I'm really starting to sweat. She says her parents aren't home so let's go on up to her apartment. We open the door and, damn, they came home early from shopping. She gives it that 'Hi, Mommy' shot and takes off. Now I'm really dying.

"Well, she solved everything. We get in that elevator. It's one of those jobs with the fence you pull closed. We go up a floor, I grab the fence, pull it open a little and the elevator can't move. Now she pulls up her skirt, pulls down her pants and I ball her right there in the elevator. That was a pretty fancy fuck for a twelve year old, right?"

Belinsky never saw his young friend again. He did see a lot of older girls around the Bronx apartments.

"There were some nasty old broads around in those days," he said. "I knew what they were after. I had to stay away from them. When I'd see one of those dirty old ladies I'd walk around the block the other way."

Belinsky was thirteen or fourteen years old, a lean, hungry-look-ing kid with a cigarette dangling from the corner of his mouth like Bogart, when he opened the door that was to change his life. He walked into a neighborhood pool hall in Trenton. In a matter of days, under the guiding hand of a rumpled, cigar-smoking man with bloated chest and cheeks, known as the Goose, Bo Belinsky found the second love of his life. It was almost as much fun as holding the elevator closed with thirteen-year-old girls.

"Shooting pool is a game," he says. "Winning is hard work. You never hustle anybody in pool. They hustle themselves. You go in a pool hall and you play and you win. That's easy. Walking out. That's hard."

Every afternoon in the fall, while schoolmates studied math and science, Belinsky studied bank shots. Every afternoon in the spring while kids his age were reading sports magazines and practicing Stan Musial's batting stroke, Belinsky was practicing his English. Every afternoon in the summer, after a pickup game of baseball or a little stickball in the playground on Jerome Avenue near Grandma Millie's, Belinsky walked the streets of Jerome Avenue looking for new pool parlors and new pool players.

"I practiced a hell of a lot," says Belinsky. "I worked out the game until I could hardly see the table and my eyes were red and tired. The Goose really helped me. He wasn't a good player but he en-joyed the game. He enjoyed winning a buck if he could."

Pool players play a circuit just like baseball, football, and basket-ball teams. They work the neighborhood pool halls and stay one step ahead of the other hustlers. They fan out in all directions, looking for new action, new entertainment, new challenges to their skills and nerve. Belinsky was sixteen when he made his first road trip. The Goose decided Bo was ready to move up. He had con-quered all comers in Trenton and he was getting to be a familiar face. Nobody would play him for money. A pool hustler's best weapon is his anonymity.

"How would you like to drive on over to Hightstown with me, kid?" asked the Goose.

"Sure, when?"

"Now. Let's see if we could get a game."

Hightstown, a small town of some 4300 people, a few miles east of the state capital at Trenton, was a perfect training ground for the young hustler. He was a new face, innocent, smiling, younger looking than his years, with long, black hair, a straight set of clean white teeth, and the angelic smile of honesty. Bo and the Goose sauntered into a neighborhood pool hall. The Goose had worked the room before. He was scouted stuff, good enough for a close game with the proper player and the right spot, but too advanced in years, too uncertain of his touch to take on anything for meaningful money.

Bo smoked a cigarette, leaned against a wall and watched a few games. The Goose asked for a table from the boy of the house. The light was turned on, the Goose picked up a rack of balls, and Bo took off his jacket.

"I chalked up and dropped the chalk. That's always a good way to start," Belinsky said. "We played two or three games, just lollypopped around, the Goose winning most of the games. We played eight ball or nine ball, Chicago, anything, just to vary the action. Just shot quietly, smoked a few cigarettes and minded our own business."

"How about a game, Goose?"

The challenger was about thirty, with high cheekbones that made him look Oriental, and an ugly scar running down the left side of his face. They called him the Masked Marvel.

"Sure, Marvel, how much you give me?"

"Twenty balls."

"Not enough."

"Hell, Goose, I haven't played in a month. Been on a goddamn trip with my old lady. She wanted to see some relatives in Iowa. No action in Iowa. They don't even have a goddamn movie in Iowa."

"Fifty balls."

"Your ass."

"Why don't you let me and the kid here finish our friendly little game."

"Does the kid play?"

It was twenty years ago and tens of thousands of pool halls later, but the memory of the challenge brought a gigantic smile to Belinsky's face. He leaned back in his chair and stared out of the motel window. He took the bottle of vodka off of his table and poured some of it over the ice in his glass. He swallowed a gulp slowly, letting most of it run carefully down his throat. He placed the glass back on the table.

"Yeh, the kid plays a little, but Christ, he's only fourteen years old."

"I'll play him for fun, just to see how he handles it. What do you want, twenty-five balls?"

"Twenty-five? The kid just learned how to play a week ago. Give him seventy-five and we'll play for ten bucks."

"I'll give him fifty for five bucks."

"Just for fun anyway."

The Goose reached into the side pocket of his pants and pulled out a dirty five-dollar bill. He placed it on the near end of the table. The Masked Marvel put his five down. Belinsky turned his back to the table.

"Go ahead, kid, see if you can win me five bucks. I'll give you a buck if you can do it. Do you understand the game? It's straight pool, just like you learned last week, and a hundred wins. All you gotta do is get fifty more before the Marvel here gets a hundred, got it, kid?"

The Masked Marvel reached up and pulled five sets of scoring disks across the wire overhead.

"If this was a fifty game I'd be the winner, right?" asked Bo. "Let's make it a fifty game."

It was Belinsky's adolescent humor at work. The Masked Marvel chose to ignore it as he chalked up. The Goose just pointed his finger toward the table, tapped Belinsky with the cue on his thighs and said, "Go ahead, kid, shoot."

Belinsky had learned his lessons well. He broke badly and the Masked Marvel knocked off ten balls before Belinsky could shoot again. Bo made a long shot at the far right corner of the table, cut a hanger into the left corner pocket, and blew a cross bank shot. The Masked Marvel moved out quickly with a run of eight. Belinsky had his best run of the game as he dropped five in a row in, almost all easy shots. In a few minutes it was over. The Masked Marvel had his hundred balls and Belinsky was still at seventy-two. He had scored twenty-two on his own while the Masked Marvel had made a hundred.

The Masked Marvel picked up the two five-dollar bills, was about to put them in his pocket when he looked at Belinsky's sad face. "You want twenty-five balls for the ten bucks, kid?"

Belinsky had his first hustle.

"It's all psychology," Belinsky says. "It's an ego thing. A guy beats you and he isn't sure just how good you are. He has to know. He has to beat you again and again and again. Soon you know it's going to be a freezeout, that's what you're after. That's when the whole thing is on the line, that's when you beat him for all his money. But you can't make it too obvious. You gotta remember the laws of hustling. You never hustle anybody, they hustle themselves. You never try to snow a snowman. And you gotta find out early if there is an exit to the street through the bathroom. Nothing does you any good if you don't carry it out of the hall."

The Masked Marvel won the next game by seventeen balls. He put the twenty down on the table and the Goose matched it without a word. It was the end of a beautiful friendship. Nine days later, on a late summer afternoon of his sixteenth year, Robert Belinsky spotted the Masked Marvel fifty balls and beat him one hundred to ninety-eight. The Goose picked up twelve one-hundred-dollar bills off the table, nodded to his young find and walked out of the pool room with him. Bo Belinsky never played Hightstown again.

The word had gotten back to Trenton before Bo did. He was a hero for the first time in his life, an instant celebrity, a guy who belonged someplace at last. Bo still played baseball when he felt like it, but he shot pool even when he didn't feel like it.

"I enjoyed the guys and the games. It was fun. You came and went the way you wanted. No questions, no bullshit, play, don't play, do what you want. It suited me more than baseball. I was my own man, win or lose on my own. I didn't have to worry that some jerky kid playing shortstop, thinking about getting into the pants of some little broadie down the street, would let a ground ball go through his legs and they would get eight runs off me. The pool was great. I didn't have to ask my mother for money anymore, either."

In the summer of 1954, at seventeen, Belinsky met Cincinnati Phil. He was to give Bo his first taste of life on the road.

"All the guys who worked the road had nicknames. Cincinnati Phil was the name I knew him by. Hell, I don't know, maybe he was Chicago Phil in some other town or Pittsburgh Peter for all I know. Minnesota Fats used to be New York Fats before he got famous. They never gave me a nickname. It was just good old Bo," he said.

Belinsky spent six weeks with Cincinnati Phil. He shot pool in a hundred towns, in a thousand pool halls, in a dozen states, moving in and out of pool halls faster than he could count the winnings in one town or blow it in another. He slept in the car most of the time. Once in a while Phil would splurge and rent a room someplace so they could wipe the grime of the road off their skin. They ate greasy hot dogs and burnt hamburgers, drank soda pop and beer, pissed on the side of the road when the garages were too far apart. Belinsky loved every single second of it.

"I was seventeen," he said. "I was on the road with a grown man, doing what grown men do. I was knocking off a broadie here and there, seeing different things, talking to different people, learning the wonders of the world. Sure, it was dirty and smelly and unpleasant, but when you're seventeen nothing is unpleasant. It's just new."

Belinsky came home at the end of the trip with a few bucks in his pocket and two more inches on his fast ball. He was almost full grown now, a straight, angular six foot two, and well muscled at 175 pounds. He wore his hair thick and full grown at the sides. His complexion was swarthy, his eyes deep and brown, his eyebrows full. Robert Belinsky was a man in every sense of the word.

His father, Edward, tried to push him more and more into sports, less and less into pool halls. He encouraged him to play more baseball and was disappointed that he still refused to go out for the high school team in his senior year.

"I didn't know what the hell I wanted to do," Bo says. "It really didn't bother me, either. I knew I would eat every day and if you do that, what the hell else really matters."

In the spring of 1955 Belinsky graduated from high school. Then he met the Farmer.

"This guy had a name, Norm Weber, and they sometimes called

him the Lemonade Man. He would stand around the pool halls like a kid working a lemonade stand, just waiting for action. He was skinny and had a sharp nose and was a young guy about twenty-five or thirty or so who looked like he was forty-five, all lines in his face and used up. He was called the Farmer because he walked around with a piece of straw in his mouth. He had these crazy outfits that he played in, coveralls, or a truck driver's uniform with Coca-Cola on the shirt or RC Cola or Joe's Service Station. You'd go into a car with him and he'd be wearing an RC Cola shirt and he'd pull over and go in the men's room. He'd come out and he'd be wearing some crazy shirt that said Sam's Bowling League or some such crap. He was wild, man, I'll tell you."

Belinsky hooked up with the Farmer. They worked Baltimore, Philadelphia, Wilmington, Washington, D.C. They moved into a town at dusk and out at dark.

"He taught me the basic rule of shooting pool on the road," says Belinsky, "and that is to never carry your own cue. That makes you look like a hustler. Use the house cue every time and drop the chalk at least once a night."

Belinsky and the Farmer piled into his 1948 green Chevrolet that summer of 1955 and worked the eastern seaboard. They were as far south as Kinston, North Carolina when the Farmer announced, "We're going down to Florida, Bo, to visit my brother. He's over in Orlando and we'll be able to stay with him while we play ourselves a few games."

Florida. The very sound of the name of the state brought excitement to Belinsky's mind. He had heard about Florida from Grandma Millie and her friends. Florida meant only one thing. Money. Oasis in the desert.

The Farmer put his foot down hard on the gas pedal, the Chevy belched some smoke, and Belinsky was on his way to Florida for the first time in his life. It would be an unhappy beginning to some very happy hours.

The Farmer had a lot of talent with a cue but none with a car. The Chevy broke down every one hundred miles or so and every time he tried to fix it, things got worse. The five-hundred-mile trip took over three days.

"We got to about the outskirts of Orlando. For two days I hadn't eaten anything but cupcakes and O'Henry bars. Finally another tire blew out again."

"Let's go change it," the Farmer said.

"Ahh, fuck it," said Bo, "I'm tired of cracking my nut on those tires."

"Well, we can get a hitch on into town, and my brother will drive us out later."

"It's better than lifting the jack again and rupturing myself."

Nobody picked them up. They waited an hour and finally walked three miles to Weber's brother's place. He was painting his house. He told Weber he would pick up the car and get it fixed, put Bo and the Farmer up for a couple of nights and feed both of them. There was only one catch. They had to help him paint the house.

"He gives me a pair of those white coveralls and I kept looking down on the ground from that ladder. Scared the hell out of myself. Painted everything in sight. I even got a little paint on the house."

In two days Bo and the Farmer were ready to hustle. They sauntered into a small bar in town. They wanted a sandwich, a beer, and if lucky, a game. The bartender, a friendly sort, asked them if they were new in town.

"Yeah," said the Farmer, "just got in."

"What do you guys do."

"We paint."

"Yeah?"

"Yeah. But we didn't come here to talk. We just want to shoot some pool for an hour and relax before we have to get on to our next job."

"Well, Christ, I'm not busy, I'll shoot a game with you."

The match was made. The first stake was five dollars. Bo and the Farmer had twenty-five dollars. They put it on the table. It was a freezeout. They knew their man. They lost the twenty-five to him.

"Hey, before you guys go, what would it take to paint this place?"

The Farmer started searching the corners of the bar with the eye of a professional. He tapped the walls. He put his finger on the dust. He walked back and forth, deep in thought, not about paint, but about just how much this guy might be good for.

"Well, since you seem like a nice guy, we'll do the job for a hundred twenty-five."

"Tell you what. I'll put up a hundred twenty-five and you put up painting the place and we'll play a freezeout."

The bartender moved to the door, turned the "open" sign around to "closed" and pulled the shades. The game was on. It went all through the night and on into the morning. When the sun broke through, the freezeout was over. The Farmer put $1120 into his pocket.

"Well," Weber said, as he and Bo started for the door, "we'll see you around."

The bartender banged his hand on the table. Belinsky stiffened near the locked door.

"I thought this was it. He was standing close to the bar now and I was sure he had a gun in the cash register. I figured he was going to take his money back for sure. I was just worried that he would shoot our asses up. Then he made his big move," Belinsky said.

"Wait a minute," shouted the bartender. "What about painting the place?"

The Farmer accepted the painting job, announced he would be back that afternoon to start work and walked out with his money and his Bo. "Isn't that the craziest damn thing you ever heard?"

Like any honest hustler, the Farmer was true to his word. He showed up with his brother's paints and brushes at four o'clock and painted the room and collected his $125.

"Did a hell of a job, too," said Belinsky, "for a guy who couldn't paint."

Belinsky admired the Farmer's style. He liked the challenge of the hustle, the mind-over-mind battle, the excitement and pressures of a good hustle. The Farmer had been born in Maine, was a college man, could use English words as well as pool table English.

"There was an air of excitement to scamming. A scammer who can make a hundred dollars legit would always rather make twenty-five scamming," Belinsky says.

The Farmer knew how to live high when he wanted to. He ran up bills he never paid. He could hustle credit on clothes, on food, on cars, on goods. Lawyers would chase him down. He would change his name, move, work another town, stay ahead of the bill collectors.

"He always owed three or four thousand dollars, all the time," said Belinsky. "One time some lawyer caught up with him. He started hitting him with legal letters, real nasty things: if you don't pay up, you'll go to jail. All that crap. One time he gets this letter saying he owes a guy four thousand dollars. He sits down and writes the guy an answer, a beautiful letter. 'Dear Sir: Received your very nasty note saying I owe you four thousand dollars. Do you know that my dry-cleaning bill alone is more than four thousand dollars. If you don't become more civilized I will take drastic action. Every Saturday night I put all my bills in a fishbowl. My friends blindfold me. I reach in and pull out one bill. That guy gets fifty cents. If you don't stop sending me those nasty letters your name will be pulled from the fishbowl drawing and you will never hear from me again.' Then he mailed the letter and prepared to move out of that apartment."

Belinsky became a recognized pool expert, played throughout his minor league and major league career, but never seemed to be able to get together with Dodger manager Walter Alston or Leo Durocher, then a Dodger Coach, long regarded as baseball's finest pool players. He played often with his running mate, Dean Chance, but was able to whip him when it counted.

"Dean's a better cardplayer than a pool shooter," says Bo. "That's his hustle. But he knows all the great pool players across the country."

Belinsky has retired from the game of pool. He says the game is too demanding at his advancing age. It sounds like a hustle.

I like his body.

—*BASEBALL SCOUT REX BOWEN ON SIGNING BO BELINSKY*

It's Better than Prison

On May 15, 1956, seven months short of his twentieth birthday, Robert Belinsky agreed to a baseball contract with the Pittsburgh Pirates farm team at Brunswick, Georgia, for a salary of $185 a month and the bus ticket from Trenton, New Jersey, to Brunswick.

"There was a local bird dog for the Cardinals who had seen me pitch. He was in the insurance business and he suggested the Cardinals sign me. They refused because I hadn't any high school records to go on. They wanted guys who had done something outstanding in the Mickey Rooney leagues, like Dean, with his high school no-hitters. They don't care if you can pitch. They care if they can tell people you can. The Cardinals had no interest, but that Rex Bowen of the Pirates had seen me a couple of times in the sandlots and came out one day; and I had a good game, fifteen strikeouts, good control, a hell of a game. That night he was over the house and he sold my mother and father on the idea.

"I know we can't give him a bonus," Bowen said, "but I like his chances. He'll get stronger and heavier as he gets older. I like his body. He's left-handed and that is always an advantage."

"My father told him to come back the next night. I pulled out a map and looked for Brunswick, Georgia. I saw that it was on the ocean. I figured it would be a kick. What the hell else was I doing? I think I was working in an overalls factory that day, shooting pool, fooling with the broads. I always liked older broads. I was eighteen, nineteen, and I would take out these twenty-two-, twenty-three-year-old broads. They used to make me laugh, though. You could fuck them in a car. That was okay, but if you mentioned a motel to them, they'd go out of their minds. Anyway, I figured baseball would be just as good as the overalls factory. I knew I would go as far as my arm would take me. Nobody would help me. I knew that if you want a helping hand in this world look at the end of your arm."

Belinsky was never a baseball fan. He never dreamed about hitting that memorable home run in Yankee Stadium or pitching that perfect game in the World Series. The only player he ever admired was Hal Newhouser, who was later to teach him the spitball as a minor league pitching instructor in the Baltimore organization. And Belinsky may have liked Newhouser because he was the only left-handed pitcher he had ever heard of.

"I never looked in the mirror and watched myself pitch no-hitters. The game was fun to play; when it was over, it was over. A lot of things are fun to do and you don't go around dreaming about them all the time. I figured if I didn't like it in Brunswick, Georgia, I could always cut out to Florida."

So Robert Bo Belinsky began his professional baseball career at the Trenton Bus Station on Broad Street on a bus marked *Atlanta*, with a brown bag in his hand. His mother had prepared two chicken salad sandwiches for the trip.

Belinsky's bus from Trenton to Atlanta arrived in the early evening and he switched to a bus for Brunswick for the final hours. It was almost midnight when he arrived in the Georgia port city, hard by the Atlantic Ocean, with the smell of fertilizer, chemicals and burning paper from a pulp factory clogging his nostrils. He checked into the Oglethorpe Hotel.

"You know the hotel in the television program 'The Munsters,'" said Belinsky. "That's what the Oglethorpe was like. Rooms falling apart, old, broken stairways, chairs that creaked when you sat on them, beds that sagged to the floor. This was the glamorous life of a baseball player. In the morning I ordered pancakes for breakfast, hit one with my fork and it bounced up and smashed me in the eye. It wasn't a hotel, it was a concentration camp compound."

A small thin man named Frank Oceak, who had been an unsuccessful minor league ballplayer, was the manager of the Brunswick Pirates of the class D Georgia-Florida League.

"We hit it off immediately," said Belinsky. "He hated me and I hated him.

"He dreamed of the time when they would make him a coach in the majors. Besides managing the team he drove the school bus we used, a rickety old thing with a hundred thousand miles on it. Seats weren't big enough for you to fart in. Oceak's most memorable quality was his lack of humor. He didn't like to laugh and he didn't like anybody else to laugh."

Oceak finally made it to the Pittsburgh Pirates as a coach for Danny Murtaugh. His most memorable moment came in the 1971 World Series against the Baltimore Orioles. The Orioles had a pretty, blonde fifteen-year-old girl, Linda Werheim, who had a cute act during the fifth inning. She worked with the ground crew, swept the bases and ended up by lightly tapping the third-base coach in the behind with her broom for a laugh or kissing him nobly on the cheek. On national television, as Linda moved toward him, Frank Oceak gave her a swift kick in the ass.

"That team was filled with those bonus babies," said Belinsky. "Oceak really had to play up to them. He knew the big club watched them. Me? Hell, he didn't know my name or care. If one of those bonus players got hurt or a pitcher got a sore arm, he'd baby the hell out of him or even call in a local doctor. But, if I had to be honest, he was no different in that than any other minor league manager. If I was hurting, he'd just send me out and tell me to pitch it out."

Belinsky pitched in eleven games for the Brunswick Pirates, won two and lost three, struck out twenty-nine batters and walked only twenty-four—a ratio that impresses baseball people—and had an earned run average of 7.36. Belinsky, of course, had a good excuse. He couldn't digest the food in the Oglethorpe Hotel.

"After a while I moved out and went into a boardinghouse. The bed was a little better and they served a home-cooked meal. But I was going stir crazy in that town with no wheels and a hundred eighty-five a month salary. I'd latch on to one of those Southern mamies and we'd drive down to Jacksonville for a few laughs. You'd knock them off in the back seat of the car and they'd pull over and buy a bottle of Seven-Up in one of those Seven-Eleven stores. Then they would use the Seven-Up for a douche. I have to break up now when I hear that uncola cola commercial. It's uncola, all right."

Two months later Belinsky had his fill of Brunswick, Georgia. He jumped the club and went to Jacksonville.

"I spent a few days down there hustling the sailors in some pool games. This one guy was weird. He made me shack up with his old lady while he watched before he would shoot pool with me. I didn't care much for his wife, but he was an easy hustle so I did it. A few days of that and I went back to the ball club."

"Where you been?" asked Oceak.

"I was out robbing old ladies' purses so I can eat. Who the hell could eat on the money you pay me? I'll have to go on relief."

Oceak saw no humor at all in the situation and fined Belinsky a half-month's pay. Belinsky stayed around two more weeks and then jumped the club for good. He went back down to Jacksonville and hustled a few more sailors. He took up residence with some local prostitutes. He hung around the bars and played darts and cards. Then he headed north to New York.

"I lived in a few joints on the West Side," he said. "I got in with these boosters, you know, guys who boost junk out of somebody's window and then pawn it off. I didn't do any of the boosting. You had to be trained for that. I just did some selling for them. I stayed with some cats, black and white, all over town.

"Then I met this one girl who really dug me, and moved in with her. She said she didn't make enough dough to support me. She said we'd have to live Dutch treat. We'd go out to a joint to get a sandwich and I'd tell her I'd flip her for the check. I had this two-headed coin and she'd always call tails. What the hell, if she didn't spend it on me, she'd spend it on somebody else. She was a good woman. I think whores got a lot more class than some straight broads. You know where you stand with them. There are only three kinds of women in this world: givers, takers, and destroyers. You really have to watch out for those big destroyers."

Belinsky went back to Trenton and continued on his merry way. He got in with the neighborhood thugs, never in the mainstream of the action, but always close enough. They were into numbers, dope, robberies, assaults, car jobs. Belinsky worked in a pottery factory part of the time. His friends told him it didn't hurt to have a job as a cover.

One day he received a letter from a man named Fred Davis of Pensacola, Florida. Davis said he was starting up an independent baseball club in Pensacola, had seen Bo pitch at Brunswick and was willing to offer him three hundred dollars a months.

"I didn't realize how deep the guys I was hanging around with were into drugs and robberies and numbers. Things were starting to get hot in town with word getting around that the cops had picked up this guy or that one. When they started questioning people, I got shaky. I looked on the map and saw Pensacola wasn't too far from some swinging spots in New Orleans. I had never been there. I figured it was worth a shot. I wrote the guy a letter, told him if he would pay me one month's salary in advance I'd join him."

Pensacola was a pleasant surprise for Belinsky. He liked the beaches and the girls in bikinis. The bars were live. The town was friendly. Local merchants made it easy for ballplayers to buy good suits, shoes, and sweaters at cheap prices. Belinsky pitched well and his salary zoomed to $350 a month.

"I seemed to have matured there," he said. "It was the first time I had a real good fast ball."

He struck out 202 batters and walked only 90 men in 195 innings, was 13–6 on the season with a 3.00 ERA. The Baltimore Orioles had a working agreement with the Pensacola Dons and Belinsky was marked down, for the first time, as a "prospect."

"The difference between prospect and suspect is the difference in the way they treat you. A prospect gets his arm rubbed. Of course, the guy should be rubbing camshafts, but at least it's something. And a suspect gets nothing," Bo says.

The owner, Fred Davis, turned out to be a fine fellow, and his manager, Lou Fitzgerald, treated Bo pleasantly.

"Fred took good care of me," Belinsky said. "I came up with tonsilitis and was out a couple of weeks. Davis paid all the bills. A lot of other minor league clubs would send you home. We even had a better bus there and the manager didn't drive it."

Things weren't completely smooth. Belinsky was in a bar one night and eyed some sailor's girl friend. The sailor broke a beer bottle over Belinsky's head. When Bo recovered, he smashed the guy's face down hard on the bar and broke his nose. The Shore Patrol arrested Belinsky.

"The sailor was a huge guy with tattoos all over his arms and body. Those are always the crybabies. You hit those guys and they scream for the cops. I called Davis from the bar. He rushed down and bailed me out. He gave me some dough and told me to take a week off in Mobile, Alabama, until things cooled down. The guy dropped the charges and I was back on the beach at Pensacola in a week. I only missed one turn."

Belinsky continued to pitch well in Pensacola, on and off the field. His best move came late on a Friday night.

"I was sitting in this hotel, at the bar, talking to a couple of my broadies," Bo said, "and I glance over at the other end of the bar and I see this gorgeous, beautiful, incredible-looking Oriental girl. Everybody was looking at her. She was just out of this world. She had on this Chinese dress, with the Suzie Wong slit right up to her shoulder. She had that whole bar flipping out. I had to rescue her."

"Hey, let's get out of here before you drive this whole place bananas."

She looked at Bo like he was a madman. Then she looked again at the dark, sensuous eyes, the long, smooth black hair, and the full smile.

"Sure," she said. "Let's go."

Her name was Zenida. She was Filipino-Chinese, about five feet two inches tall, with a marvelous body and cream-colored skin. Her husband had been an air hero in the Korean war, met her in Seoul, married her and brought her back to the States. He commanded a flight squadron out of Pensacola, but he no longer commanded

Zenida. She had filed for divorce and was vamping her way through Pensacola. It was love at first sight. Belinsky moved in that night.

"She was all woman. Some females don't have the gumption to be women," Bo says.

Zenida followed Bo around the league. She would show up unexpectedly in a town, spend the night with him in his hotel, and disappear just as unexpectedly at daybreak. She never interfered in his life or in any other action.

"I could tell her to get lost for two hours if I had something else going, and she wouldn't piss or moan; she'd just go and show up two hours later," he said.

In 1962, after he had pitched his no-hitter with the Los Angeles Angels, Belinsky was driving around in a candy apple Eldorado Cadillac. Zenida called one day and said she would like to see him if he was free. Bo told her to wait for him in the parking lot of Chavez Ravine after the game. He described his car. Now, Albie Pearson, the diminutive outfielder of the Angels, a religious, straight-living young man, had only one vice. He also drove around in a candy apple Eldorado Cadillac.

"Here comes Albie out of the park with his wife. He's walking toward the car. He sees Zenida sitting on the car, her Suzie Wong dress up to her ass, her legs twitching all over the place. She's halfway across the parking lot and can't really see who it is, so she's waving because she knows it's a ballplayer with a broad coming out of the players' entrance and who could it be but me? When Albie gets a little closer she stops waving, but by that time it's too late. Albie is white as a ghost and his wife is just pissed."

In 1959 Belinsky was serving his second tour of duty in Pensacola.

"One night I make it with this young girl in the motel. She tells me she is eighteen and I don't ask her to prove it. A few days later she shows up at Zenida's place, starts screaming she is only sixteen and is going to have my ass on a statutory rape charge if I don't marry her. You should have seen a guy pack. Zenida hustles her out of the place and I call Davis. I explain the situation to him and he's shook up when I tell him the kid's name. 'Christ, her mother is a school crossing guard in town and the chief of detectives is laying her. The old lady will have the cops on you in a minute. You'd better get out of town.' "

Zenida and a couple of friends covered Belinsky with a blanket, pushed him into the back seat of her car and drove across the border to New Orleans.

"A week later my contract had been assigned to Aberdeen, South Dakota. That's as far away as I could go. The manager was Earl Weaver. I bet he had no idea how he suddenly came up with the new left-hander that late in the season."

After his strong season in 1957 with Pensacola, Belinsky moved up in 1958 to Knoxville in the Sally League where he was 0–2, and Aberdeen in the Northern League where he was 10–14. Then came Amarillo, Stockton, Pensacola, and Aberdeen in 1959.

"My career wasn't going anywhere," said Bo. "The Orioles had two young left-handers that I played with that they liked a lot more. The first was Steve Barber. The other was Steve Dalkowski. We pitched together day and night. They were both as crazy as me."

Belinsky spent the winter of 1958–1959 in New Orleans.

"My folks thought I should quit baseball and get an honest job," Bo said. "I was having too much fun."

He lived with a prostitute in New Orleans. Every time she did a trick Belinsky had to go out and get some coffee. He did it because he liked the girl and needed the money.

"One day I bring the coffee back and three guys jump me. They had beaten the girl up for her dough and now wiped me out. They did a proper number on me. It took me three weeks to recuperate. I'm there in this girl's pad and who shows up but Zenida. She was making it with some guy who drilled for oil. I told her she better stop coming after me. I was a loser and would only cause her grief. Never stopped her. She gave me some dough, cut out again, and showed up the next season in Aberdeen."

At the end of the 1959 season, after four years in professional baseball in eight cities, Belinsky decided to quit. He didn't know what else he could do, but he knew what he didn't want to do. He didn't want to play baseball any longer.

"The season had a few more days to go and I put in a call to Harry Dalton, the farm director, back in Baltimore. I told him I was busted up in a scuffle, wasn't going anywhere in that organization, and was quitting baseball. He told me to think about it. The next day Weaver calls me into his office."

"The Orioles want you to report in Baltimore to them. They want you to pitch batting practice. It's a big break," Weaver said.

The Aberdeen season ended and Belinsky started driving east from South Dakota with a young outfielder. The two teammates drove across country without incident until they got to Chicago. Then things got tough.

"He was just a country kid and the idea of being with the big city boy all alone was too much for him. He started to get drunk and started screaming, 'I wanna get laid, I wanna get laid.' He wanted me to stop on the road someplace and find him a broad. I think he started screaming somewhere around the Missouri line. By the time we reach Chicago he's out of his mind. 'I gotta get laid, I gotta get laid.' So we drove on into Chicago. Now he figures the only place for a sure thing was in the black section. So he's hanging out of the car window yelling, 'Where are the whores, where are the whores, I wanna get laid.' I thought we might get blown up.

"Finally we park on some dirty street, a pimp comes over to the car and we deal. I'm walking around later on, looking for the car and I look up at a hotel window and there's this guy, blind drunk, hanging out of the window yelling, 'I got laid, I got laid, I got laid.' I thought they were going to drop him right out of the window. He finally comes down and we find our car. That's all we find. They broke a window, stole all our clothes, and smashed the trunk trying to get in there, too."

The now more experienced outfielder was contrite and sober most of the rest of the trip. At three on a Friday morning in September of 1959 Belinsky and his pal walked into the lobby of the Southern Hotel in Baltimore.

"We're with the ball club," Belinsky says. "We have reservations."

"I got one room. Yeh, that's it."

"What do you mean, one room? We just drove all the way across country. I gotta have a room to myself so I can rest."

"One room, that's all I got."

"Okay, dammit, we'll take it. What the hell."

"It's a single room," said the clerk. "One small bed. That's all I got."

Belinsky looked at the reservation slip upside down. "Godammit, I'll call Dalton. Let's get this straightened out. What kind of an operation is this?"

Belinsky went to the one pay phone in the lobby and called Dalton.

"Yes?"

"This is Bo Belinsky, Mr. Dalton, from the Aberdeen club. We just got in. All they got here in the hotel is one room, and not in my name either. Where the hell am I supposed to sleep, on the floor?"

"It won't hurt for one night," Dalton said.

Bo Belinsky slammed the phone down hard, grabbed his bag from the aged hotel clerk, walked out the door, and retired from baseball.

Several days later Dalton placed a call to Belinsky's home in Trenton. He asked Bo's mother to get him to reconsider. The Orioles wanted to send him to the instructional league team in Clearwater. The sound of Florida in winter was a lot more appealing than Trenton. Belinsky accepted the offer and reported to the Clearwater club in the middle of November in 1959. His teammates included Steve Barber, Boog Powell, Buster Narum, and a tall, handsome, raw-boned eighteen-year-old right-handed pitcher from a farm near Wooster, Ohio, named Wilmer Dean Chance. They were to meet later in Los Angeles with more exciting results, but for now they were only casual friends.

"Dean was a real hayseed," said Bo. "He had this big high school reputation, had signed for a sixty-thousand-dollar bonus and was being touted as a star. I was always forced to prove myself. I was twenty-three already. I figured I had no chance to be in the majors. I just liked Florida instead of Trenton."

Luman Harris was the manager of the club. He was easy on the young players. Belinsky spent a lot of his off time making money in the pool halls of Clearwater.

"I went into this one joint and they tell me that the best they had ever seen was Eddie Waitkus. I laughed at that name. He was the ballplayer who had gotten himself shot by a broad who came up to his room when she told him she loved him. She loved him, all right, with a bullet in his lung. He had left his engraved cue in this place and they let me use it. It made me a lot of money." Belinsky said.

Bo lived with Steve Barber and a pitcher named Ralph Schell.

"Schell was like a guy in the Nazi youth movement. He got up every morning, did his exercises, did everything by the book. He ran his ass off that whole winter season. Had a hell of a fast ball, too. Only trouble was it was straight as a string and everybody hit it over the fence."

One afternoon, after a workout in Clearwater, a girl in a green Chevrolet parks near the players' entrance. She spots Belinsky coming out, gets out of the car and walks over to him.

"You're Bo Belinsky, aren't you?"

"Yes."

"Can I have your autograph?"

Belinsky immediately told the pretty girl he never signed autographs in front of ball parks.

"Let's go have a cup of coffee some place, and I'll sign anything you want," he said.

Belinsky made a date to see the girl that night. He gave her the address of the apartment where he was staying. A couple of ballplayers were entertaining two girls when Belinsky's girl showed up. While one sat with the two girls in a back room, the other ballplayer jumped Bo's girl friend.

"When I finally get to the apartment the girl is hysterical. She had been raped and her dress was torn and she is screaming. This nut was laughing. I had a hell of a time soothing that broad that night," Belinsky said.

Belinsky went to spring training in 1960 with the Orioles—who made a brilliant run at the Yankees that year, before blowing the pennant in three late-season games at Yankee Stadium—and was cut early. He was assigned to Vancouver, pitched in a few games, and was called up for Army reserve duty with the Dixie Division. He was sent to Fort Knox, Kentucky. On his first night off, he met a tall girl who wore her stringy hair in a boyish cut. She was Penny.

"When I meet a broad," says Bo, "I never ask questions. I'm not running a true confessions pad. If I dig you and you dig me, that's it."

Penny dug Bo and Bo dug Penny. They spent weekends in Miami or New Orleans. Penny paid for everything. They made the Fountainbleu, the Eden Roc, worked on their Florida tan and drank, and made beautiful music together. One afternoon she showed up at Fort Knox.

"Your wife is here," an officer told Belinsky.

"My what?"

"Your wife. She's right outside the cadre room. Says it's an emergency."

Belinsky walked out of the office door in his army fatigues and Penny gave him a huge kiss, announced that the baby was sick, and asked if he could get a day off to see him.

"Why haven't you written?" she asked.

"Too busy with the army, sweetheart."

Belinsky was given a forty-eight-hour pass. Penny had the car waiting outside and they spend a pleasant two days in Myrtle Beach, South Carolina.

"One day she had a pile of bills in her pocket. I just couldn't hold my curiosity any longer. She always seemed to have all kinds of money and she never seemed to do anything to get it. Finally I asked her where the bread came from."

"Oh, didn't I tell you? My husband was very wealthy. He was a big industrialist and left me a great deal of money. I'm also a high-salaried interior decorator. Why, I can make a thousand dollars with one consultation."

Shortly before Belinsky was to be separated from the service he received a visit from an army captain.

"I'm with the Criminal Investigation division. We're preparing to prosecute you and your wife. She signed bad checks for four thousand dollars in Columbia, South Carolina."

Belinsky instructed the captain to inspect his file, to learn that Bo was a single man, that he had nothing to do with Penny's paperhanging, and that he would be happy if he could forget the whole thing. The Federal Bureau of Investigation questioned Belinsky, cleared him of any implication, and prosecuted Penny. They found

her one evening in Trenton at 244 Hewitt Street in the living room
of Edward and Anna Belinsky.

"My mother," says Bo, "is a compassionate woman."

Two years later, Belinsky was sitting in a bar in Little Rock,
Arkansas. He got into conversation with a man wearing civilian
clothes. The man revealed that he was a general in the army re-
serves, and at one time had commanded the Dixie Division. He told
Bo how his wife had cleaned his bank account out one day of four
thousand dollars, left him and two children behind and disappeared. The man hardly seemed upset. He said his wife was now in
prison in Trenton. She had been cashing bad checks most of their
married life. She had, the general learned, taken up with some
ballplayer. In a moment of supreme honesty and humility, Belinsky
revealed that he was the party of the second part. The general never
even raised his voice. For the next two hours they drank to Penny.
Then Belinsky got up to leave.

"If this is any satisfaction to you, sir," said Bo, "we had a hell of
a time on your four thousand dollars."

Belinsky was discharged from the army in July of 1960 and joined
the Vancouver club of the Pacific Coast League. He got into shape
quickly, pitched well in relief, and for once seemed motivated.

"It was better than the army," said Belinsky, "and everyone knew
expansion was coming. There would be more jobs in the major
leagues."

The Vancouver club, managed by George Staller, had some good
young players. One of the best prospects was a huge black man
named Walter Bond. He was to be dead of leukemia before his
thirtieth birthday.

"You see a thing like that," said Bo, "and you know why I live each
day for today."

The Vancouver club was young and talented. They were a bunch
of free spirits, led the league in hotfoots, and stayed up late partying
and drinking in their rooms at the Blackstone Hotel on Granville
Avenue.

"The favorite hangout was an after-hours club called the Penthouse. It was a rough place, filled with whores. If I was with a whore

and some other whore made eyes at me, both of them would ad-
journ to the bathroom. One would come back with a hole in her
head from a bottle. One time I'm in there and I get set to leave and
I see that my coat is gone. Somebody tells me a guy who took it is
sitting across the street in the Peter Pan coffee shop. I walk across
the street with Howie Goss, one of the guys on our club. I see this
guy. He's acting like he's drunk. I just walk over nice and slow, grab
him by the back of his neck, move a dinner plate in front of him and
mash his face into it. Then I ask him if he has my coat. Just then his
partner walks over. I asked him, 'Where's my coat?' He says he
doesn't know anything about any coat. I tell him I want to see his
car. He says, 'What car?' Hell, he's carrying the goddamn keys in his
hand. I grab the keys, walk out, and pick up my coat. Then I go back
in. The guy says, 'You got your goddamn coat, now beat it.' I hit
him with my left hand flush on the side of his face. I propped him
up on the wall and then I left."

The next day Bo left for a road trip to Salt Lake City. He told the
manager, George Staller, he couldn't pitch on the trip. Staller called
him to his hotel room.

"Why can't you pitch?"

"I hurt my hand."

"How did it happen?"

"I was running," Bo said, "and I slipped in the outfield."

Just for that, Staller suspended Belinsky without pay.

"I'll always remember George for that. He was the third-base
coach of the Orioles when I pitched my no-hitter against them in
1962," Bo said. "I enjoyed watching him each inning."

Belinsky finished the 1960 season at Vancouver with a 1–3 mark.
Considering that he had to duck a bad-check charge, wasted six
months in the army, and "hurt his hand" while running in the
outfield, it wasn't that bad a season.

"At least," he says, "I survived without being sent to Saskatche-
wan. That's where the whores who got into trouble in that town
were sent. The cops would arrest them and instead of sending them
to jail would ship them on the railroad out to the plains. They got
off that train and were greeted by a few dozen boozed-up cowboys
who hadn't seen a girl in six long months. Now, that's what I call
having a bad season."

When anything goes wrong around here, Belinsky, you're the first one I suspect.

—PAUL RICHARDS

The Beaver Freaks

A gorgeous dark-haired, dark-eyed girl from Bogota, Colombia, won the Miss Universe pageant and was rewarded with a week in Miami at the McAllister Hotel in early March of 1961. The Baltimore Orioles trained in Miami. They stayed at the McAllister Hotel. Two of their young prospects were left-handers Steve Dalkowski and Bo Belinsky. The manager was Paul Richards.

Richards was a Texan, who had begun his baseball career as a seventeen-year-old infielder in the Brooklyn Dodgers organization. Like most hitters with a .227 lifetime average in baseball, Paul Richards had spent the next two decades proving that he was smarter than anyone else in the game. Baseball people generally recognized the taciturn Texan as one of the intellectual giants of the game despite the fact that he never managed a major league team to a pennant and never was the general manager of a team that won a pennant. Richards's stock in trade was his aloof, arrogant style, his ability to convince young players of his past successes, and his self-confident stubbornness.

In 1960, under Richards, the Orioles had suddenly developed

into a contending team. They were a game behind the Yankees in late September with an impressive young pitching staff led by Milt Pappas, Jack Fisher, Chuck Estrada, Jerry Walker, and Steve Barber. The pitching staff became known as the Baby Birds and excited all baseball. Most of the credit for their development went to Richards who took these young, strong-armed kids, taught them an off-speed pitch called the slip pitch, and made winners out of them. The fact that they were all under twenty-five and could throw bullets hardly seemed to matter when the accolades were tossed out.

Baltimore blew its chance at an upset pennant when they collapsed in a three-game series in Yankee Stadium, the first really big series of their young lives. The crucial play came in the very first of the three games when two young infielders, Ron Hansen and Brooks Robinson, collided under a popup and Hansen dropped it.

Richards was determined that such foolishness would not be repeated in 1961.

Belinsky and Dalkowski were determined that there would be more foolishness in 1961.

As fate and the gods would have it, Belinsky was assigned to room 812 in the McAllister Hotel when he reported for spring training. That night, in the very next room, 814, preparing for a joyful and triumphant tour of Miami, was Miss Bogota, Miss Colombia, and Miss Universe, all wrapped up in one delightful bundle, size 36-24-36. Bo was ready to fall in love until he got a look at her mother, a strong, moon-shaped, somber-looking woman, whose mission in life seemed only to be to keep the animals of South and North America away from her pure-bred, well-brought-up daughter. The hassle was too much for Bo. He never bothered.

"There were so many pretty girls in Miami that it didn't matter to me. I really didn't care. I saw her in the hall a couple of times and smiled to her. Her mother was right there, so she didn't even smile back. I had really forgotten about her."

Steve Dalkowski and Steve Barber, who had played together at Aberdeen and Pensacola with Belinsky, made a date to join him for dinner. Dalkowski showed up at room 812 just as Miss Universe was leaving 814. Dalkowski almost passed out with excitement.

"Bo, Bo, for crissakes, did you see the broad in the next room?"

"Oh, Juanita, sure. Nice, heh?"

"Are you getting any of that?"

"I'm too busy."

"Too busy? Bo, you gotta be out of your mind. She's the greatest thing I've seen since I've been ten years old."

"How would you know? You haven't seen her!"

Dalkowski had to admit that the passing glance in the hall really couldn't be considered a close scrutiny.

"God, when there's beaver like that next door I gotta see it, I just gotta. How the hell am I going to catch her."

Barber, Belinsky, and Dalkowski hatched a magnificent plot. Dalkowski was to be the main man but all three and the rest of their teammates would enjoy the activity equally.

Dinner was postponed and Dalkowski raced downstairs to the maintenance room of the hotel. He slipped past the unlocked door of the room and slipped out with a drill. He raced back up to Belinsky's room. Then he went to work. He began drilling holes in the wall. The holes were large enough for an eye to rest comfortably upon and see everything in the next room. Dalkowski drilled twenty holes in the wall, all at different levels, the entire length of the wall. He left nothing to chance.

"I can see everything in there," Dalkowski announced. "Now we just have to wait for her to come back."

Assuming that Miss Universe went out to dinner with her mother, the three players canceled their plans for a large steak dinner and settled for a hamburger in the hotel coffee shop. Then they returned to Belinsky's room, watched television, and waited. Shortly before ten o'clock they heard footsteps coming down the hall and some light chatter in Spanish. They moved into position. They were not disappointed. Miss Universe immediately took off her shoes, took off her earrings, and pulled her dress over her head. Her mother sat clothed in a chair and turned on the television. Barber and Belinsky watched and laughed. Dalkowski panted. The mother moved into the bathroom, undressed, and came out with a saggy pair of pajamas on. Miss Universe sat at the dressing table, combed her long, dark hair endlessly and seemed to be asking the mirror who was the fairest of them all. A mirror would have to be a nut not to say, "You are, sweetheart."

The next afternoon, Dalkowski described his evening activity to the rest of the players on the Orioles. By ten o'clock the next night, a dozen Oriole players had gathered in room 812 to socialize with Bo. One of them carried a flashlight so that his beaver shooting would not end at lights out.

"She creeps into bed, turns out the light and rolls over. This one guy fires the light into her room. He's moving it around just as she rolls over toward our side. When the light hits her, she lets out a scream. Now we know we are in trouble."

Belinsky, Dalkowski, Barber, and friends disappeared out of Bo's room and took off into the Miami night. They were back just before the midnight curfew. Several notes were in Belinsky's mailbox asking him to call manager Paul Richards.

Miss Colombia had called the hotel security and in the matter of minutes a full investigation was on. The security men unlocked Bo's door and quickly discovered the peepholes. They immediately called Richards who was chagrined at the spectacle. The hotel wanted compensation and they wanted the culprits arrested.

"Miss Colombia was an invited guest of the United States," says Bo. "It looked like we were in the middle of an international incident."

Belinsky, Barber, and Dalkowski returned to their separate rooms. The phone rang and Bo answered in a sleepy voice. It hardly mattered that he was fully clothed. He thought he might convince whoever was on the phone that he had been sleeping quietly all night.

"This is Richards. I want you down here immediately."

Then he hung up. It was too early in spring training to be shipped out, so Bo knew it could be only one thing. Miss Colombia had squealed.

Belinsky sauntered into Richards's room a few minutes later. Dalkowski and Barber were already there.

"Now I'm going to get to the bottom of this," Richards said. "When anything goes wrong around here, Belinsky, you're the first one I suspect."

"What are you talking about, Skip?"

"The holes, who drilled the holes in your room?"

"Holes? What holes?"

"The holes in your wall."

"Oh, those holes."

The security men stood off to a side. Richards had promised them he would handle the matter, find the guilty party, and make him responsible for the act.

"Were you looking in those holes at the next room?"

"I don't know, I might have. I forget. I just got back from dinner."

"Did you drill the holes before you left?"

"Skip, I'm telling you the truth. I didn't drill a single hole."

Now Richards turned to Dalkowski.

"Did you drill the holes?"

"Uhh, yes, I think maybe I did."

"How many holes did you drill?"

"Oh, I don't know, maybe two or three."

"How many?"

"Oh, I don't know, Skip, maybe eight or ten."

"Did you look through those holes at the girl next door?"

"No, Skip, I didn't do that."

The veins in Richards's neck were standing out. He looked about eight feet tall as he stared down at Dalkowski.

"Why in the hell would you drill holes in a wall into a girl's room if you didn't intend to look through them?"

"Oh, I don't know, Skip," said Dalkowski. "I just like to drill holes."

The club paid the hotel for damages and Belinsky and Dalkowski were shipped to Little Rock. Barber stayed with the Orioles. He was a better pitcher than either of the other two.

"I never knew why they picked on me," says Bo, his eyes all innocent and charming. "They think because the holes were in my room that I had something to do with it. If they were mad at every guy on that club who had been in my room to see Miss Universe they would have to have a new team that season."

Belinsky excuses girl watching—beaver shooting, as ball-players like to call it—as a manly everyday sport for young, virile athletes.

"It's harmless and it's fun," he says, "and it sure does help to pass the time. There are a lot of boring, lonely hours in baseball."

Belinsky says he remembers only one time when anybody ever got hurt from beaver shooting. "Not really hurt," he says, "just sort of out of his mind."

He was playing with Pensacola in 1959. There was a young outfielder on the club from Shreveport, Louisiana.

"A dull guy, really," says Bo. "All he ever did was stand around the lobby and shoot beaver. He had just gotten married and claimed he was straight. Only his wife could turn him on. In fact, he used to brag about how she never wore pants and what a hot number she was. But he still loved to look. He got so wild he bought himself a beaver-shooting kit for road trips. He got a heavy pulley and some heavy rope and use to boost himself up the hotel door with the rope and pulley so he could shoot beaver or watch other guys in action. He was a real beaver freak, goofy over it. That's why we were glad when he got his. Nobody deserved it more."

The beaver freak had decided to drill a few holes in the back wall of the dugout in the park in Pensacola. The dugout was slightly elevated and the back of it rested against the bottom of the front row of seats. It gave players a perfect vantage point for any legs that might be sitting behind the dugout.

"This had been going on for a few days," Bo said. "He would drill a hole, look through at the people behind, then fill up the hole with a cork so no rain or wind would come through it. This one day, just before the game started, he pulls out the corks and makes his rounds. Then all of a sudden he goes crazy. He catches a set of legs without pants on. He begins to quiver and shake. Then he calls everybody over for a look. The team runs on the field and they play the national anthem. He is still in the dugout shooting beaver. Then he finally runs out adjusting his sunglasses as if that was the reason he didn't go right on the field. He's out in right field and the game starts. Everybody on our bench is taking turns during the top half of that inning looking through the holes in the dugout. I must admit, she was a hell of a sight."

The inning ended quickly and now the right fielder raced in toward the dugout for a second chance. He was coming in hard when he got just inside the infield dirt. Then he looked up and saw a pretty girl waving to him from the stands. He almost swallowed his glove.

He had been looking at his wife's legs through a hole in the dugout and so had everybody else.

"He had forgotten she was coming to the game that day," Bo said. "I don't think I ever heard him mention anything about shooting beaver again."

After being sent out by the Orioles, Belinsky considered quitting baseball again before reporting to Little Rock. He was now twenty-four years old, was not getting any better as a pitcher, and had little motivation for the game.

"I guess the only reason I went to Little Rock was because I had nothing else to do and this was a new town," he said.

But the Orioles management still had hopes for him. He had given them some headaches off the field, but he showed promise on the field. He was a left-handed pitcher in an organization that was hungry for left-handed pitchers. He seemed to be developing a strikeout pitch as he matured and that year wound up leading the Southern League in strikeouts with 182 in 174 innings. His old pal Paul Richards had left the Orioles on August 31, 1961, to become the general manager of the new Houston Colt .45s. Luman Harris, a low key, soft-spoken man, who had managed Bo's instructional league team at Clearwater in 1959, finished the season as the new Baltimore field manager. Belinsky had gotten along well with him. There were some good signs all around. Belinsky finished the season with a 9-10 mark and a 3.72 earned run average.

"Little Rock didn't have a very good club that year. Most of the good players were already up in the bigs," he said. "I probably could have won a few more games with better defense. I also missed two weeks of the season. I was laying low in Hot Springs when I should have been pitching."

Belinsky's enforced summer vacation in Hot Springs began one night in a downtown club in Little Rock.

"It was one of those real small joints," he said. "Supposed to hold about a hundred people and they have three hundred in there on a busy Saturday night."

Belinsky decided to fight the crowd this one Saturday night. He was with Bob Walls, a young outfielder on the Little Rock team.

"We needed the recreation," Bo says. "We had just come off a road trip. In that league it wasn't easy. It was all those goddamn bus rides, sixteen, eighteen hours at a time, no food, just bouncing on the bus. That league ruined more kidneys than anything I had ever heard of."

Walls and Belinsky marched into the club shortly before midnight.

"We stood out right away," Bo says, "we were the only guys in the joint with shirts, ties and jackets. It was a real casual southern-fried-chicken place with all these creeps in sweaty T-shirts dancing with the broads. At first I felt out of place, but after I looked at some of the girls I figured I belonged."

Walls had only one problem in the small, smoke-filled room. He couldn't see.

"He wore contact lenses. He was blind without his lenses, really blind. When he took them out at night in the room he would walk into the door when he got up in the middle of the night. I could never get any sleep with that guy around. In this place, with the smoke and the dirt and the bad lights, he really was dying. His eyes started burning so he takes out his contact lenses."

"Hey, Bo," said Walls. "I can't see a thing. When a nice broadie passes by let me know, so I'll ask her to dance. I don't want no dogs."

Belinsky and Walls were dancing most of the night away with the Southern belles, all peaceful, calm, and loving.

"These tables are real crowded, you see, and the dance floor is jammed. So I'm just about leading Walls back and forth on the floor. He's so blind he can't even get a broadie back to her seat. Now he decides to go to the bathroom. That's where all the trouble starts."

Walls gets up to walk toward the men's room and brushes into a guy sitting at the next table with a pock-marked friend. The friend leaps from his chair, grabs Walls's arm, and forces him back into his chair. The other guy moves next to Bo.

"I know you guys are Chicago hoods," the pock-marked hero announces. "I want you to clear out of this place and now."

To emphasize his point, he reaches into his pocket, pulls out a switch-blade knife and opens it up under the table. The knife sits inches away from Walls's balls.

"I'll tell you," said Bo. "I really didn't know what the hell to do. I was angry that we were getting handled by these creeps, but I was worried about Walls's balls. If I made one move that guy might have sliced him up right there."

Belinsky moved calmly and deliberately. He placed his hands on the table and began talking gently to his new friends.

"Hey, look," said Bo, "you have us all wrong. We're just a couple of guys looking for a dance. We didn't come here for any trouble. We just want to have a good time. If you don't want us in your place, we'll just move. Right, Bob?"

Walls, knowing the exact location of the knife to the inch, just held still and stared at his assailant. He expected Bo to make some kind of a move. He wanted to be ready to make one of his own. He would let Bo do the talking.

"Look, I've got my hands on the table. I don't have anything. Let us just get up and walk out quietly. We don't want any trouble."

Belinsky smiled pleasantly and everybody relaxed for an instant. That was all the time Bo needed. The left-hander quickly raised his left forearm under his man's chin and caught him at the Adam's apple.

"His eyes began rolling in his head like one of those kewpie dolls. I thought they were going to pop right out of the sockets. His partner never moved. He sat open-mouthed. Then I caught him with a right hand and knocked him off his chair. The knife dropped on the floor and we got up and ran the hell out of there."

Belinsky never saw his attackers again. He thinks he would recognize one of them if he did.

"I might not remember his face," Bo says, "but I would know him from the size of his Adam's apple. I believe that fellow will have an esophagus problem the rest of his life."

Belinsky immediately notified the club that he had been attacked and had responded in kind. It was suggested the ballplayers journey to Hot Springs for some soothing baths while tempers cooled.

Hot Springs is a resort town where millionaires congregate for sun, baths, fun, girls, cards and pool. It was Bo's kind of town. He spent ten days there, mostly in his shorts, ready for any of the aforementioned activities.

"It was a town where you had to have bread," he said. "You didn't see many young people, just old, bald-headed guys with fat bellies and young broadies. These old guys all wanted to go out in John Garfield style, banging a broad, getting a heart attack on the spot and being pried loose with a smile on their faces. I did see a couple of them go out but it wasn't quite that way."

Belinsky was in one pool game that he will remember forever. It convinced him that nine ball was a young man's game. He was engaged in the sport with this chubby industrialist from Arizona who was with a tall, blonde beauty. While she sunned herself at the pool, Belinsky and the money man got into a friendly game of pocket billiards.

"He could play," Belinsky said, "but not as good as he thought. It's a hell of a lot easier hustling a rich guy than a poor guy. Rich guys put up money faster and have more pride. They never believe they are beaten until you go for a freezeout. We had just started playing, maybe I was a couple of hundred ahead and we're playing nine ball. I've cleaned the table out and now I'm ready for the nine ball. It's a tough shot, deep in the corner against the rail but it's no problem. I know I'll make it. I chalk up and bend over the table. This guy begins coughing and I stand up. Who the hell can shoot with a guy coughing blood on the table? I'm still behind the nine ball and I'm ready to sink it and pick up my money if this bird is going to spend the rest of the night coughing. Now he falls on the table, brushes the nine ball with his hand and goes down on the floor. Now I'm figuring maybe I've been had. This might be the greatest con ever. They call the cops, an ambulance comes and takes him away. Later I find out he's D.O.A. I couldn't help but laugh at that one. He died but he beat me out of the two hundred anyway."

Like most ballplayers, Belinsky handles himself with poise and skill across a card table. Except for sex and baseball itself, ballplayers spend more time playing and talking about cards than any other activity. They play just about everything for high stakes. Rookies have been known to lose most of their salaries playing with stars and trying to keep up with the price of the game. Poker is the clubhouse favorite, played on a training table or a foot locker, with coaches, managers, and sportswriters sometimes joining in. The stakes become high enough in some cases to disrupt the efficiency of the team's operation. High-stake card games may have as much influence on the happiness of a ballplayer's marriage as extramarital sex. Extramarital sex is a proven, harmless pastime for most players: what the little woman doesn't know doesn't hurt her. But card losses are a lot harder to hide. Johnny Superstar has an awful tough time convincing the old lady his pay is a thousand dollars short because he was fined for not running out a ground ball.

Card games are played in the clubhouse, in the hotel rooms, on the airplanes, where the nonplayers are cursed for having to disrupt the game by going to the bathroom, and on the team bus. The sight of a half dozen handsome young athletes playing poker in the nude in the middle of a baseball clubhouse is a scene to behold. Some teams specialize in other games, hearts, whist, some pinochle and gin. Always for money, always for a lot of money, though the scores are usually kept on paper and money is never publicly passed.

Most managers, when questioned about the games, excuse them as a harmless diversion. "You don't see any money, do you?" they say. Some managers, for their own reasons, actually ban card games in the clubhouse. On those clubs, players keep games running for days on road trips. The card game is interrupted only to go to the ball park and resumed immediately after the ball game. Sometimes a player gets four hits in a game and is grumpy. Sometimes a player strikes out three times and hits into a double play and is all smiles. The game in the hotel may be going a lot differently.

"I've always played cards," says Bo. "It passes the time. And if you win a few bucks it passes it even more quickly."

In Hot Springs Belinsky played in some of the biggest card games he had ever seen.

"It was mostly gin there," he said. "They played Hollywood, twenty-five cents a point. You could go for a bundle that way. This one guy was playing and he was having a hot night with the cards. Everything he picked up was perfect. He didn't make a wrong move. He's got this one guy blitzed in two games. The other guy was beginning to sweat. He was getting white as the game went on. Now this hot guy picks up a card, smiles, discards, and announces, 'Gin!' His opponent collapses right on the table with the cards tightly held in his hand.

" 'Gin, gin,' the hot guy is yelling. 'How many points does he have in his hand? It's a blitz, he can't do this to me, he can't lie down. I got gin.' "

The stricken man was pushed off the table and settled on the floor. Somebody put a jacket under his head. He still held the cards in his right hand. The house security men rushed over. A crowd gathered.

"I don't care what's happening to him," the guy is shouting. "I gotta see his cards. I gotta see how many points he has. I blitzed him, I gotta be paid."

"He was a wild man," Bo said. "A half hour after they took the dead man away he's still running around the room, yelling he blitzed the guy. He's holding the dead guy's cards in his hands. He's screaming for his money. I'll tell you, some of these guys took their card games seriously."

Belinsky didn't take anything seriously. He enjoyed his vacation in Hot Springs and rejoined the Little Rock club in Atlanta, Georgia, for the start of a long road trip.

While Belinsky was playing in Little Rock that summer of 1961, things were happening three thousand miles away that would have a profound effect on his young life.

As far back as the early 1950s, baseball owners began envisioning new horizons in the far west. The population centers were shifting and the airplane made travel west easily accessible. Walter O'Malley, the owner and president of the Brooklyn Dodgers, one of baseball's most successful franchises, began exploring the possibility of moving his franchise to California. The Dodgers played in historic, romantic Ebbets Field. They had outgrown the facility, and O'Malley envisioned a massive new publicly built ball park in Brooklyn or, better yet, in the virgin territory of Los Angeles. When the city politicians stuttered and stammered on the question of a new Brooklyn park on Atlantic Avenue in a depressed, mostly black part of the borough, O'Malley moved quickly to solidify his hold on Los Angeles. Through complex machinations, with driving determination, O'Malley acquired territorial rights to Los Angeles and cleverly convinced the city and county to build him a magnificent new ball park in an area called Chavez Ravine in a striking setting high above the Los Angeles hills. He needed one more thing—California competition; and he convinced his New York competitor Horace Stoneham, whose New York Giants played in the withering Polo Grounds, to go west with him.

In 1958 the Brooklyn Dodgers and the New York Giants died of a malingering illness. In their place were born the Los Angeles Dodgers and the San Francisco Giants.

Warren Giles, the chubby, glad-handing, ineffective president of the National League reacted stoically to the news of the move west, "Who needs New York?" Mayor Robert F. Wagner did. He created a committee led by an aggressive attorney named Bill Shea to explore the possibility of moving an old franchise to New York or creating a new one. With Shea's drive and political connections, baseball opened its doors to all new territories. What had started as the move to new territory became an open-door expansion policy. Owners, who had stubbornly protected the rights to franchise territory, were forced by congressional study to open all territory in the United States to potential franchises for fear of congressional antitrust action.

A new league, called the Continental League, was established on paper. One of the teams was the New York Mets. When the paper league crumpled in a paper heap, the Mets were accepted into the National League along with the Houston Colt .45s. The era of expansion was upon baseball.

The American League, under former Boston shortstop Joe Cronin, had been angered ever since 1958 by the move west by O'Malley and Stoneham. The territory was so attractive that they had envisioned an even split with the National League getting Los Angeles and the American getting San Francisco. But O'Malley, too slick for his opposition, ended that idea when he came west with Stoneham in his pocket.

Now the Continental League began making noise. The American

League decided to get back at the Nationals for stealing Los Angeles and San Francisco. Baseball people are that way. At the winter meetings in November of 1960, Joe Cronin stepped out of a locked hotel room suite and announced to waiting reporters, "Gentlemen, we have decided to expand immediately. The American League will play with ten teams in 1961. Two new franchises have been accepted as equal members of the league, Minnesota and Los Angeles."

In a triangular move, the ancient Washington franchise, under the Griffith family, which had included such brilliant stars as Walter Johnson, Bucky Harris, and Joe Cronin himself, moved to Minnesota. A new franchise in Washington was created. The third team was Los Angeles. Bill Veeck and Hank Greenberg, who had promoted so successfully in Cleveland and Chicago together, had investigated the Los Angeles territory for the American League. Unhappily for baseball, the American League's owners found Veeck's witty, antiestablishment style (he had sent a midget to bat for the St. Louis Browns wearing uniform number ⅛) and Greenberg's directness too uncomfortable. They awarded the franchise to Bob Reynolds, a former Stanford All-American football player, and his partner, Gene Autry, the singing cowboy star.

The Los Angeles Angels were to play in O'Malley's ball park in Chavez Ravine. Fred Haney, who had managed Milwaukee to two pennants in 1957 and 1958, was named the team's general manager. After Casey Stengel, who had been fired by the Yankees in 1960 for being seventy years old, turned down a request to manage the team, Bill Rigney was given the job.

The Los Angeles Angels, led by youngsters Albie Pearson, Lee Thomas, Leon Wagner, Ken McBride, and Eli Grba, and veteran pitchers Tom Morgan and Art Fowler, won sixty-seven games, lost ninety-five and finished in eighth place, ahead of the new Washington franchise and the established Kansas City franchise. They would very likely be even better in 1962.

Late in 1961 the Angels dispatched a scout by the name of Tuffy Hashem, a pleasant, mild-mannered gentleman, to search through the prospects in Triple-A baseball for a possible draft selection by the Angels. Hashem covered several thousand miles in August and September, made charts on hundreds of players, talked to dozens of managers, watched hundreds of games in tired, old ball parks. He arrived back in Los Angeles late in September, met with Haney, Rigney, and the other scouts several times. He was invited by the Angels to watch the World Series in Cincinnati with the New York Yankees and evaluate some of the talent that might be made available. When the Series was over he flew back to Los Angeles and sat down one more time with Haney and Rigney before going home for the winter.

"One name keeps cropping up in my conversations with the managers and coaches in the minors," Hashem said. "I've seen the kid pitch twice. I think he's a prospect. He's a left-hander and he might help us. I think he's worth a look."

"What's his name?" asked Haney.

"Belinsky," said Hashem. "Robert Belinsky. They call him Bo."

"I think I've heard the name. Was with Little Rock, right?"

"That's right, we had reports on him last year. The Orioles liked him, but they didn't bring him up because he missed most of the 1960 season in service. He's got a good fast ball, very good control for a left-hander, and throws a dinky curve."

"How old is he?"

"He's twenty-four, I believe. I still think we should take a chance on him in the draft."

"Why hasn't anybody picked him up beofre this? Does he have a bad arm?"

"No, not at all, very strong, wiry kid, can pitch in turn without any problems."

"Do you know anything else about him?"

"Well," said Hashem, "you hear the same things about him when you ask around. You say Bo Belinsky, they all smile, look at you like you are nuts, and tell you, 'Yeah, I know Bo. He's got a million-dollar arm and a ten-cent head.' "

I'll make an exception for you. He can leave with you. The parrot is clean.

—*VENEZUELA'S MINISTER OF HEALTH*

The First Word You Learn Is Adios

Roger Maris had hit sixty-one home runs for the New York Yankees in 1961 to break Babe Ruth's single season mark of sixty. The controversy over the record raged most of the summer as Maris was compiling a home run record in a 162-game baseball season while Ruth did it in 1927 in a 154-game schedule. Said Maris, "A season's a season." Said Commissioner of Baseball Ford C. Frick, "It must be marked with an asterisk." On Monday, October 9, 1961, while the Yankees were ending the Series and Maris was answering the same questions over and over again in the clubhouse at Cincinnati's Crosley Field, Mrs. Anna Belinsky answered the ring at the front door of her Trenton home.

The letter from the office of the Baltimore Orioles looked important. Mrs. Belinsky called Bo at Russo's.

"Telephone, Bo. Your old lady."

"Another crazie broadie has landed at my house."

Mrs. Belinsky explained to Bo that an important-looking letter had just arrived from the Baltimore Orioles.

"Open it and read it to me," Bo said.

She began slowly, "The Baltimore Orioles have assigned your contract outright to the Rochester Club of the International League effective this date."

That was the final blow for Bo. He had been pitching professionally for six years. He had just completed a reasonably successful season at Little Rock, led the league in strikeouts, and certainly deserved a chance to make the Orioles in spring training in 1962. Now he was assigned again to another minor league club, would not go to spring training with the Orioles, and saw no more point in continuing this charade.

That evening he called Harry Dalton, the farm director of the Orioles.

"Harry," he said, "I'm quitting. What the hell do I want to go to Rochester for?"

"Don't be so hasty. Give it one more shot. We still might ask you to come to spring training. We have to examine our roster a little more closely next month."

Belinsky was fed up with what he considered a runaround. Despite some fairly impressive pitching, the Orioles obviously did not consider him a major league prospect. It wasn't his arm they didn't like, it was his head.

"Look, Bo, you have a good fast ball, good curve. What I think you need is another pitch. Would you be willing to pitch winter ball? I might be able to get you a job. If you don't make our ball club, maybe somebody else will pick you up in the drafts. Several clubs have inquired about you."

Belinsky said he would pitch winter ball for the right team and the right money. Two days later Dalton called back and said the Pompero Rum team in Caracas, Venezuela, wanted him. They would pay him $1600 a month, round trip expenses, and arrange for reasonable rent on a pensione in downtown Caracas.

"It was more money than I had ever made in a baseball," Belinsky said. "The Caracas people had heard of me, knew I could pitch, and knew that I would put people in the stands. It sounded like a good deal for them and for me. Besides, I hadn't made that South American scene yet and with a good sunburn on my dark skin I could easily pass for a local and make it with all the dancing señoritas."

Four days later Belinsky arrived in Caracas and began getting in shape to pitch in the Venezuelan League, whose season had already been under way for nearly a month.

At the same time, in Los Angeles, the Angels had been working on their draft choices for the baseball winter meetings scheduled for November 27, 1961, in Tampa, Florida. They had made a list of their twenty top choices in order of preference. That was the order in which they would draft if the players named were still available when the Angels' turn to pick came up.

At ten o'clock in the morning of November 28, 1961, in the main ballroom of the Tampa Terrace Hotel, the roll of clubs began with the Washington Senators, the expansion team which had tied for last in 1961 with Kansas City and had won the coin toss for the first draft. For twenty-thousand dollars they could draft any player in the country off any minor league team.

George Selkirk, a tall, handsome, gray-haired man, who had been babe Ruth's successor in right field for the Yankees, was now the general manager of the Washington Senators. He stood up when Washington's name was called and announced, "The Washington club drafts player Ken Hamlin, shortstop, from the Toronto roster."

There was a great deal of murmuring in the room. One of the favorite pastimes of baseball people in the winter is guessing what the other guys will do. Hamlin was a mild surprise. He had been a weak-hitting infielder for the Angels in 1961 with a .209 average. He had been assigned to the Toronto club over the winter and was now being grabbed off by Washington. Baseball people are not known for their unerring evaluation of talent.

Philadelphia was next, drafting Billy Consolo from the Vancouver roster. Another marvelous choice. In two years he would be running a barbershop. Kansas City was third. They picked outfielder Gino Cimoli. Now here was a fine choice. Cimoli had been with the Dodgers, was as good-looking a ballplayer as had ever put on a uniform, and had gained everlasting fame as a member of the Pittsburgh Pirates by needling the Yankees after his team had beat them in a wild-hitting Series in 1960 by saying, "They made all the runs and we won all the games." Then he promptly dumped a huge bowl of potato salad over the head of Pittsburgh Mayor Joseph Barr.

When Los Angeles got its turn next, Fred Haney stood up and announced, "The Los Angeles club drafts outfielder Marlan Coughtry from the Seattle club." Then he sat down with a satisfied smile on his face. Coughtry was the first man on the Los Angeles list. He rewarded such faith by managing to hit .182 for the Angels in eleven games before being traded away.

The draft droned on most of the morning. When the Angels got their second turn they selected infielder Felix Torres. At twelve-twenty-five with most of the room empty and lunch dates being kept all over Tampa, Los Angeles was called again. Sixty-two minor league players had already been selected by the twenty major league teams. Haney stood up, looked at a printed sheet in front of him and announced in a gravelly voice, "The Los Angeles club drafts pitcher Robert Belinsky from the Rochester roster." Haney turned to manager Bill Rigney and said, "Let's go eat."

In Venezuela, unaware that he had just been given a free ticket to the wonderful world of Hollywood, Bo Belinsky worked on his new pitch.

"I had a fast ball, a curve and a little changeup," he says. "The only off-pitch I had at the time was a spitter. It wasn't a very good pitch for me because I couldn't control it like some of the good ones."

The spitter is an illegal pitch in baseball, outlawed in the 1920s in baseball's quest for cleanliness and approval after the infamous Black Sox scandal almost wrecked the game, and used ever since only by its most skilled practitioners. Some of the better spitball pitchers in recent times included Gaylord Perry of the Giants, Don Drysdale of the Dodgers, Jack Fisher of the Mets, Dean Chance of the Angels, Belinsky, and Lew Burdette.

"Hal Newhouser, my hero, taught it to me in 1959," says Bo. "He tried to teach it to all the kid pitchers in the Orioles system. Some picked it up and some didn't. Every pitcher has fooled with it at certain times. Only a few have ever thrown it in a game because it's a dangerous pitch if it isn't controlled. If it doesn't drop, it just hangs up there like a balloon and the hitters knock it out of the park. The best I ever saw was Lew Burdette's. When we were together in Philadelphia in 1965 he really worked with me on it. He got the spit from his mouth and cupped the ball in his palm. He did a lot of other things, just as an act, like rubbing his forehead, rubbing his uniform shirt, rubbing his cap, fooling with his pants, but somewhere along the line, despite all the other moves, he had simply spit on the first two fingers of his right hand. Then boom. The balls falls off a table and some hitter strikes out screaming.''

Belinsky's favorite artist at work was Whitey Ford of the Yankees, considered by many to be the best pitcher in baseball in his time. The tough managers in baseball generally agreed that if their life depended on winning one game, they would want Whitey Ford to pitch it for them.

"Whitey specialized in the mud ball," said Bo. "He would spit on his fingers and then lean down to pick up the resin bag from the ground. He'd flip the resin bag into his palm and pick up dirt with the fingers. When I was with the Angels and pitching against the Yankees in the Stadium, I loved to watch Whitey strike out our last hitter in an inning with his mud ball. Then Elston Howard would roll the ball back to the mound. I would go out there, pick up the ball and see this big wad of mud glued to the ball. My first pitch to the first Yankee hitter was usually a beauty. If they fouled it off and I had to get a new ball, I was immediately in trouble."

In Venezuela, Belinsky worked quickly to get into shape. He knew he would not be paid the glorious salary of $1600 a month very long if he wasn't able to pitch quickly. Five days after he arrived he was told he would pitch.

"I can't," he protested. "I'm not in shape. I need a week more to get ready."

"Tomorrow," said the manager, "you are pitching."

Belinsky took the ball as ordered the next day and began warming up. He had nothing. His arm still hurt from the inactivity of the last month and the quick return to action. He couldn't throw hard. So he threw easily.

"I figured I might get by a few innings with soft stuff. I began turning the ball over with my wrist and it broke away nicely. I did it a couple of more times. Then the game started and I used a slow curve to left-handed hitters and this new pitch, the screwball, to right-handers. That pitch was made for me. No pitch and no pitcher were ever better made for each other."

In fact from then on, Bo was known in plenty of places as the screwballing left-hander. His screwball became an instant success. He was a hero almost from his first start. He won his opener 4-1. Then he pitched a shutout. Then he won 7-1. The crowds began coming out to see the American screwball pitcher. Then he started getting stronger as his arm came around and now he was throwing a hard fast-ball to go with that screwball. In his fourth game he struck out seventeen batters. The major league record was eighteen.

"That made me a superstar," said Bo. "After that it was a fishcake."

Belinsky was a celebrity in Caracas. Wherever he went small boys and pretty girls followed. He moved out of his pensione into an expensive apartment. His name was in large letters almost daily in the local newspapers. Businessmen, lawyers, engineers, industrialists came to the park to be introduced to the new hero.

"One day I met this guy, Lou Vega, one of the richest men in the country. He had been a doctor and had been involved for years with research in leprosy. Now he was into a lot of other things, mostly things that made a lot of money. We only played four days a week down there so I had a lot of time to go on trips with him into the jungles and the Amazon. On one trip he caught a monkey and we took it back to my apartment. He was a funky monkey and was a real ham. I had this pad with a large balcony. He would go out there and do flips all over the railings. He could draw a crowd just by doing a couple of back flips over the railing. What he really loved was looking at himself in the mirror. He used to break himself up. He would race over to the table, jump up on it, look in the mirror, start playing with himself and laughing like hell."

Belinsky also acquired a multi-colored parrot on one of his excursions into the jungle. He named the parrot Loretto.

"When I was ready to go back to the States I wanted to take Loretto with me," Bo said. The health people wouldn't allow it. I made a couple of phone calls to friends and we got a clearance. The guy said he would make an exception for me after he examined Loretto. He took him away for a day, brought him back, and said he was clean. Hell, I got the papers to prove it. He still lives with my folks now in Trenton."

Caracas, a cosmopolitan city, was Bo's style. There were Germans, French, Canadians, Mexicans, Danes, Swedes, and Indians throughout Caracas. Many gathered daily to sip wine at the outdoor cafes, take the sun, and drink champagne and eat caviar.

"Once a week," said Bo, "I'd pick up the tab for a champagne party. We'd take a whole cafe, get twenty guys and twenty broadies, and have ourselves a ball. They were all groovy people, students, tourists, businessmen, everything. We'd get some of the local musicians to play for us and have a hell of a time."

During one champagne party, a mild, thin, sensitive-looking young man with glasses, walked by the cafe. He watched Bo dance for a while and then asked if he could sit down and join in.

"His name was Jerry Rogers from some tall town in Nebraska. He had come to Venezuela on one of those YMCA-sponsored tours. This was a free day on the tour and he had wandered downtown with his little camera. When he sat down I gave him a glass of champagne."

"No sir, thank you very much."

"Well, hell, if you are not going to join in on the fun, there's no use sitting here."

"Well, I'll take a little sip then."

Rogers sipped and sipped and sipped. Soon he was dancing with some of the dark-eyed beauties. That night he lost his camera in another cafe, and his virginity in another apartment.

"He was beautiful, said Bo. "He came to our parties every week for about a month. Then he didn't show up. I thought his tour had gone back to the states. That wasn't it. One of the girls told me he had met some rich señorita, became her stud, and settled in the hills near Caracas."

Venezuela was in the midst of great political turmoil when Belinsky pitched down there in 1961. The strong military government was having trouble with a rebellious Castro-type movement that was sweeping the country. Anti-American feeling was running high from both sides of the South American political spectrum. One of Venezuela's *ex-presidentes* had left the country suddenly one night as tension increased.

"I was going out with his girl friend," said Bo. "She had inherited his car when he left. It was one of those glass-topped jobs with bullet-proof windows and metal sides. I think they are made especially for South American politicians and come off an assembly line by the hundreds. All the bigs shots down there have them."

Belinsky was riding down the Sabana Grande, the main thoroughfare in Caracas, one evening when a small truck filled with soldiers pulled up. The *presidente*'s ex-girl friend was driving. Bo was in the passenger seat in the front. Guards holding machine guns surrounded the car and examined the plates.

"I'm a ballplayer, an American, Belinsky," he smiled. "You know, Belinsky, screwball left-hander——"

"Papers."

One of the soldiers was using his machine gun barrel as a pointer. Belinsky thought his finger would do.

"I pull out my wallet and hold it out in front of me. The guy lifts it out the window of the car with the end of the gun. If you think that didn't scare hell out of me. . . ."

There was some excited conversation among the guards, a flashlight examination of Belinsky, and then finally, angrily, one of the soldiers motioned for the girl to drive on. Belinsky sat back in his seat and muttered to himself and a guard looked at him angrily and then smiled. He made a pitching motion with his left hand while his right held firmly to his gun. "Bas-a-ball," he said. "Adios," said Belinsky.

Belinsky pitched and won the next night and then took off into the jungles of the Amazon for a weekend rest. He went with some oilmen who introduced him into some native culture.

Belinsky said the chewing of leaves for medicinal purposes was as commonplace as breathing.

"I tried it," he says, "I'll try anything. I'm not a user of drugs, but I don't want to be ignorant of anything. I've tasted LSD, tried all the hard stuff, smoked pot. Pot doesn't do anything for me; it's like a downer. I don't like it."

Belinsky said greenies, the green-colored pep pills distributed in all baseball clubhouses, were used extensively by most pitchers he knew in his career.

"If you're a pitcher and you take a greenie, you'll blow it by pitching. Some days you just can't get your body going. The manager gives you the ball and says, 'Here, pitch.' He doesn't ask you if you have a headache or stayed up late the night before. So a greenie gets the juices going. In baseball you have to do your job today. You can't worry about *mañana*. If you don't win, you're gone. The reason so many guys are popping greenies is because they need that extra lift."

Belinsky came back refreshed from his rest in the jungle and resumed pitching.

"I knew it was better to pitch in town than to pitch in the jungle. Out there they showed me one clearing where they used to play some softball. They told me one story about the time a guy hit a ball into the brush and the outfielder went into the trees to retrieve it. Three days later they discovered his body. The jaguars had been waiting behind the outfield to have him for lunch."

Things weren't that dangerous in town but they were still pretty active. Rumors of new American-backed invasions of Cuba, and against other Central and South American countries sympathetic to Castro, filled the air.

"People in Caracas really took all of that revolutionary stuff in stride," said, Bo. "Unless they were getting shot at they tended to disregard anybody else getting shot at. One day we were having our weekly champagne party. It was a real nice day and we had some of the best broadies in town. Then I hear this big clamor off in the distance. It sounded like somebody was banging pots and pans together. Then I see some people coming down the boulevard, running like hell, and diving into the hallways. The guns go rat-tat-tat, rat-tat-tat, and we all dive under our tables. There is a whistling sound and a shell hits the building next to us, about fifteen feet away, and some windows are smashed. The cement starts falling from the building and I could hear the bullets ricochet off the ground and cut into the awning of the restaurant. It's getting a little close.

"I look over and one of the local guys is under his table and he's pouring some champagne for a girl under the next table as if they were out at a beach party someplace. It was a crazy scene. This broadie smiles at me from under her table. I figure if the natives can cool it, why not me? I smile back at her, roll a bottle of champagne down to her, and we drink. We still had a couple of bottles left after the shooting to use at her pad when I was making it with her that night."

Belinsky continued to pitch well as the Pompero Rum team qualified for the playoffs and the Caribbean World Series in San Juan, Puerto Rico.

Belinsky landed in Philadelphia and drove on to Trenton for a little rest on January 8, 1962. In less than five weeks, Belinsky was supposed to report to the spring training camp of the Los Angeles Angels at Palm Springs, California. He arrived home and was presented with a standard major league contract which had been mailed to him by the Angels.

All major league contracts are exactly the same except for one, small section. Under the section labeled payment it reads, "For performance of the Player's services and promises hereunder the Club will pay the Player the sum of $ . . . . . . in semimonthly installments after the commencement of the playing season covered by the contract." In the long space for the amount, a secretary in the office of the Angels had written the figure provided to her for this contract by general manager Fred Haney. It called for six thousand dollars, the minimum salary allowed under baseball law and the standard stipend offered to a rookie who had not yet played a day in the major leagues. Most rookies sign it gleefully and send it back.

Robert Belinsky was not most rookies. Hollywood would soon realize that.

Bo is just a delightful rogue.

—*IRV KAZE, PUBLICITY DIRECTOR OF THE LOS ANGELES ANGELS*

Poolside Philosopher

The Los Angeles Dodgers owned California. They had come from Brooklyn in 1958, won a pennant in 1959, and were baseball's most glamorous team with Sandy Koufax, Don Drysdale, Maury Wills, Ron Fairly, and Tommy Davis. Hollywood actresses, stars and starlets, were rumored to be linked with the players romantically. Dozens of beauties sat in plush, cushioned seats behind a screen next to the Dodger dugout. Milton Berle was the team's unofficial mascot. Doris Day was an almost everyday presence at Dodger Stadium. Producers, directors, and agents maneuvered daily for introductions to the baseball players. Any Hollywood party that could produce Koufax, Drysdale, Wills, or any lesser Dodgers immediately gained significant status. It was one big happy whirl for the virile young men of Los Angeles who wore the Dodger uniform.

The Angels were lost in the shuffle. Hollywood is a front-runners' town. Win and be partied. Lose and be ignored. Academy award winners would be riding high on the social scale one season and be phased out the next. The Angels were a baseball team of rejects, has-beens, never-will-bes. They played to friends, family, and real fans in their first season. The Hollywood set stayed home while the Dodgers were on the road and the Angels were in Dodger Stadium, a ball park they called Chavez Ravine. In the publicity battle and ticket battle, the Angels were a sorry second in Los Angeles.

They were about to throw their big gun, an untried left-handed pitcher named Robert Belinsky, into the breach.

"We had heard of Bo when we drafted him," says Irv Kaze, a dapper, witty, spirited, publicity man, who handled public relations for the Angels then and is now business manager of the San Diego Chargers football team. "We knew he was flaky and we knew he had been around and would be good copy. We were in direct competition with the Dodgers for tickets and we knew Bo would sell us some. We had no idea just how famous he would become and what a drawing card he would develop into. After all, my God, he hadn't played in a single major league baseball game yet."

While Kaze, Fred Haney, and other Angels officials plotted their publicity campaign for spring training, Belinsky sat back comfortably in Trenton. The Angels did not realize Bo would do them more good in Trenton than all the players they had ready for the opening of spring training in the romantic setting of Palm Springs, California.

"When the first contract came," said Bo, "I thought it was a joke. I had played all those years in the minors and they were offering me the minimum six thousand dollars like I was some kid with no record anyplace. I wasn't going to sign anything like that. I figured if they didn't give me at least eighty-five hundred I'd forget all about baseball. The hell with them. I had a few good things going in Trenton."

Spring training was scheduled to open February 24. On Washington's Birthday, Fred Haney called Belinsky at his parents' home in Trenton. That was his first mistake. Nobody cons a con man over the phone.

"Now look, Belinsky, you are only a rookie and that's what we pay rookies."

"I've been around. I want eighty-five hundred. Not a penny less."

Haney hung up, angry. Belinsky left his home, went down to Russo's, made fifty bucks in an hour, and drove up to New York.

He met a girl and stayed incommunicado with her for two days.

The Angels opened spring training in Palm Springs. They were headquartered at the Desert Inn. All players were present and accounted for except for Belinsky.

Bud Furillo, a quick-talking, fast-dealing, hustling reporter for the *Los Angeles Herald-Express,* was the first to smell something out.

"I guess," Belinsky laughs, "I was good for him and he was good for me. I made him famous and he made me famous."

Furillo, slightly jealous that his paper played the doings of the Dodgers over the Angels, decided to strike back with vengeance. He would create a story that nobody could ignore, not even his own newspaper. He would make Bo Belinsky an instant hero, well before Belinsky landed in Los Angeles. He called Bo in Trenton.

"You're a holdout now. How much do you want?"

"I'm not coming in for a penny less than eighty-five hundred, and you can tell that to Haney."

"What are you doing to pass the time?"

"I'm shooting a lot of pool and laying a lot of broads," Bo said.

Furillo's story the next day was a beauty. He had Bo entered in a big-money pool tournament in New York. He suggested that Bo was too busy with pool and making too much money to bother with baseball. He indicated Bo would quit baseball unless the Angels made him a better offer. He cleaned up Bo's quote about the girls just enough to get into a family newspaper, but not enough to lose the flavor of the event or Bo.

The *Herald-Express* bannered it on page one with a handsome picture of Bo. The Angels had found a devil.

Charlie Maher, one of the country's finest sportswriters, was the Associated Press's man with the Angels. He took Furillo's discovery, used it as background, called Belinsky for more colorful quotes on wine, women, and song, and wrote an engaging story that ran in more than one hundred papers across the country. The legend of Bo Belinsky was being built in New York and Kansas City, Albany and Encino, Terre Haute and Rock Island.

Braven Dyer, an elderly, humorless, baseball reporter with the *Los Angeles Times,* was the next to jump on the bandwagon. He was to meet up with Bo and Dean Chance later under some exciting circumstances, but for now he recognized the publicity value of Belinsky. He took the club's side in the contract dispute but immediately increased the interest in Belinsky with his story in the *Los Angeles Times*. Other reporters, including Phil Collier of the *San Diego Union*, Ross Newhan of the *Long Beach Independent-Press-Telegram*, Bud Tucker of the *San Gabriel Valley Tribune*, and Dick Miller of the *Santa Monica Outlook*, pounded out thousands of words daily for more than a week on Bo Belinsky.

"He was," says Kaze, "the most heavily covered player we ever had before he ever set foot in our camp."

While all this journalistic excitement was going on three thousand miles away, Belinsky remained aloof from the scene. He shot pool, slept late at home, played a little basketball, chased a few girls, and treated each day with equal respect. It hardly bothered him that the Angels had been in camp for a week now and that a rookie's chances diminish with each day he misses at camp.

"I didn't care about that," said Bo. "I didn't think I was going to make their club anyway, especially after I asked for more money. If I got the contract I wanted I would make eighty-five hundred dollars no matter where I played even if I got sent to the minors."

Irv Kaze, sitting back in his San Diego office now, thinks back to those days of early Belinsky.

"He was the greatest thing to ever happen to us," Kaze says. "He put the Angels on the map. But he never really cared about pitching good and winning. He never seemed to care about anything. He had a great arm, he could have been a star, but he wasn't motivated. He is the only baseball player I have ever met in my life who really didn't care whether he played in the major leagues or the minors."

Eight days into spring training Haney moved. He had been angered that Belinsky hadn't immediately signed his first contract. Now he didn't like the stories in the press suggesting that he was cheap for not offering Belinsky more money on the strength of his long and distinguished minor league career. Haney wasn't as impressed with Bo's pitching as he was with Bo's wooing. Baseball people admire that skill in a player though they will never admit it publicly. Haney also realized quickly that the massive press coverage was helping the Angels. He needed Belinsky in camp quickly before the writers tired of conducting long-distance telephone interviews. He called Bo at home that evening. Bo was out. He returned home at 4 A.M. A note was on the table to call Haney immediately. Bo called him and got Haney out of a deep sleep.

"Did you call me?"

"Uhh, yes, I called. We want you to sign."

"Are you giving me the eighty-five hundred?"

"Uhh, look, I can't make that kind of decision. We just can't pay a rookie more than the minimum."

"Then why did you call? You know I won't sign for less than eighty-five hundred."

"Uhh, look, Belinsky, why don't you come on out here and we'll talk about it. You can sit down with our owners and maybe get some more money."

Belinsky had won the first skirmish. Owners don't talk contract to rookies. They deal personally only with the very biggest of players —like Willie Mays, Frank Robinson, Sandy Koufax, Hank Aaron, and Bob Gibson. General managers handle all signings of underlings.

"Okay," said Bo, thinking of some California sun instead of the Trenton snow. "I'll catch the next plane out tomorrow."

Arrangements were made for Belinsky to fly to California and arrive at Palm Springs in the early afternoon. Haney notified Irv Kaze and told him to announce to the press that Belinsky had agreed to terms and would report. Belinsky hadn't agreed to anything except to report to Palm Springs, but baseball people never let facts get in the way of their operation.

"I figured I would get more money if I reported than if I stayed home. Once I was in camp they wouldn't want to send me back home without a contract and pay my way out twice," Bo said.

Irv Kaze gathered the writers together shortly after the Angels finished their morning workout. He announced that Belinsky, the well-known rookie pitching prospect, would be arriving in camp later that afternoon. He also announced that he would make Belinsky available to the press for a late-afternoon press conference as soon as he arrived in camp.

"I knew there had been a couple of stories written about me," said Bo, "but I had no idea what was happening. Those guys were starved for news, starved for somebody to write about, anxious for me to help them beat the Dodger writers with big stories. They used me; but what the hell, I used them too."

Belinsky flew across country like an innocent pigeon. He expected the same treatment he had always gotten in the Orioles training camp. He was always ignored by the manager, ignored by the regular players, not used often in training games, and dismissed by the team for some minor league port of call toward the middle of March. The instant Irv Kaze decided to hold a press conference for Belinsky he decided to meet him himself at the airport. That would guarantee his appearance. Nothing would be left to chance. Haney and his assistant, Marvin Milkes, made themselves available for the press conference in case the question of contract difficulty with Belinsky came up.

"I had never met Bo, and when I saw him get off the plane I knew I had a winner," Kaze said. "You could just smell out a guy who will be good copy. He was too beautiful for words."

Belinsky stepped off the plane into the bright sun. Kaze didn't need a scorecard to recognize him. His long black hair ran down the back of his neck. His sideburns were as long as Rulolph Valentino's. His dark eyes were covered by the largest pair of sunglasses Kaze had ever seen. He wore a yellow sport shirt, open at the throat, tan, body-fitting pants, and alligator shoes. He had on a loose cashmere sport jacket. A cigarette dangled from the side of his mouth.

"I'm Kaze, welcome to California."

"Christ, I thought you were Autry."

"He's a handsome son of a bitch," Kaze says, "there's no getting away from that. He's got that lean and hungry look they all like to mother. You can almost feel the animal sex in him. It didn't surprise me that he could turn on the girls. And when he opens his mouth, he's charming as hell. A lot of it is bullshit, a good line, but Bo knows it and everybody else knows it. But you can't help liking the guy. He's a rogue, but he's a delightful rogue, an entertaining guy to be around."

Kaze drove Belinsky to the Desert Inn. He tried to question him about his past, about the pool tournament he was playing in, about his reputation in the minors, about his pitching repertoire. Belinsky was only interested in knowing what kind of a place the Desert Inn was.

"Old broadies or young ones?" he asked.

"All kinds," Kaze said. "I believe you will be happy here with us."

Arrangements were completed at the pool of the Desert Inn. Two sliding carts, filled with bottles of Scotch, rye, bourbon, vodka, gin, and accessories, were set at poolside and manned by bartenders. Two waiters circulated at the pool with trays of hot and cold hors d'oeuvres. Several tables filled with sandwiches were unwrapped for action. Hollywood waited for the star.

"The great man appeared with a smile on his face and a large ring glistening in the sun. He gave them what they wanted and just charmed hell out of all of them. I sat there and thought how lovely it would be," said Kaze, "to see the Dodgers covered at the bottom of the paper in two paragraphs."

Belinsky laughs when he recalls the grilling he got that afternoon.

"It was like an Edward G. Robinson movie," Bo says. "They sat me down against the pool, poured me a drink and took off. They wanted names, dates, and phone numbers of all the broadies I had laid. I told them there wouldn't be enough room in their papers for any other news if they printed that. They wanted to know about the pool tournament. Hell, there was no pool tournament; I was shooting some friendly games, and they got the idea I was in some great contest. I let it ride. They had heard about some of the fights in the minors and some of the adventures in Venezuela. I built it all up a little. Then they asked about the contract. From the questions they asked I could tell which ones were for me and which ones work for the club."

When the Dodgers had come to Los Angeles they had purchased space in the newspapers in some immoral ways. They never put writers on salary as such, but they saw to it writers made extra money from writing program pieces at high prices, from receiving tickets to games they could sell, from performing statistical services, from all sorts of gratuities for space received. Ball clubs try hard to work with their writers and throw them a small pittance from time to time or a Christmas gift to keep things harmonious. No club ever developed it to such an art as the Dodgers did. One writer even had the club's public relations man doing legwork for him and writing stories for his paper when he was otherwise occupied. It was a beautiful relationship for all concerned.

Kaze, being professionally trained in New York, where such activities would generally result in writers murdering the club in print, thought he could make it on hard work, understanding, and simply good stories. He didn't have to pay anybody to write about Belinsky. He just had to make him available.

"I realized that from the first day," said Bo. "These guys didn't want the truth. That wasn't as good a story as something I could make up. So I went along with them. I answered all their questions the way they wanted. When they asked about broadies, I built it up. When they asked about pool, I made out to be the best player that ever picked up a cue. When they asked about my contract, I made it sound like I wouldn't sign under any conditions unless Autry begged me personally."

Belinsky was assigned to a room at the Desert Inn with a hulking, veteran first baseman named Steve Bilko. Bilko was thirty-four years old, had once hit fifty-six homers in the minor leagues for the Los Angeles Cubs, was easygoing, and liked to drink beer.

"I got up the next morning," said Belinsky, "and Bilko had been out and back to the room by then. He bought all the papers and had spread them out on a table opened to the sports pages for me to read. I spent all morning reading those stories. None of it was true."

Bilko turned to Belinsky and said, "Well, rook, it looks like you're famous."

"Is this me? Who the hell are they writing about?"

"All you gotta do now is pitch and then go straight into the Hall of Fame."

Led by Bud Furillo, the press onslaught continued. Belinsky was followed around wherever he went. He spent three wild days in Palm Springs without spending a dime or buying a drink or signing a contract.

Late on the third day, after several unsuccessful meetings over the contract question with Haney, Belinsky was summoned to his room.

"You sign this contract right now or we send you home on the next plane," Haney said. "This can't go on any longer."

Belinsky had decided he liked this team and this town. He had come all this way, been wined and dined for three days, and didn't have anything going at Trenton.

"If you promise me you will renegotiate my contract in midseason," said Bo, "I'll sign."

"If you make the club we'll take a look at the contract again in midseason. I can't promise anything but if you don't sign you're gone."

Bo signed.

"I didn't get any more than the six thousand dollars they had originally offered me, but I had missed the first ten days of camp, had become a celebrity, and was certain of getting a chance. No ball club builds a guy up the way the Angels built me up and then doesn't give him a chance."

Belinsky went to work on the practice field and got himself into shape. His arm was tired from the long winter of pitching in Venezuela and he threw easily until the strength started slowly coming back to it. The writers continued to chronicle his every move.

"Bud Furillo called me Superstud and Wonderboy and he was writing about me every day. A few of the other writers like Charlie Maher and a couple of others were kind. But then there were eight or ten wolves around, led by Dyer, who kept writing that I was a rookie who hadn't done anything and what the hell was the fuss all about."

Soon, the mail began pouring in to Belinsky. It was of two distinct kinds. The first kind were the love letters and mash notes from girls, offering their bodies to Bo at the drop of a coin in a phone booth. He stayed clear of most of that stuff. Experience had taught him that most of those young ladies were demented.

The other collection of mail was of a more serious nature. It blamed Belinsky for ruining the Angels. He had not yet pitched a game for them.

One letter began, "Dear Bo: This used to be a nice team until you joined it with your pool-playing and girl stories. I have been an Angels fan ever since the team began. I will now switch to the Dodgers where young, wholesome gentlemen play the game of baseball." About the only difference between the "young, whole-some" men on the Dodgers and Belinsky was that the Dodgers had a better team than the one Bo played on.

Spring training was a struggle for Belinsky. His arm came around slowly. When he got a chance to pitch he was wild and ineffective. The writers continued to write about him as a character, but none would venture a guess that Belinsky was the second coming of Lefty Grove. The pressure began to build about the end of March for a decision on Belinsky. The Angels decided he wasn't worth the trouble. Fred Haney called the Orioles and offered them Belinsky back for $12,500, half of what they had paid for him in the draft. He didn't look like he could pitch and he wouldn't be worth the aggravation. Besides, the other players were being distracted by Bo's nighttime adventures. The Orioles nicely said no, thanks, no Bo.

"Palm Springs is a hell of a town," says Bo. "It didn't take me long to realize the training camps in the major leagues were a lot better than the regular towns in the minors."

Gene Autry and Bob Reynolds, the owners of the club, liked Belinsky's style. Autry, a big Hollywood name, believed that Bo would sell some tickets and be good for the club if he could hang on until the season began. He never pushed but he urged Haney to give him a little more time.

"Haney was a pretty good guy," said Bo. "He had been a winner with the Braves, had some great players there in Warren Spahn, Lew Burdette, Eddie Mathews, Hank Aaron, and Joe Adcock, and took things in stride. He had a great sense of humor. There were times when we argued contract that I really had him breaking up. He was trying to be serious but he would bust out laughing. He was a good man about the whole thing. Fred Haney has a lot of class in my book."

Things weren't as smooth between the manager, Bill Rigney, and Belinsky as they were between Bo and Haney.

"Rigney's got that white hair and everybody called him the White Rat. He's Joe Hollywood. Wears those dark shades all the time and tries to let you know he is in with everybody, a real big man about town. That first spring he was busy building up Jim Fregosi, that was his discovery, to the writers. He didn't have time for anybody else.

Rigney's big with the golf course and the golf clothes and likes to show himself around the hotel lobby and at the bar. He likes people to notice him. I think that's why Rig and I never really got along. I think he was jealous of all the attention I got. Rigney likes that ink himself. He had never really been much of a player himself, but he wants to show you he can be bigger than any guy on the team."

While the days left toward the end of spring training dwindled down to a precious few, Belinsky pondered his fate. He didn't think he would make the club.

"I knew I didn't have an ally in Rigney. He was waiting to show his hand. I think that he probably would have been a little warmer to me if I had pitched well. He wanted to win, that was one sure thing about him and he could manage the hell out of game. I think the writers pushed him into giving me a chance," Bo said.

Belinsky did have one guardian angel in that camp, the big bear of a pitching coach, Marv Grissom.

"He comes on tough and loud like he's going to cut your head off, but it's all an act. He's got a good heart. He's a good boy. We got along fine."

Haney, Rigney, and the coaches, Grissom, Jack Paepke, Del Rice, and a delightful guy named Rocky Bridges, sat down together in Rigney's suite at the Desert Inn during the first week of April to cut the Angels squad down to the player limit. Rigney wanted to send Belinsky back to the minors, but Grissom urged another look. Haney thought it would be useful if they kept him around at least through the first weeks of the season when they could carry twenty-eight players.

On April 8, 1962, the Los Angeles Angels broke camp and headed for the opening game of the season against the Chicago White Sox in Comiskey Park. They would work out April 9 in Chicago, and Ken McBride would pitch the opener for them against the White Sox on April 10. The roster was cut and there would be two memorable additions to the Los Angeles squad on that first roster of the 1962 season, a twenty-year-old right-hander from Wooster, Ohio, named Wilmer Dean Chance and listed on the roster as Dean Chance, and a twenty-five-year-old left-hander named Robert Belinsky, listed on the roster of the Los Angeles Angels as Bob Belinsky.

"Me and Bo," said Chance, "were on our way to the bigs."

The bigs would never ever be the same again.

The Angels flew to Chicago and were quartered in the posh Sheraton Chicago. Belinsky immediately went to work on his major league career.

"We had this left-handed pitcher with us," remembers Jim Fregosi, an Angels rookie that season. "His name was Ron Moeller and he had been in service and was being carried with the club with a chance to make the team. We were short of left-handed pitching. Everybody knew Bo had been around baseball for a while and Moeller was sure Belinsky knew all the broads in all the towns in America. He asked him for a number."

Belinsky told Moeller he had a great number for him and if he gave him a chance to make a phone call to check it he would give it to him. Moeller, getting excited already, assured Bo he wouldn't move while Belinsky checked his phone list. He gave Moeller a number, told him to dial it and ask for room 617. Moeller went right to a phone and dialed the number.

"You could see the smile on his face," said Fregosi. "This was a guy who had put all his faith in Belinsky's basket."

The phone rang and a male voice answered.

"Yep."

"Hi. I've been given this number to call Cheryl. Is she there? I'm a friend of a friend of yours."

"Who the hell *is* this?"

"Who the hell is *this?*"

"This is Rigney. Now, who's this?"

"Moeller dropped the phone like he had been shot," said Fregosi. "He never asked Bo for a number again. A couple of days later Rigney must have gotten on to his voice. He was gone before he really had a chance to pitch."

Belinsky had a way of making left-handed pitchers disappear into thin air.

The Angels opened the season and Belinsky never moved from his seat in the bullpen. The team traveled on to Minnesota and Belinsky played catch with Del Rice in the cold of a place called Bloomington, a suburb of St. Paul and Minneapolis, where a new ball park had been built. On April 13 the Angels began a three-game series at Minnesota against the Twins. They flew back to Los Angeles on the night of April 15.

Belinsky moved into a place called Ernie's House of Surface, a swinging spot along the beach. It was highly recommended by several of his teammates, notably a right-handed relief pitcher named Ryne Duren, who told Bo it had one of the best bars in the league. Duren was one of the best bar men in the league. He had once pushed a cigar in the face of Yankee coach Ralph Houk after a pennant celebration, and Houk had smashed Duren's face with a slap. The stunned Duren didn't understand the ferocious response to his gentle kidding.

"Some guys," explained Casey Stengel, "just get whiskey slick."

Duren, Art Fowler, basketball player Hot Rod Hundley—a Belinsky in shorts—and several other Angels made this spot their home base. The nights were fun and the hours were long. Belinsky was still being written about almost daily in the Los Angeles papers but hadn't yet been in a game. It seemed as if the Angels were just keeping him around for publicity value and then would quietly drop him when the season became serious.

"With all the writers around," said Bo, "it probably wasn't a bad thing that I didn't pitch early. The pressure was enormous. As I look back now I wonder how anybody could have gone through what I went through and still played baseball."

The Angels were scheduled to open their home season in Chavez Ravine against Kansas City on April 17, a Friday night. They had a Saturday night game and a Sunday day game scheduled. They also had a pitching problem. Ted Bowsfield, their one reliable left-handed starter, was bothered with a sore arm. On Saturday, Rigney was asked who his starter was for Sunday. He said he would announce it after the game.

The Angels won on Saturday and Rigney was in a garrulous mood as reporters interviewed him after the game.

"I'm going to throw the ball down the middle of the floor in the clubhouse," said Rigney, "and whoever picks it up is the starter. It's too early in the season to be out of arms, but we are out of arms. Bowsfield can't pitch and I'd like to start a left-hander against this club."

There was only one other left-hander on the club who could start. It was Robert Belinsky, who had not yet pitched a single inning in a major league game. The writers demanded the name of the starter.

"I think I'll give the kid, Belinsky, a start tomorrow," Rigney said.

Belinsky had become so famous among Los Angeles fans that the writers wrote more about Belinsky's starting assignment than they did about the game on Saturday. Every California sports fan knew that the left-hander from Trenton would get his first start.

Irv Kaze sat late in his office that Saturday night thinking about Belinsky's debut. He knew that if the rookie could win he could be promoted into a drawing card in a hurry. Nobody had turned on the California writers faster than Belinsky had. He had not yet pitched an inning of major league ball but had a folder of clippings in the morgue of the *Los Angeles Times* larger than some Dodger players who had been around town since 1958.

Haney's assistant, Marvin Milkes, an exuberant, enthusiastic man, envisioned wonders for Belinsky.

"If he wins," said Milkes, "he could be the biggest drawing card we ever had. We play the Yankees in New York on May 22. I can see it now. All that New York publicity and Belinsky shutting out Mickey Mantle, Roger Maris, and the Yankees before seventy thousand people in Yankee Stadium."

"If he loses," said Irv Kaze, "he might be in Hawaii by May 22."

Kaze was kidding. He knew that Belinsky was making his job easier. He was keeping the Angels in the papers and helping to sell tickets, especially on the road. People like to see the heroes of the other team. Everything about Belinsky was commercial, even his mixed background, Jewish mother and Polish father.

"When he wins," said Kaze, "we'll tell everybody he's Jewish. When he loses we'll tell everybody he's Polish."

On Sunday, April 19, 1962, Robert (Bo) Belinsky of the Los Angeles Angels started his first major league game. He trained for it as he trained for most games in his career. He stayed out until he found something worth staying in with and then he did his thing. Then he took her home.

"I guess I got to bed about four or five in the morning," said Bo. "I got my six hours sleep. That's about all I ever needed. Sex always helped to relax me. Nobody ever died from it, you know. That is, if you don't want to count John Garfield.''

Belinsky arrived at the ball park shortly before eleven o'clock for the one o'clock game. Pitching coach Marv Grissom gave him a shiny new baseball and a very old lecture.

"Win, kid," he said, "or you're gone."

"There was no subtlety," said Bo. "I knew that I was just hanging on. I knew that I would have been long gone if the writers hadn't made such a fuss over me. The writers made me a celebrity and the front office pressured Rigney into keeping me around a lot longer than he would have if nobody had written a word about me. I knew Rigney wasn't thrilled with me and if I got bombed I was gone. If you are a quiet, mild guy in this game and play politics with the manager you can hang around a little longer even if you don't win. If you have a big mouth like me, it's win or see-you-later."

Irv Kaze remembers that first game well. The press and the front office and the writers were all excited about it. Belinsky sat on the bench smoking a cigarette and entertaining his teammates with stories about his adventures in South America.

"In all the time I knew Bo," Kaze says, "I never saw him get excited, not about anything, not about a game or a play or even a broad. He just laughed about everything and kept rolling along."

Kaze said that Belinsky is the one person he met in sports who seemed to be exactly the same whether he was on top or way down on the bottom.

Belinsky admits he did a good acting job that Sunday afternoon. Everybody thought it was good old Bo, just starting another game, cooler than hell.

"That's nonsense," says Bo, "I was scared to death. I thought I was going to throw up I was so scared. It was like a fairy tale just being out there on that mound. I kept it hidden but I was a wreck."

Ten days after the 1962 season began, Belinsky walked to the mound for the first time in Chavez Ravine and received a good hand and scattered boos as he threw his warmup pitches.

"All I wanted to do was concentrate on the hitters," he said. "I knew if I could work on them without thinking about anything else I would do well. I knew I had major league stuff."

Belinsky threw his good fast ball, mixed it with his screwball, and floated up an occasional changeup. He led 3–2 with two out in the eighth when Rigney came to the mound.

"Nice going, kid," he said. "I'm bringing the old guy in to save it."

Art Fowler, thirty-nine-year-old right-handed relief specialist, came in, got the third out, retired three straight batters in the ninth inning and Belinsky had his first major league win.

"I was sky high when I got back to Ernie's House of Surface to change for dinner. I walk in the door and they got a champagne table set up for me. It was a hell of a night."

Four days later Belinsky got his second start and defeated the Cleveland Indians. Five days later he pitched nine innings for the first time in the major leagues and defeated the Washington Senators 3–0. The Los Angeles sportswriters were going wild.

Bud Furillo nominated Bo for Rookie of the Year. Charlie Maher suggested the expansionist Angels, in their second year in the league, might win the pennant. Even crusty old Braven Dyer thought Belinsky might be a pretty good pitcher if he started going to bed earlier.

Through the efforts of Furillo and Hot Rod Hundley and veteran players on the Angels, Belinsky began making contacts with the Hollywood set. He was a steady customer at the Whiskey A-Go-Go, dancing deep into the night. The pretty girls waited for him outside of the Los Angeles clubhouse and craved his favors. He met girls at parties, at nightclubs, at the ball park, at discotheques, at every conceivable spot in Los Angeles.

"There's no problem meeting girls in baseball," Bo says. "They come to your room and knock on the door or they introduce themselves in the lobby of a hotel as friends of friends or they walk up to you in a restaurant and drop their phone numbers on a handkerchief and walk away."

Girls are just people, only more so. They like winners. In the early sixties when they were winning, the arrival of the New York Yankees in a hotel would result in a crowd scene of good-lookers. As a losing team, odds are that most pretty girls meeting the Yankees in their road hotels are wives, their own wives.

With each victory, the pretty girls around Belinsky increased in number. The avalanche was yet to begin.

"I was going so good on and off the field," said Bo. "I figured I could do no wrong."

He proved just how right he was the very next evening.

"It was May 4, 1962," Bo remembers. "I can't ever forget that date, a Friday. I was scheduled to pitch the next night, May 5, against Baltimore, my old team, for the first time. It was some sort of a Mexican holiday and the strip was jammed with tourists. I see this one doll and we strike up a conversation. We go into this joint for a couple of drinks and a couple of dances. It's a Mexican holiday and they are playing all this wild Mexican music. I can hardly hear what she's saying because I'm too busy eyeing her tits. She was tall and really built. I figured it was time to move. She figured the same thing. 'My pad or yours?' She said hers was nearby and very private so we made it to hers. She was fabulous, those long legs and all, that long black hair. Fantastic. Now it's four o'clock in the morning and I have to pitch the next night so I figured I'd better blast off. She wishes me good luck and I'm out the door before I remember to thank her for the swell evening. I come back and offer her tickets for the game. She tells me she has a date that night but she might come some other time. I tell her I'm at Ernie's and she can call me anytime, any old time at all."

Belinsky would never see this dark-haired beauty ever again but the events of the next evening would make her an immortal in his mind.

No-Hit Bo and the Late, Late Show

The Angels had gotten off well in the 1962 season after their opening year of 1961 and an eighth-place finish. In early May, on the
strength of the sudden emergence of Belinsky as an undefeated
starter, the rapid development of Dean Chance, the progress shown
by rookie Jim Fregosi, and the quick starts by veterans Lee Thomas,
Billy Moran, Albie Pearson, and Leon (Daddy Wags) Wagner, Los
Angeles was threatening to become a contender in the pennant
race. All of the excitement meant little to the fans of Los Angeles,
who seemed wed to the Dodgers, and attendance was unimpressive.
On Friday night, May 4, the Angels played the Orioles in the first
of a three-game series, and the attendance was 5341.

"It was an insult to the whole team," Belinsky said.

Belinsky arrived Saturday at Chavez Ravine after his happy night
along the Strip in time to see coach Marv Grissom put the baseball
in his left shoe, a ritual he had followed each time Belinsky was to
pitch. He dressed quickly and went out for batting practice. It was
a mild night, temperatures in the low seventies and the sky clear.
Belinsky had slept twelve hours, according to some people the

wrong twelve hours, but he felt rested. He was anxious to impress the Orioles, the team that had finally given up on him and allowed him to be drafted by the Angels.

Baltimore was in a state of flux. They had almost stolen the pennant from the Yankees in 1960 with a young pitching staff and finished second. In 1961, Paul Richards had resigned in August to take over in Houston and they finished third under Luman Harris. Harris had moved to Houston with Richards as a coach in 1962, and Billy Hitchcock, a mild-mannered, pipe-smoking gentleman, had been named manager. As always happens to gentlemen like that, the players took advantage of his good nature, stayed out late, didn't work hard, and Baltimore was to finish seventh—nineteen games behind the pennant-winning Yankees.

The Orioles, that Saturday night of May 5, were a mixture of veterans with Johnny Temple at second base, Dick Williams (who was to win fame as the manager of the world champion 1972 Oakland A's) in left field, Jackie Brandt in center field, and Gus Triandos catching. Youngsters in the lineup included Brooks Robinson at third base, Jim Gentile at first base, Dave Nicholson in right field, Ron Hansen at shortstop, and of all people, Bo's old pal Steve Barber on the mound.

"I guess I was as high for that game as any game I had ever pitched in my life," Belinsky says. "I really wanted to show them I could pitch."

To make things more interesting, George Staller, who had managed Belinsky in the minors and suspended him for a fight, was coaching at third base.

Belinsky had won three straight and had become as much fun to watch on the mound as he was to read about in the papers. Except for opening day, it was the best crowd the Angels had drawn. More than sixteen thousand people paid to see Bo pitch.

"I wanted fifty thousand," Bo said. "A good crowd works up to excitement."

During batting practice, Barber kidded Belinsky about his new success.

"I thought the only thing you ever did in the minors," said Steve Barber, "was chase broads. When did you have time to learn how to pitch?"

"I didn't," Bo said. "It's just that the hitters up here are all fishcakes."

Belinsky took a deep breath, walked to the mound, and threw his eight warmup pitches. His arm felt strong and the ball moved with that extra good hop. He knew if he made good pitches he would have a fine game. The ball was alive and well this night. Chavez Ravine is a pitcher's park. The long fly balls somehow sit quietly in the outfield until they are caught. Well-hit balls have a way of losing their power before they ever reach a wall. Belinsky liked the distant fences and the heavy air.

"Let's go with the screwball early and save the fast ball for later when they're tired," said Belinsky.

"Just keep the ball down," said catcher Bob Rodgers. "Especially to the right-handers, Triandos and Hansen. They can hit it out."

After 152 professional baseball games, Belinsky knew all the rules, down and in to good hitters, up and away to weak hitters, move the ball, throw strikes, hard stuff inside and slow stuff outside. The only thing that mattered was execution.

The crowd stood for the national anthem. Belinsky moved around nervously on the mound, tapping his toes to the organ music. He ran his left hand through his greasy hair and got ready to pitch. The extra grease on his hand would give the ball a little extra dip. Johnny Temple stepped in. Belinsky was ready. He took Bob Rodgers's sign for a fast ball and the game was on.

Temple hit a fast ball off the end of the bat and grounded out. Dick Williams and Brooks Robinson had trouble with the screwball and were easy outs. The Angels got a run in the first inning and Belinsky led 1–0. The Orioles went out easily in the second and the Angels scored again for a 2–0 lead. Belinsky retired Nicholson and Hansen in the third but walked Barber. He blamed it on lack of concentration against his old pal. He was in trouble in the fourth when he walked Gentile, Brandt was safe on an error, and Triandos walked. Three on, none out, and Rigney pacing the dugout, scratching his white hair and signaling frantically to the bullpen for somebody to get ready. Marv Grissom told Ryne Duren and Eli Grba to start throwing. "Jesus Christ," Belinsky said to himself on the mound as he spotted the frantic action in the bullpen. He had won three straight games, hadn't allowed a hit in this one and was now on the verge of a hurried shower if the Orioles got a hit here. "Jesus Christ," said Bo. Then he struck out Nicholson on a high fast ball, got Hansen on strikes with a screwball, and got his pal Barber on a soft fly to center field.

The Orioles were hitless through the fifth, the sixth, and into the seventh.

"That's when it started," said Bo, "the noise, the excitement, the cheering, everybody pulling for me. It sounded like a hundred thousand people were in that park."

No hits through eight innings. Belinsky had now retired the last seven men he had faced, all on fast balls. The Angels finished batting in the eighth inning and Belinsky reached for his glove and leaned over to Rodgers. "Fast balls," he said, "nothing but fast balls."

As he was walking to the mound, Jackie Brandt passed him on his way to the dugout.

"Nice game, Bo," he said, "but it's over. I'm going to lead off with a bunt single."

A flake in baseball jargon is a weird person, a far-out person, a kidder and a comic, a man capable of incredible stunts just for a laugh. Jackie Brandt was baseball's original flake. He roomed with an outfielder in St. Louis by the name of Wally Moon. Moon suggested that Brandt was so wild his brains were falling out of his head, flaking off his body, hence, a flake. Only a flake would kid a man about a no-hitter while he was trying for it. Casey Stengel once kidded Johnny Vander Meer out of his concentration after Vander Meer had pitched two consecutive no-hitters, the only time in baseball history for such a feat, by reminding him the feat was impossible. Casey Stengel was a flake. So was Brandt.

"I didn't take Brandt seriously," said Bo. "I knew he was goofy."

Brandt refused to bunt and flied out. Two outs to go and the crowd screaming. Gus Triandos was next. He grounded to Joe Koppe at second and was an easy out. Two out. One more to go for a no-hitter, for the first no-hitter in California big league history, the first ever by an Angel, that little devil Bo Belinsky. Now came Nicholson again, often reported to be the strongest man in baseball. He once turned the shower faucets off in the Miami clubhouse at the

Baltimore spring training camp and the Orioles had to hire a plumber to turn them back on.

"He was a strong guy but he didn't know the strike zone," said Bo. "If you could throw a fast ball up and in on him you'd have him."

The count went to 1–1 on Nicholson. Belinsky took the sign from Rodgers, peeked over at coach George Staller staring dispassionately at him from third base, pumped twice, lifted his right leg high in the air, came around with his left arm and fired a fast ball up and in. Nicholson swung at it, caught it on the handle of the bat, and lifted a foul ball off third base. Felix Torres, a thirty-year-old infielder from Ponce, Puerto Rico, rescued from the minors in the same draft that claimed Belinsky, glided over from third toward the stands.

"The ball went up like a balloon," said Belinsky, "and seemed to hang there like some little kid's bubble. It was if the whole world stood still. There was an instant of silence in the place while the fans searched for the ball. They spotted it, spotted Torres under it and started to scream and applaud and cheer. I goddamn nearly got goose bumps until the thing came down."

The ball settled comfortably into Torres's glove for the final out. Belinsky had a 2–0 no-hitter, the first in California history, the fifty-eighth in the history of the American League, and was in the record books with such luminaries as Bob Feller, Allie Reynolds, Bob Lemon, Virgil Trucks, and Bill Dietrich. Two other boys named Bo had turned the feat: a rookie by the name of Alva L. (Bobo) Holloman with the St. Louis Browns in 1953 and Louis N. (Bobo) Newsom with the Browns in 1938. Newson, a real Bobo, managed to allow a hit in the tenth inning of his no-hitter and lost the game to the Boston Red Sox.

Belinsky watched Torres catch the ball, accepted the baseball from him, shook every hand on the Angels, laughed to himself when Bill Rigney raced out to greet him, tipped his cap to the fans in the stands ("Hey, look at the blonde with the big tits," he said to Rodgers), and raced into the dugout to hold court for the gasping members of the press.

"Bo, when did you start thinking about the no-hitter?"

"This morning," said Bo, "about four o'clock."

That one went over the writers' heads but they pursued their questioning.

"Did you know you had a no-hitter?"

"Yeah," he said, "the Orioles kept yelling at me, 'Hey, Bo, you got a no-hitter.' That's how I knew."

For more than an hour the questioning went on, Belinsky standing against the wall of his locker, his white uniform shirt with the large number thirty-six soaked gray with sweat, his hair falling down his forehead, his eyes open and attentive, his smile constant and charming.

A friend of Bo's, Andy Spagnola, who ran the Thistle Inn on Glendale Boulevard, announced that a champagne party in the new hero's honor would begin as soon as he could shake the reporters and get to his place. Bo moved slowly. He enjoyed the spotlight too much to cut it short. It was almost two hours later before Bo walked in to the Thistle Inn, was hugged and kissed by some curvaceous beauties hoping for Bo's favors this special night, and applauded by the men in the crowd.

"I was trying to be cool about it," said Bo, "but it wasn't easy."

Belinsky had a drink and excused himself to make a phone call. Instead of setting up a date for the night or arranging something for the next night, Belinsky dutifully called his parents in Trenton to share this happy moment with them.

"We heard it on the radio," his mother shouted. "Your father couldn't stand it. He had to go out for coffee. When will we be seeing you?"

"We'll be in New York at the end of the month. I'll see you then."

Belinsky returned to the party and danced the rest of the night away. Then he tapped one of the lovelies and left with her.

"I picked her," Bo laughs, "because she could cook breakfast better than any of the other broadies."

Belinsky awoke a national celebrity on Sunday morning. His picture was on the front page of the *Los Angeles Times* and his career was spread in stories across all the Los Angeles papers and sent out across the country by Charlie Maher in the Associated Press stories. It would never quite be the same again. Everything Belinsky would do from that day on would be big news. No-hit baseball pitchers are never again nonpersons.

"Everybody wanted me at every Hollywood party," said Bo. "Playing baseball seemed only incidental. I was just on a mad whirl, day and night. It was even a little much for me."

Several days later Bud Furillo introduced Belinsky to a Beverly Hills attorney named Paul Caruso. He would open new doors to Belinsky. Caruso handled contracts for many Hollywood people and was on first-name basis with most of the important names in Hollywood—actors, directors, producers, agents. The easiest way for a starlet to get her name in the gossip columns in May of 1962 was to be seen with Bo Belinsky. Items began appearing daily about Bo's dates. Some of them were actually true.

The biggest and most elegant party Belinsky attended was a huge dinner in his honor at Caruso's palatial home in Beverly Hills. The Beautiful People were all there, Jane Wyman, Merle Oberon, Maureen O'Hara, and directors, producers, and agents by the dozens, coming in and going out all night, drinking fine wines and eating far-out hors d'oeuvres.

"After hustling in pool halls and living on O'Henry bars this was something else," Belinsky said.

The party was winging along nicely. Caruso grabbed Bo by the arm and brought him over to a dapper little man with white hair, tailored suit, and a sunburned face. Belinsky had finally made the big time. Walter Winchell wanted to meet him.

Winchell, sixty-five years old, his star descending, was still an important and feared man in journalistic circles. Especially in Hollywood and on Broadway. He had begun his career as a vaudeville hoofer before World War I, switched to journalism as a serious reporter, and drifted into a gossip column with the *New York Graphic* and the *New York Mirror* in the late 1920s. He prided himself on being big with the cops and did arrange for several gangsters, notably the notorious Louis "Lepke" Buchalter, to surrender to him for police delivery, thereby gaining a scoop for his paper and a boost for his ego. He began a Sunday night radio show that became a fixture in American life with his famous opening, in his fast-paced, gravelly New York voice, accompanied by a ticker-tape sound, bellowing out, "Good evening, Mr. and Mrs. North and South America and all the ships at sea. Let's go to press." He created a journalese all his own, chronicling marriages, divorces, births, and deaths of show business, sports, or political people in his own vernacular. He hung out in the name Hollywood places, Jerry Lewis's restaurant, Dino's, the Peppermint West Lounge, Chasen's, La Scala, and in the biggest New York places, Toots Shor's, the Forum of the Twelve Caesars, 21, and the Copacabana.

"Walter," said Caruso, "I'd like you to meet Bo Belinsky."

"Hello, Walter," said Bo. "Nice to meet you."

Belinsky had made his move. Nobody called Winchell by his first name on their first date. Belinsky didn't follow protocol. Bo was his own man, set his own rules, no matter whose ball park he was playing in.

"Walter was all right," said Bo. "He was a funny old guy and we had a lot of laughs together. He knew every broad in town that counted. He could call up an agent and have the guy turn out fifty girls in half an hour, each more better looking than the next.

"One time Winchell decided to throw a party for the ball club at the Coconut Grove. He calls me up and tells me to invite everybody on the team for that night. He reminds me to make sure they all come alone. He would have all the broadies there for us, all knock-outs. I spread the word around the club and we are all set for that. I get there early with Dean and there are about twenty beauties waiting there for us, smashing broadies, it was like being a kid let loose in a candy store. Now here come the players. I almost drop dead when they walk in. They all brought their own girls. Some of the idiots even brought their wives. So there I was with twenty beautiful girls all to myself. That's even too much for old Bo.

"All those guys on the team wanted to just meet Winchell and Eddie Fisher. He was playing there that night. We all got friendly with Fisher and a few weeks later he invited us all over to his place for a farewell party. He was taking off for a singing date in London. He left the party early and it went all night long, a hell of a bash. I wound up taking Juliet Prowse home or she wound up taking me home, I forget which way it went."

Belinsky was a fixture at Hollywood parties, cool by nature, handsome, poised with the biggest of company and a national sports figure at the top of his game.

"These agents and producers were always trying to get me to take out their newest girls," Bo says. "We'd go to some joint, the owner would pick up the tab, there would be an item in the paper the next day and everybody would be happy. One day, Bill Banks of Hollywood Newsreel calls me up, tells me he's got the greatest chick in the world for me to meet. I tell him I'm too goddamn tired, I wanted to stay home that night. He insists. So I go. He introduces me to Tina Louise, a hell of a broad. We went together for two months. I was really crazy about her."

Belinsky ran his pitching record to 6–1. The Angels were anxious for Bo to go slow off the mound, knowing full well that losses would start following these late nights. It was difficult for Rigney, Haney, or anyone else from the team to control Bo, especially since he was still winning.

Winchell began hanging around the ball park and Rigney suggested that he please keep himself out of the clubhouse. Walter didn't take too kindly to that. Bo remained loyal to Walter, invited him, and also suggested Walter watch the games from the press box, supposedly off-limits to non-card-carrying members of the Baseball Writers Association and positively off-limits to females, even ones as pretty as Tina Louise.

"Bo fell hard for Tina," Winchell says. "That was his thumb-to-nose insult to the Angels' brass, who tried to get him to stop hanging around with Winchell's speedy set. I took Miss Louise to a game one night and was told she couldn't come into the press box. That was news to this fugitive from Broadway, so we went into Dodger owner Walter O'Malley's private box."

After the game Winchell wanted to take Bo downtown to meet Joe DiMaggio, who was in town visiting with his Marine Corps son. "You know," Winchell said, "Bo meets Joe. Joe meets Schmobo."

Belinsky turned down Winchell's invitation for a meeting with Joe D. He decided he would much rather be alone with Tina. No schmobo, Belinsky.

"I dated Ann-Margret for a while," Bo says. "She was sexier looking than she really was. But it wasn't a total loss. I was getting movie and television offers then and I was advised to get an agent. I knew if I became a big movie star I would have to change my name. I already decided what it would be I'd change it to Lance. Lance Belinsky."

"I dated Connie Stevens. I already knew her from spring training. Great girl, but I wound up dating her nineteen-year-old cousin. She was freaky, really out of sight."

Belinsky even had a date with a real live queen.

"I don't even know how it came about, but I got a date with Queen Soraya of Iran. I think it was after her marriage with the Shah had busted up and she was trying to make it in the movies or something. She was nice but she was a little weird. She was into all that mystical stuff, witchcraft, everything far out. She had blown her crown because she didn't have a son for the Shah, and now she was asking the witches for all the answers. But really a nice broadie."

Things became too hectic for Bo at Ernie's House of Surface, so he started looking around for a more impressive apartment. He was introduced to Alex Borisoff, a master cellist and composer, who had written the score for *Mutiny on the Bounty,* and his wife, June Starr, a famed Hollywood voice instructor. They liked the idea of sharing a little of the sports spotlight with such an accomplished figure as Robert Belinsky, so they leased an apartment in their Hollywood Hills home on La Pressa Drive to Belinsky for two hundred dollars a month.

Belinsky was given the top part of the house, a separate apartment with a gigantic lavender-colored bar, an orchid-colored bed, black sunken bath, huge, deep rugs, and glass-enclosed roof.

"One night I was fast asleep," said Bo. "I'm all by myself and it's very quiet. There was a narrow ledge around the apartment, just barely wide enough for somebody to walk on. I hear this pitter-patter noise. I figure it's some goddamn burglar or something. I'm ready to call the cops. I look up and see this delicious-looking broad hanging over the edge and peeking into the glass roof. What could I do? I had to invite her in just to save her life."

As Belinsky's fame spread, all sorts of people came to him bearing gifts. That's the way it works with sports stars. Clothing dealers give them clothes if they sign a few autographs. Groceries hold special-events days for them, draw large crowds to shopping centers, and pay them off with huge bags of groceries and free milk delivery for a year. Even expensive items, such as cars, fall into the grab bag of a successful athlete.

"I was blowing a lot of money on cabs," said Bo. "Some of the chicks had cars but I still needed my own wheels. Hollywood isn't a town where you want to be left without a car."

Belinsky had been doing so well on the field that he decided now was the time to talk to general manager Fred Haney about getting a raise in salary from his $6000 minimum salary. Haney agreed that Bo was worth more than the minimum and informed him that as of the next paycheck he would be making the grand sum of $8500 a year with more to come if he continued the good work all season.

"This one automobile dealer had contacted me. He offered me a free car, any car in the place. All I had to do for it was sign autographs every Saturday in this place for the rest of the season for an hour when the club was home. It was a piece of cake and I was going to get a three-thousand-dollar candy apple Eldorado Cadillac for these autograph sessions. It seemed like a hell of a deal."

Belinsky got the car with license plates "BO" and was driving merrily back and forth to the ball park and on his appointed rounds each day. He made one autograph-signing appearance, pleasing the car dealer and the fans.

"One day I'm in the clubhouse after a game," Bo says, "and Autry comes down with a couple of his cowboy friends to say hello. It had been a big win for us and he had been up in his private box all night and now he's feeling no pain. He tells me the club had decided to give me a raise and I should go to the office the next day and pick up my check. I had already agreed to a raise with Haney. I didn't know if I was getting more money or he just didn't know about the raise. I didn't say anything. I figured he was having his little joke with his friends.

"Now he says to me, 'Bo, I hear you have a new car.' I tell him I do. He says, 'Fine, we'll pick up the payments on it.' I tell him about the autograph deal but he insists the club is buying me the car. I can tell the guy I won't be coming around for autograph sessions anymore, and he can send the club the bills. I didn't want to do that to the dealer, I had made a bargain with him to show up, but I didn't want to hurt Autry's feelings either. I was working for him, not the car dealer, so I said I would go along with it. Autry said he would get Haney to call the dealer the next day and spell it out."

Belinsky stopped showing up on Saturdays for his autographing sessions assuming all arrangements had been completed by the club. Then he got his first surprise, a statement of a back bill on a new candy apple Eldorado Cadillac.

"I figured it was just a bookkeeping error. They sent me the bill instead of to the club. I ignored it, figuring they would catch up by the next month. Now comes the next bill. This time it says if it isn't paid the car will be repossessed immediately. Now I race into Haney's office with the bills to clear it up."

"What about this car bill, Fred? It hasn't been paid."

"What car bill?"

"On the Cadillac that Autry said the club was paying for."

"Well, Bo, we gave you the twenty-five hundred raise on your salary. That was supposed to be for the Cadillac."

"What? That was agreed to well before the Cadillac. Autry said the club would pick up the bills for the Cadillac. I was getting the car free for signing autographs. When I stopped, the club was supposed to pay it. Autry said it was his gift for the no-hitter and my good pitching."

"Bo," said Haney, "you know baseball rules prevent us from giving you a gift. All we can do is write you a new contract. We did that. The club is straightened out with you."

Belinsky knew he had been had. He stormed out of Haney's office.

"I had been in baseball a hell of a long time," said Bo, "and a lot of things happened to me, but you never really learn. There's always something new."

The candy apple Eldorado Cadillac that Belinsky was supposed to get free for signing autographs on Saturday mornings wound up costing him more than $3200 in costs and charges.

Belinsky wrote off the automobile experience as just another learning adventure. He continued to drive to work in his big car and met all the payment bills himself. Most of his dates liked the idea of whirling around Hollywood in the candy apple Cadillac. Except for one show girl who proved to be rather difficult.

Bo had been making the early breakfast scene almost every morning and the Angels began cracking down. From a 6–1 record he lost six of his next seven games and suddenly wasn't as successful on the field as he would have liked. The girls in town still remembered the no-hitter, so business didn't fall down in that department. The Angels tried to warn Bo about his excessive night life. Rigney fined him for missing curfew one night on the road. He warned the rookie he'd better mend his ways. He ordered traveling secretary Tommie Ferguson to keep Dean Chance and Belinsky apart with different roommates. Belinsky was assigned to catcher Ed Sadowski. Sadowski went his way and Belinsky went his. Then Rigney came up with an idea. He assigned pitching coach Marv Grissom to room with Belinsky. It was a beautiful idea. Except Bo needed no roommates in Hollywood.

Winchell had arranged for a nice quiet party with some forty or fifty girls in attendance and maybe half that number of guys, two ballplayers, Chance and Belinsky, and a group of young actors and agents.

"It was a nice party until it was time to leave," said Bo. "When Dean and I decide to split, these two girls ask us for a ride home. Against my better judgment I decide to do it. Now we are tooling down Wilshire Boulevard and everything is fine. Well, one thing led to another, and this girl starts mouthing off about she loves me and will stay with me and wants to cook breakfast and all that bull. I'm really in no mood for that, so I tell her to keep her big mouth shut or I'll throw her out."

Chance was in the front seat. Bo was driving the car, his girl friend and the other girl were in the back seat. Belinsky pulls the car over to the side and orders the girl out. She resists.

"We're on some side street," says Bo, "and I lose my temper. I begin pulling her out of the car and she is holding on to the doorknobs. I'm pulling her over the front seat and out the door and she's hanging on to the handle. The next thing I know she smashes her head against the window and cuts herself up pretty good. She's screaming, yelling, carrying on pretty good, and I'm screaming right back at her. Just then the cops hear the noise and a squad car pulls over."

Chance, who had just sent his pregnant wife home to Ohio, didn't like the idea of getting caught at five o'clock in the morning with a girl in a car even if it was merely an innocent ride home.

"He sees the cops and he takes off," says Bo. "He decides he's going to beat it the hell out of here before the cops see him. I figure he's nuts because those L.A. cops are nobody to fool with. He starts moving away just as the cop comes around the corner and sees us. He halts Dean and threatens to shoot him if he moves an inch. Dean slows up and finally walks back."

As a rule ballplayers and police get along remarkably well. Each knows that belting a girl around in a car is just clean, wholesome fun. The cop also knows the player can't stand having any such experience make the newspapers. One ballplayer, a pitcher for the Philadelphia Phillies some years back, put the mutual understanding to its supreme test one early morning on a Chicago beach. He was undressed with his girl friend when a cop flashed a light in his face and informed both parties that they would have to come downtown for such conduct.

"Look," said the pitcher, "I'm a ballplayer with the Phillies, a married man with children, and I can't afford having this kind of thing make the papers. When I get up I'm going to pull on my pants and starting running like hell. The only way you can stop me is by shooting me in the back."

Then he took off. The cop pulled his gun from its holster, held it high in the air, shouted a warning, and then laughed. He knew and the player knew that no policeman would shoot a ballplayer in the back for doing what anyone would probably do in the very same circumstances.

Belinsky's cop was of a different breed. He was forced into action by the sight of the bleeding girl on the street. He took Bo, Dean, and the girl down to the infirmary where the girl was sewn up and repaired.

The police were attempting to get the girl to sign a complaint against Belinsky for assault. She considered it and then told Bo, "I won't sign if you promise to stay with me all week."

Belinsky thought discretion was the better part of valor, so he agreed to her untenable demands.

"You think she showed any gratitude?" said Bo. "Hell, no. Three

months later she gets a smart attorney and sues me in a civil action
for one hundred and fifty thousand dollars. My lawyer had to give
her a few bucks to get her out of town and shut her up. You just can't
trust broads.''

The story made headlines the next day in the Los Angeles papers
and Belinsky and Chance were called into the office of general
manager Fred Haney and each was fined five hundred dollars for
that episode. Reporters asked Haney if the fine was for fighting with
the girl or for being up at five o'clock in the morning.

"At home," said Haney, "there is a common sense curfew. Neither Belinsky nor Chance observed it. Neither of them know just
how close they have come to being shipped to the minors."

Belinsky told the press he would be a good boy from now on. He
reported to the ball park on a Sunday morning, three days after the
incident, with a sore throat.

"I've had three straight nights of normal rest," he said, "and this
happens to me."

Chance started the game that afternoon in Chicago against the
White Sox, lasted until the sixth inning, left with the score 5–3 in
favor of the Angels and saw Belinsky save the win for him with a fine
relief effort, his first in the major leagues. The rest of the bullpen
didn't miss the opportunity to hail Belinsky's arrival when he came
out to warm up.

"Ahh," said catcher Ed Sadowski, "the prince, Mr. Belinsky, is out
here."

Belinsky told the Los Angeles writers after the game that they had
seen the last of that wild man from Hollywood. He wouldn't stop
going out, of course, but he would control his night life and help
his team win more games.

"Hollywood can be too much," said Bo. "It's like cocaine. After
a game somebody invites you out and you say you'll go for an hour.
Next thing you know it's four hours or, if you are real lucky, it's all
night."

When we got caught out at five o'clock in the morning with those crazy broads, Bo took all the blame. He said, "The kid here had nothing to do with it." That's what I call a friend.

—*DEAN CHANCE*

The Dean of Them All

The snow covers the farm fields of eastern Ohio in the late winter of 1971. The beef cattle rest snug in their barns in the 202-acre Wooster spread of Wilmer Dean Chance, gentleman farmer. The land, the cattle, the modern equipment, the house, the goodwill, would go for something like $300,000 if Dean Chance of "Dean and Bo" wanted to liquidate.

He is away from his farm now, sitting in a cold, dimly lit building on a downtown street in Akron. Wooster is sixty miles from Cleveland, a good place to have a farm. Akron is a million miles from Madison Square Garden. That is where Dean Chance has his hopes. He is a fight promoter and his best boy, a heavyweight named Ernie Shavers, is on the threshold of the big time.

"I'll promote it in Las Vegas," Chance says. "It will be bigger than Clay-Frazier, a major event in American sports history, the biggest social event of the season with planeloads of rich guys flying in for five hundred dollars apiece to gamble, to drink, to eat in the restaurants, and to see the biggest fight in the history of boxing."

He is into bowling alleys and real estate around Akron. He promotes fights in his own gymnasium, a dark building on a grimy Akron street, but large enough to hold three hundred people paying three bucks apiece for a fight promoted by Dean Chance Enterprises. He had just paid his ex-wife Judy $65,000 in cash as a divorce settlement and pays $300 a month in child support for his son. He once made $60,000 a year playing baseball, was the youngest Cy Young Award winner in the history of the game, and was making $47,000 a year as a twenty-three-year-old pitcher.

"Yeah, I remember Bo from that first camp in Clearwater in 1959," said Chance. "He was the guy giving everybody a hotfoot. He was famous for something else then. He never ate. He lived on coffee and cigarettes. I had to laugh when he was big in L.A. A place called Dario's named an Italian sandwich after him, the Bo Special, all piled up with meat and cheese and tomatoes and the works. The last guy in the world to ever eat one would be Bo."

Chance talks with the ease and confidence of a man who hasn't a worry in the world. He has plenty of money, a full, busy life out of baseball, no wife and enough pretty girls to keep him happy.

"Nobody," said Dean, "made it with girls the way Bo did. I never learned his secret. I just enjoyed watching him operate. When I roomed with him, it was like rooming with a suitcase. I'd never see Bo at night. Into a town and gone. Albie Pearson roomed with him and said he had two jobs, one playing baseball, the other as Bo Belinsky's answering service."

Chance grew up in Wayne County, Ohio, on his parents' 166-acre dairy farm, milking cows in the early morning, playing ball until late afternoon. As a right-handed pitcher and basketball forward for Northwestern High School in Wooster, Chance was an athletic legend. He was an all-state basketball player with over one hundred colleges offering him scholarships. He was 51–1 as a high school pitcher in four years with eighteen no-hitters. Twelve of the sixteen major league clubs wanted to sign him in the summer of 1959. He was all the things in high school Bo Belinsky only heard about. The Orioles signed Chance for a thirty thousand dollar bonus.

"I met Bo in 1959 at the Orioles rookie camp in Clearwater. I think the attraction then was the fact that I had a car and Bo didn't. I had gotten a car with my bonus money. I let Bo use it anytime he wanted. We used to go into a few joints down there together, but I always had a problem. I was pitching well for that Clearwater club and every time I won a game there would be a story in the paper starting off, 'Eighteen-year-old Dean Chance. . . . ' Well, it was pretty impossible for any bartender not to know I was under age, so I couldn't get a drink anyplace. It really didn't matter. I didn't drink much and Bo didn't either. It was just a place to go.''

Ten days after he began spring training with the Angels in 1962, he saw Bo again.

"He was a celebrity even before he showed up," Chance said. "Everybody was talking about him. The players were interested in him because we had heard a lot about him and because he was holding out as a rookie. That just isn't done. We kept close to that situation because we wanted to see just how that one would come out."

Belinsky joined the Angels, and he and Chance immediately resumed their friendship. Chance was now almost twenty-one years old, could almost drink in any bar and still had a car.

"We both got off pretty good in 1962 and then Bo pitched his no-hitter. That really turned the town on. Here comes Walter and all the rest of them. I'll tell you, after that no-hitter, Bo didn't get much rest. One thing about Bo, though, everybody was excited about Bo, but Bo. He just played it cool like that was the way he had always been treated."

Chance protests that he was married during his stay in Los Angeles and was only a silent partner in Belinsky's adventures.

"Bo always had broads around, always; but after the no-hitter they were just better looking and a little more famous. I think the only girl from those days he really loved was Mamie. I think a lot of them loved him, though. There is no question in my mind that Tina Louise was in love with Bo. If Bo had asked her to marry him she would have given her movie career up in a minute for Bo."

Chance says that Winchell was Belinsky's agent for beautiful Hollywood women.

There could have been a great deal of jealousy on the Angels over Belinsky's activities, but none of it surfaced. The other players were amused and amazed by Belinsky's method of operation.

"One time we were on an eastern trip and we got back to Los Angeles at three thirty in the morning. I mean we were dragging. We get off the plane and there's Winchell waiting in the lobby with three of the best-looking girls you ever saw in your life. Bo doesn't even wait for his bags. He just gets somebody else to pick up his suitcases and takes off into the night with Walter and the girls. As they walked off, everybody cheered. We all knew Bo would have some good stories for us the next day."

By midseason Belinsky was traveling big all around the league. The team plane would arrive in New York; everybody would grumpily board a bus for the hotel, and Belinsky would casually walk to a waiting limousine and be driven to Jilly's or Shor's or the Spindletop. "Those places wanted Bo to stop in. They would send the limousines for Bo. Bo had a way with people."

After Chance and Belinsky had their early morning escapade with the girls and the cops on Wilshire Boulevard, Chance had to be a little more careful with his spare time.

"As soon as I could get to the phone the next morning I called my wife. I told her there might be something in the papers about me the next day, but not to believe any of it. I was just out for a ride with Bo. Then I called my folks and told them not to believe anything they see, hear, or read about me. It was just a lot of unfortunate circumstances. I didn't even know how it got in the papers. I guess the cops must have called the press. The next afternoon Haney called us into his office and told us we had better be prepared for the press. He said, 'Everything you guys do is big news.' I learned that all right when I walked out of Haney's office and there were twenty reporters and television and radio guys waiting for a statement. I don't know what I said, but I'm sure it had something to do with being a good boy after that."

Chance said that once his name and Bo's became linked nobody believed he could just be alone in his room watching television at night.

"One time we traveled to Washington. We were walking into the lobby of the Shoreham Hotel. There were these beautiful girls sitting there as the club comes in. Everybody thought sure they were for me and Bo. They were wrong. I wasn't going that good. They were for Bo and one of his sportswriter friends. Bo sure did share the wealth."

At the end of the 1962 season, Belinsky paid Chance a visit at his Wooster farm. It lasted one day.

"Bo just took a look at those fields and those cows and announced that farms just weren't for him. He needed the bright lights," Chance said.

Later on that winter, Chance got a call from sportswriter Bud Furillo who had been asked by the producers of *Damn Yankees* at Melodyland in Anaheim, just outside the entrance to Disneyland, to obtain the services of Dean Chance or Don Drysdale of the Dodgers for a part in the show. Furillo immediately decided on Chance.

"They'll pay seven hundred fifty dollars a week," said Furillo.

Chance decided that wasn't enough money for a show business career. Then he thought about the opportunity to make a few bucks for Belinsky, who never seemed to have enough.

"I told Furillo that if he could work out a deal where they would take me and Bo and pay us fifteen hundred dollars each I might consider it. He got back to me and said the producers would go for it. I immediately called Bo. I thought he would be excited at making fifteen hundred dollars. He didn't care about it."

"That's no money," Bo said.

"That's a lot of money for me. I'm taking it even if you don't."

"Well, if you want me to help you out," Bo said, "I'll go along with it."

Dean and Bo played Melodyland for two weeks to huge crowds. Bo didn't use his stage name Lance. The signs simply read, "Bo Belinsky and Dean Chance."

Chance was fast asleep in his room one morning before a performance when he got a phone call from Belinsky. He was frantic. He needed Chance to play cards.

"Bo had been living with this girl, Barbie," said Chance. "She liked to play cards. She had gotten Bo into a gin game and had taken him for three hundred fifty dollars, all the money he had in the world. Now he calls me. 'Dean, get your ass down here. I want you to play cards for me with Barbie.' I tried to tell him it was three o'clock in the morning but he wouldn't listen. He kept screaming for me to get down there and take his money back from Barbie. I had seven hundred fifty dollars in my pocket."

Chance dressed and went down to Belinsky's room. Barbie and Bo sat at a card table with the cards spread out in front of them. They had been playing for hours.

"I think it was three thirty when Barbie dealt me the first hand," said Chance. "I won it and figured I would clean her out in an hour, give Bo back his money, and get to sleep. Three hours later the game was over. She had cleaned me out of seven hundred and fifty dollars."

Barbie paid the price for her big win over Bo and Dean.

"He kicked her out after that," said Dean. "But he sent her home in a cab. Bo had class. She went out without a fuss. Bo waved to her and said, 'Barbie, you're a real lady.' "

By the beginning of the 1963 season the Angels accepted the fact that Belinsky and Chance were close friends and agreed to room them together.

"Everything went along just fine," says Chance, "until the very last game of spring training in Palm Springs. We had been out for dinner the night before, nothing special, and went to bed at a reasonable hour. We were breaking camp that day and heading home so we had to be at the park early. We forgot to put in a wake-up call and we got up an hour late. By the time we got to the park we were about two hours late for the workout. Rigney was pretty mad about that. He fined us five hundred dollars each for that one. I was giving back more money in fines than I was making."

Chance was 14–10 in 1962 with an impressive 2.96 ERA. It impressed the Angels enough to give him several more chances after a few skirmishes with Belinsky.

"They kept reminding me," Chance said, "that I had two more options left and I could wind up in the minors at any time."

While Chance's pitching career flourished in 1963 and 1964, Belinsky ran into difficulties. As a result, he was to find a new home in Hawaii, scene of the Los Angeles Triple-A farm team.

"The first time he was sent out," said Dean, "we had the biggest bash for him at the El Rancho Club anybody had ever seen. It just went on and on all night long in honor of Bo. It really was some sendoff. So great, in fact, that Bo blew the plane to Honolulu."

Belinsky came back to the Angels late in the 1963 season and Chance and Belinsky developed some big plans for the off-season.

"By now everybody knew that we liked to shoot pool," Chance said. "So this guy comes to me with an idea for a fantastic pool tournament in the United States, Europe, and Japan, going all over, shooting for this guy's company, making a lot of dough, and having a hell of a time. The thing was all set to go, but Bo backed out at the last minute. Just didn't want to tie himself down to something like that for so long a time. If Bo gives his word on something he does it. But the trouble is you can't get him committed to anything. He just likes to be loose all the time, on the move, just rolling along wherever his feet take him."

In the spring of 1964 they were reunited again as roommates. It was to be their last year as teammates.

"We both had a different attitude toward the game that year. We both wanted to pitch better, win more, and really move into that big money," Chance said.

Belinsky pitched well. Chance pitched spectacularly. At the age of twenty-two he had become the best pitcher in the American League and a keen rival for the incomparable Sandy Koufax. Chance established a major league record for the most 1–0 games that season, six; won twenty games and lost nine for the Angels, had a fantastic 1.65 ERA and led the league in innings pitched with 278. In July of 1964, Chance was selected to pitch the All-Star game at New York's Shea Stadium against the National League. More than fifty thousand people jammed the ball park in Flushing, New York, to get a glimpse of the marvelous pitcher with the tricky, corkscrew motion. Chance had been so good that year he had made Mickey Mantle a defensive hitter.

"Every time I see his name on a lineup card," Mantle said, "I feel like throwing up."

On the evening of July 6, 1964, he sat in the favored spot at Toots Shor's restaurant and was important enough now for the boss man, the irrepressible Shor, to greet him as a "crumb bum," his highest accolade, and point him out to show business personalities in his

joint. Then Chance moved on to Jilly's for some late evening entertainment and excitement. At about two o'clock in the morning he
fell asleep. He was to start the All-Star game in less than eleven
hours. At three thirty in the morning the violent jingle of the phone
jolted Chance awake. He was annoyed at himself for forgetting to
tell the hotel to turn off his phone. He thought it might be some silly
sportswriter calling from Los Angeles for a late story on his activities before the All-Star game. He fumbled with the light switch and
made it to the phone.

"Uhh, hello."

"Dean, we just wanted to call you and wish you luck tomorrow.
Have a good game, buddy."

"Bo, do you know what the hell time it is?"

"Time? Yeah, I guess it's—let me ask. Hey, what time is it? Dean
wants to know, he's in New York. It's twelve thirty, Dean, is that
okay?"

"Bo, for crissakes, that's L.A. time. It's three thirty here and I'm
pitching here, not there."

"Yeah, that's why we called, to wish you well tomorrow against
all those big bombers in the National League."

"Hey, Bo, that's nice of you, but I got to get to bed. Thanks for
calling."

"Good luck. We'll be watching you on the tube. Have a good
game. We'll be rooting for you."

Belinsky hung up and Chance, the twenty-two-year-old right-
hander from Wooster, Ohio, couldn't fall asleep again the rest of
the night. He kept thinking of those big bombers from the National
League.

He started the All-Star game against Don Drysdale, pitched three
scoreless innings, and left the game ahead 1–0. The Americans
managed to lose the game 7–4 but Chance had impressed all the
National Leaguers who had seen him for the first time. He was the
lead story in all the Los Angeles papers as he rejoined the club that
night.

"Bo pitched good enough to make the All-Star game, but they
never picked him. It's a shame. I think the All-Star game would have
been a perfect scene for Bo."

Chance finished the season in a blaze of glory in 1964. He was awarded the Cy Young Award, symbolic of the best pitching in the league, and the first to call and congratulate him was Bo.

"Bo is a thoughtful guy," said Chance. "He had a lot of good times, but he was always kind, considerate, and understanding. I'm not ashamed to say it. Bo was the best friend I ever had in baseball. He would have made a lot of money if he had been more serious about the game. I always did pretty well with money in baseball and I always tried to help Bo when I could. He just doesn't know how to hold on to money. Bo is one of those guys if you give him a hundred thousand dollars today he'll let it slip through his fingers and give you nothing back tomorrow."

For his side, if one were to give Dean Chance $100,000 today, there would be a good chance he would convert it into $200,000 tomorrow.

After their paths separated in 1964, Chance pitched two more seasons for the Angels and then was traded to Minnesota because the Angels simply didn't want him around any more. They got a journeyman outfielder, Jimmie Hall, a journeyman first baseman, Don Mincher, and a rookie pitcher named Pete Cimino for him on December 2, 1966. In 1967 Chance won twenty games for the Minnesota Twins. He held out for a $60,000 contract. When he got it, it was mid-March. By the time he was able to pitch it was mid-April and the season had already begun. Chance hurt his back rushing himself into shape and never was the same pitcher again. He was traded to Cleveland in 1970 and then sold to the New York Mets in September of that year for $150,000. The Mets sold him to the Detroit Tigers on March 30, 1971, and the Tigers released him at the end of the 1971 season.

"I wish I could get something going for Bo," he said. "Maybe I'll open a pool hall and let Bo run it for me. I'll pay him fifty bucks a week and let the rest of the money be invested for him by a professional. If I pay Bo all the money it would be gone before he got it."

Chance says the Los Angeles papers always wanted to believe the worst about himself and Bo.

"They made up a lot of stuff," says Chance. "And we never denied it. Why, one time, we even believed we could only foul up.

We're in the clubhouse in Washington and Rigney calls us into his office. 'J. Edgar Hoover wants to see you two guys.' I'm wondering what we did now that the F.B.I. would want us. We were escorted up to Hoover's office and he had a big grin on his face, wanted to shake our hands and just wanted to meet us. We hadn't done anything wrong. 'Walter just wanted me to meet you,' Hoover said. It was pretty exciting. We went all through that F.B.I. building and saw all of their latest machines, shotguns; had a great time. It was really a wonderful day. That's the way it always was when I was with Bo. We had a lot of laughs and I don't have any regrets at all about my time in the major leagues with Bo. He's one hell of a guy in my book. He'd give me the shirt off his back and I'd give him the shirt off mine. I think I'll give him a pool room. It's the least I can do for a guy who covered up for me because I was a married man. He's a good friend. When I get to be an old man, I'll think back often to those days of 1962, '63, and '64 and I'll be smiling, you can bet on that."

I'm going to have something to say to him about popping off like that when I catch up with him.

—MANAGER BILL RIGNEY OF THE ANGELS

Everything's Up To Date in KC but Bo

The 1962 season will be remembered as Bill Rigney's finest summer. The Los Angeles Angels had finished eighth in 1961, their first season in the American League, and that was considered a major achievement.

"It was certainly more than any of us had expected in our first season," said owner Gene Autry.

In 1962 Rigney was pulling off some kind of a major miracle. By midseason he actually had the Angels in the thick of the pennant race. On June 15 they were in fourth place just two and one-half games behind the New York Yankees. On June 30 they had climbed to second place, just one-half game away from the top. As late as August 3, when all pretenders to the Yankee throne are supposed to be gone, the Angels were only three games behind the Yankees in second place.

The team got some surprising pitching from Ken McBride and Eli Grba, some fine hitting from Leon Wagner and Albie Pearson, and a tight defense.

More and more as the summer wore on, the big difference between the Angels of 1961 and the Angels of 1962 had to be the fantastic pitching of the two rookies, Bo Belinsky and Dean Chance. At one point Belinsky was 7–1 on the season and Chance was 12–7. The Angels were staying in the race on the strength of these two young arms.

"Bo went into a slump," said Chance, "but he didn't let his sense of humor go down with his pitching."

It was Belinsky's habit to soothe his pitching and professional ills with parties. A pitcher had to forget a bad performance if he was to be any good to himself or his teammates next time. No pitcher could forget a bad performance faster than Belinsky. Just about the time Belinsky started having trouble winning on the field, he instituted a program off the field that was to amuse, entertain, and invigorate all of his teammates.

The Angels were going to a champagne party.

"I had always liked champagne parties," says Bo. "I can't remember where I had my first one. I know it wasn't in Trenton. No one ever heard of champagne back there."

Belinsky and Chance, as cohosts, set the ground rules for the party. The party would take place on the road, in the team hotel, in a separate room rented for that purpose. It would usually be a very small group consisting of Belinsky and Chance as cohosts, several pretty girls as cohostesses and one honored guest from the Los Angeles Angels.

"We didn't want to pick out the guy and make all the other guys feel bad," said Belinsky, "so we held a raffle. The guy with the winning ticket would be guest-for-a-night. Of course, for him, all expenses were paid.

The date, time, and place for the party were set. Belinsky walked on the field one day in Washington (champagne parties were often held in Washington because the team stayed at the Shoreham Hotel, known for the largest rooms in any hotel on the baseball circuit) and everybody was asked to pick a slip out of Belinsky's uniform hat. The slips had different words printed on them at different times for the winners. But there was no mistaking the winning tickets with words like "smile" or "bingo, now you get bango-ed" written on them. Belinsky always held the drawing before a game so he could watch his man operate during that afternoon or evening's game to see if it resulted in the man having a better or worse day than usual.

"We had this one guy on the club, an infielder, who was really a fine fielder. Well, one day he won the winning ticket in the champagne party. He got four hits that day and made some of the greatest fielding plays you ever saw in your life. I think it did a hell of a lot for him. The guy was married and was a very quiet, shy guy. He seemed like the kind of guy who would have to ask his wife permission to sleep with her. Now that he knew he would be making it at the champagne party, he got so loose he became the greatest ballplayer in the world."

The infielder started the champagne party slowly and shyly but after a few glasses of the bubbly, he went to work and had himself a memorable evening.

"I have to admit," said Belinsky, "there was quite a letdown after that. I think he went one for twenty five after that, or something like that. Every day he would come up to me and say, 'Bo, when's the next party? I gotta go to your next party.' I hated to tell the poor guy we had another rule. Nobody could make more than one appearance a season at our parties."

Parties or not, the Angels continued to romp through the 1962 season. Everywhere the team went Rigney and his players were celebrities. This was the first year of the National League expansion and the Mets and the Houston Colt 45s were where expansion baseball teams are supposed to be, in the bottom. Los Angeles, surprising everyone—mostly themselves—was right up at the top of the league with the lordly Yankees.

On July 23, 1962, with Belinsky in decline and Chance struggling slightly, the Angels decided to deal for another pitcher. It was to have a profound bearing on Belinsky's career. The Angels traded outfielder Gordon Windhorn, who had once been a Yankee farmhand with a supposed future as a hitter, for a right-handed relief pitcher named Dan Osinski. The Angels and the Kansas City Athletics also agreed that Kansas City would get another player from Los Angeles at the end of the season. The player to be named later was not identified in the papers filed by the two clubs with the Commissioner of Baseball, Ford C. Frick. The fact that a player to be named later was included in the deal was not announced to the press.

Soon the fact that another player from Los Angeles, preferably a pitcher, was to be delivered to the Kansas City club at the end of the year became a known fact. Speculation on the question followed the Angels from town to town as they played around the circuit. Each team had a candidate for a trade to Los Angeles and if the Angels were to trade off another pitcher, every other club would be ready for a trade with the Angels. Suddenly the Angels had marketable baseball players.

"We speculated about the player to be named later," said Belinsky, "but none of the speculation concerned me or Dean. We were both rookies having good years and we didn't seem like the kind of players a club would trade away for a pitcher like Osinski. I was still learning a lot about big league baseball, and I was finding out that what you do on the field may not be nearly as important as what you do off the field."

Late in the afternoon of August 28 Belinsky got into a cab at the Muehlebach Hotel in Kansas City and rode to Kansas City Municipal Stadium with Dean Chance. Bo dressed quickly and went on the field as was his custom to exchange pleasantries with the players on the other team, many of whom he had known in baseball. Ballplayers are the tightest fraternity in sports, more than half of each team having played with or against the other team's players throughout their career. They are bound together by their common problems and common antagonisms, management, the press, the fans, and the problems of the road; problems like keeping their wives back home quiet and content while they are amused and entertained by such notorious baseball followers (Annies, as the players call them) as Chicago Shirley, a one-woman ball team. She was the only woman in baseball known to have balled a whole team in one night.

"I was out near the batting cage kidding with some of the guys on the A's," Belinsky said. "We were having a few laughs and talking over some old times and some new talent. Then they blew the whistle to signify that the A's had finished their time for batting practice and that now it was our turn to hit. I pulled my glove out of my back pocket and I started walking slowly toward the outfield to shag flies."

Belinsky walked slowly across the infield and walked toward center field. Near second base he happened to cross paths with Hank

Bauer, the gruff manager of the Kansas City A's, who has been forever immortalized by one sportswriter as a man whose face "looks like a clenched fist."

"I had always kidded with Hank like I kid with everybody else," Bo said. "We crossed paths and I nodded to him and asked him how he was doing in this goddamn heat."

"Hey, Bo," Bauer said, "take good care of yourself the rest of the way. Next year you'll be with us."

"Next year I'll be with you?"

Bauer was already walking in toward his dugout and never said anything more to Belinsky. Bo continued to walk out toward the outfield and almost started screaming before he got there.

"Next year I'll be with him? For crissakes, he's in Kansas City. What the hell am I going to do in Kansas City?"

Belinsky spent the rest of the night sitting on the bench thinking about the move to Kansas City. He was to be the player to be named later for Osinski. Osinski for Belinsky. It would be a headline writer's nightmare.

The Angels went on to Washington for three games. Belinsky hadn't said a word to anybody about what Bauer had told him. He was still seething when the team arrived at the Shoreham Hotel. He was so angry he decided to have a champagne party and not invite any other players. It was a nice party, but it still didn't soothe his furrowed brow.

"We were going into New York for a weekend series over Labor Day," said Bo. "I figured that would be the place to let it out. I wasn't going to no goddamn Kansas City. They got a lot of stews [airline stewardesses] there, but what the hell do you do with them after you ball them—there's no place to go."

In less than a year in the major leagues Belinsky had made himself a major drawing card. Yankee Stadium was filled with nearly sixty thousand people for a Sunday doubleheader with Belinsky scheduled for the first game and Chance for the second.

"I was going against Whitey Ford," said Bo. "I figured I would be helped if I could pick up his mud ball after each inning before the umpires did."

Not much helped Bo this day. He was knocked out early, Chance was beaten in the other game and the Angels were finished as far as the pennant was concerned. Win, lose, or draw, Belinsky was still one of the favorite interviews for New York sportswriters. They gathered around him and Belinsky announced, "I've been traded to the A's as the player to be named later in the Osinski deal and I'm not going."

Belinsky protected Bauer and would not reveal how he knew. He just insisted that he was accurate, that the deal had been completed and that he was to be sent to Kansas City as soon as the season was over.

When the story hit the newspapers the next day, the Angels and all baseball were horribly embarrassed. Hank Bauer remained silent in Kansas City. Rigney exploded in New York. Fred Haney couldn't imagine how the details leaked out. A trade of a player to be named later is a calculated risk. If the player finds out he is to be with another club, it opens baseball to all sorts of suspicion. A man playing for one club against a second club—one he will soon join—may not try his hardest against that team. That suggests that every game may not be fought honestly and legitimately. It opens baseball up to the kind of suspicion that has supposedly disappeared since the infamous Black Sox scandal of 1919, when the Chicago White Sox threw that World Series to the Cincinnati Reds.

It rained the afternoon the story broke in the New York papers, and the Angels immediately called a press conference to deny everything.

Rigney sat in his hotel suite falling all over his heated denials. This was really a front-office matter, not a manager's task, but Rigney was the senior man with the club and took the heat. He had been on the phone all morning with the Angels front office and knew full well that Belinsky had been the man both teams had agreed to as the player to be named later. Then, doing his duty to God, country, and the Angels, Rigney lied to the press.

"This is absolutely ridiculous," he said. "No player on this club has been named to complete the deal. It just isn't so."

Rigney's face was growing livid with anger and his white hair seemed be standing up on his head in rage.

"It is true that we owe Kansas City a player," Rigney said, "but that was announced at the time of the deal."

Rigney was not questioned by any of the writers as to the fact that the player to be named later was not announced at all as the deal was made, but had been leaked to newsmen from Kansas City sources at a later date.

"Transactions like this are made in baseball all the time," said Rigney. "But we couldn't designate the player now even if we wanted to. It would be a violation of baseball law. At the close of the season we'll get together with the Kansas City club and work this out. Right now I don't know who the player will be and neither do they."

When Belinsky had announced that he was the player to be named later and was ticketed for Kansas City, the question was put to Kansas City owner Charles O. Finley.

Finley, a millionaire insurance executive from Chicago, had made a fortune specializing in malpractice suits for physicians. As his business had prospered, his ego had grown. Still, he had not received the kind of rewards he thought he had earned: mainly attention and national fame. Having been a sports fan for a long time, he decided to purchase a baseball team. He bought the A's and immediately annoyed his fellow American league owners with his publicity gimmicks, including a team jackass he modestly named Charley O. But he had finally received the national attention he craved. He got more of it after the Belinsky furor.

At first Finley decided he would neither "confirm nor deny" that Belinsky was the player to be named later. To knowledgeable fans, this immediately confirmed that the player was Belinsky. Finley knew it was but he also knew his fellow owners wouldn't take kindly to his saying so since it violated baseball management traditions.

Finley then made a statement to the press.

"We made a deal with Los Angeles in which we sent them Osinsky for cash and a player to be named later. That player is subject to approval by both clubs. We do not know if that player will be Belinsky or somebody else. I cannot come out and say we got Belinsky when we don't know if we got him or not. Los Angeles has not promised us Belinsky or any other player on the team. We might even have a lot of discussion on the subject."

It was a nice, gentle way of saying that the A's expected to get Belinsky but if they fussed about it too much, they would not. Of course, Bo had blown the whistle on the deal and Kansas City would never get Belinsky. It was too bad. Bo and Charley O. would have made a hell of an act.

Rigney seemed angrier that Belinsky had let the cat out of the bag about the deal than he was about the fact that baseball may have been caught pulling off a suspicious deal. Rigney indicated the possible danger areas.

"I think I'll have to sit down and have a serious talk with this young man. He seems to be a little mixed up. All this certainly hasn't helped the ball club. Why, we still have a shot for the pennant. For all any of us knows, he may be in there pitching for us in the World Series. How would he like that?"

Reporters checked with Commissioner Ford Frick after Rigney's press conference and immediately discovered that there had been no official mention of any player to be named later in any part of the deal for Osinski.

Commissioner Frick, a former newspaperman who had been given the job for his loyal services to the game as a journalist—a bad indictment for a supposedly objective journalist—was unavailable when reporters sought information on the contract. He had been unavailable for most sticky situations during his long tenure and covered up his inability to make meaningful decisions on ticklish questions by announcing, "That's a league matter." For that diligence, the baseball owners kept rehiring him each year and rewarding him with higher pay until they retired him with full battle honors. His achievements in office would fill the head of a pin. Upon his retirement, for this persistently loyal do-nothing service Ford C. Frick was named to the Hall of Fame. He was replaced by a retired air force general named William D. Eckert. The general's claim to fame occurred the instant of his election when Willie Mays innocently inquired, "Who he?" and Larry Fox, a *New York World Telegram and Sun* newsman, announced, "My God, they have hired the unknown soldier."

After Eckert was fired in a palace coup by baseball's young Turks, Belinsky announced that he was available for the commissionership.

"Why not?" he asked. "I couldn't do worse."

After a heated struggle between Charles Feeney, general manager of the Giants, and Michael Burke, president of the Yankees, both good and creative young men, baseball failed to agree and elected as commissioner a Wall Street attorney and Princeton graduate named Bowie Kuhn. He put on a hell of a public relations show in his first year in office, snowed the baseball owners into a new seven-year, one-million-dollar contract, and went into an immediate decline.

Baseball has not been terribly successful with its choices for leadership. It is mostly because strong, rich men own baseball teams and strong, rich men don't want strong, independent men telling them how to run their businesses.

When Frick finally got around to studying the Belinsky deal and the outrageous practice of naming players later, he ruled that he couldn't rule, that it was "a league matter" or a club matter, and everybody should wait until the season was over and see what would happen.

On November 30, 1962, at baseball's annual winter meetings, Fred Haney announced that the Angels were sending pitcher Ted Bowsfield to the Kansas City A's as "the pitcher to be named later" in the deal for Dan Osinski. Haney had a sour look on his face when he announced it. For once, the reporters were kind. They laughed a little and wrote it down dutifully. By his own public announcement of the impending deal, Belinsky had killed the trade—which is probably what he had intended to do.

Kansas City would just have to get along without Bo.

The furor over the aborted deal started quieting down in early September as the Angels stayed surprisingly close in the pennant race. All chances of catching the Yankees were just about gone, but there was a great deal of hope the Angels could finish in second place. It meant a great deal to the young Angels.

"I was making eighty-five hundred that year," said Dean Chance, "and one thousand five hundred for finishing in second place seemed like an awful lot of money. I wanted it. Bo didn't seem to care. He never seemed to care when money was involved. We started to slip farther back in the pennant race. Now we were in danger of slipping out of third place also."

The Minnesota Twins passed the Angels in the standings in early September and moved into second place. The Angels had a rough eastern trip and arrived home eight games out of first place with no chance for the pennant. They still had a strong hold on third place, and for an expansion team it was certainly an impressive position.

The Angels kept losing and the Detroit Tigers, figured to be a contender, started winning. Now the Chicago White Sox also put on a burst and panic was setting in around the Angels. Rigney got edgy and the players, tired from the pressures of staying close most of the season, didn't think they had much left.

Los Angeles arrived at the Hotel Cleveland on Thursday, September 27, for the final three-game series starting the next night. Bill Rigney called Belinsky and Chance to his hotel suite.

"We have to win two out of the next three games to finish in third place," he said. "I want you guys to go out tonight and have a hell of a time. Then get your rest for the next three days. You'll be pitching the last two games."

Rigney had bad-mouthed Belinsky to the press and now he wanted him to help him finish third. It was the kind of move typical baseball managers make. They are sweethearts when they think a player can help them and devils when they think he can't. Rigney still had hopes for Belinsky. He already knew that Chance, who had emerged as a star in his rookie season, would give him the best game he could.

Belinsky and Chance scheduled a champagne party. They knew there wasn't much else to do for excitement in Cleveland. The party went off well and Chance and Belinsky arrived early at Cleveland's Municipal Stadium the next day.

"I went down to the bullpen to get some sleep," said Chance. "I wasn't going to pitch that night so I thought I would rest."

Belinsky joined him down there. He was scheduled for the Saturday game.

"I went down there to think about those cute little creamers we had the night before," Bo said.

Cleveland knocked out the Los Angeles starter and Chance was awakened from a deep slumber.

"When Rigney waved to Marv Grissom to get me ready," Chance said, "Marv didn't believe it, either."

Chance was the man Rigney wanted. He came on in to relieve, pitched five strong innings and the Angels won the game. With Belinsky pitching well the next day the Angels won again. On Sunday the season ended and the Angels finished in third place. It was a happy flight home.

For bringing the Angels home in third place, Bill Rigney was named Manager of the Year in separate polls held by the Associated Press and United Press International. Los Angeles gathered other individual honors. Tom Tresh of the Yankees finished first in the Rookie of the Year voting, but Bob Rodgers, the fine young catcher of the Angels, finished in second place. Dean Chance finished in a tie for third place with Bernie Allen of Minnesota and Dick Radatz, the huge relief pitcher of the Boston Red Sox. Los Angeles players Billy Moran, Lee Thomas, and Leon (Daddy Wags) Wagner were members of the All-Star team.

It had been a highly successful year for the Angels. In their first season, 1961, without Belinsky and Chance, they had drawn 603,510 fans. In 1962, with Belinsky and Chance, they had almost doubled that attendance to 1,144,063. It would be presumptuous to say that Belinsky and Chance were the only or, even, the most significant factors in the increased draw. The team improved, they had a pennant run, they had a dozen fine players and the manager had an exceptional year. Still, Belinsky and Chance generated most of the excitement.

"I know one thing," says the publicity man Irv Kaze. "They may not have been the most important guys on the team but they sure helped."

"Let's face it," says Bo, with no false modesty, "I put that team on the map."

Belinsky had also done a good job of putting himself on the map. With the season ended he returned to Los Angeles and started enjoying the steady nights he couldn't enjoy during the season. When the season ended Belinsky could go where he pleased. He went Hollywood.

"I got the eye shades, let my hair grow a little longer, and spent my nights in the best clubs in Hollywood. There are a lot of people in Hollywood who like to drop names. My name was still a pretty good one to drop that winter, so a lot of people were dropping it. Hollywood is a strange scene. Show biz people will come on strong for people in other fields like sports where they won't come on strong for other show biz people."

Belinsky's nights were filled with delicious dishes presented on a platter by Winchell. By day he even managed to be invited to play in tennis matches with Dinah Shore. By night there were pool parties with Tina Louise. There were parties of every sort and stars and starlets pounding at his doorstep at all hours of the day and night.

"I was young, I was strong, I was healthy. The whole thing was a ball. I only had one rule about these broads, they had to come highly recommended. I wouldn't take out a broad without checking her references. Most of the times the broads I dated all were touted by friends of mine, Hollywood agents, directors, producers, friends of Winchell, newspaper people, guys like that, responsible, serious people."

Like all baseball people, Belinsky put a lot of faith in the scouting report. Ballplayers are scouted by trained eyes and their future abilities are analyzed and reported to the club in hopes of discovering a virgin star in the woods, like a seventeen-year-old Mickey Mantle in Commerce, Oklahoma, or an eighteen-year-old Lou Gehrig at Columbia University, or an eighteen-year-old Willie Howard Mays in Westfield, Alabama.

The most famous scouting report—crisp, concise, and completely accurate—was turned in by a Cuban scout named Mike Gonzalez to the St. Louis Cardinals after he had examined a young shortstop over a period of months in Havana. Gonzalez wired his office, "GOOD FIELD NO HIT."

The Belinsky scouting system isn't as concise and takes a little more time for thorough examination, but serves the purposes of rating some of the prospects he studied during the happy winters in Los Angeles.

TINA LOUISE —"Big redhead, great body, great legs, very sweet girl. She wasn't doing well in the movies at that time so any extra publicity she could get would help her out. She turned out to be a real nice girl, not domineering, and I enjoyed being with her. She had been to Europe a great deal and had a continental flair about her. It was nice. I really enjoyed being with her. She was equally comfortable in the society scene or down in the roughneck places with me. She was a good broadie."

ANN-MARGRET —"I met her at a party. Somebody had thrown a party for Corbett Monica, the comedian, and she was there and I was introduced to her. She was show business all the time, always on; the kind of girl that if you took her out to a nightclub to watch a show, she would manage to get the emcee to notice her and call on her, and when you looked around she had done six or seven numbers on the stage. She wasn't quite as good-looking or sexy in person as she was on the screen. I was surprised when she did that sexy stuff in *Carnal Knowledge*. I didn't think she was the type. She was a little bossy, sort of the mother type, wanted to tell you what to do all the time. She was a smart girl though. She was being handled by Colonel Parker, who had handled Elvis Presley, and she knew she would make the big time."

PAULETTE GODDARD —"Let me tell you, it was a thrill taking her out to dinner. I met her through some friends. There was no hanky-panky, just a nice, pleasant evening with an elegant lady. I think she had been my favorite actress when I was a kid and when I got the chance to take her out, I almost flipped out. We went to dinner and then out to the Peppermint West on celebrity night, and everybody treated her with great respect. She was an important and wonderful lady. I'll tell you something else about her. She was a little older than me, of course, but I never noticed. She was such a beautiful woman, so elegant, so courtly, that you never realized her age. There are some women who just never grow old. Paulette Goddard is one of them."

QUEEN SORAYA —"She was always lonely, always unhappy. When the Shah of Iran gave her up, she was certain she was cursed. She was always looking for somebody who could take the curse off her. She lived in Zurich at the time and I think she was getting fifteen thousand dollars a month as alimony from the Shah so she could live good. We went out in her chauffeured limousine. She was very elegant, a magnificent woman, beautiful to look at. She spent a lot of time in seclusion. I guess it isn't easy being a Shah's ex-wife. One thing about her, she always was heavily weighted down with jewels. Maybe she'll leave me one of those emeralds."

DORIS DUKE —"They tell me she is the world's richest woman. I went to a party at her place one time. I think they called it the Garden of Allah or something like that. Fantastic place, grounds just went on and on and on. She's an old broad but she's fun to be with. I think at that time she was going out with a Filipino piano player. Everybody knew she promised big alimony to her husbands in case it didn't work out. I wasn't interested in that. I wasn't about to be a gigolo for anybody, not even for somebody like Doris Duke who had all the bread in the world. But it wouldn't be bad having that steady alimony money coming in now, would it?"

Belinsky's list of lovelies could go on and on but he says most of them, the starlets, the cocktail waitresses, the Baseball Annies, the simple, pretty girls he met in his travels, have disappeared from the deepest recesses of his mind.

There were a lot of pretty girls in Bo Belinsky's life but the two most important, Mamie Van Doren and Jo Collins, were yet to come.

I'm pregnant.

Surfboard Serenade

The best weapon a general manager of a baseball team has in his arsenal when he begins negotiating contract with his players each season is the weather report. Snow clogged the roads in the midwest and the east late in February. High winds blew in the plains states. At the Riviera Hotel in Palm Springs, California, the temperature was eighty-one degrees on February 22, 1963. One by one, players began signing contracts for less money than they had hoped for and left home in snow, to arrive in the beautiful California sun.

Belinsky, who had been sunning himself tan all winter in Los Angeles, was not after the better weather in Palm Springs. He simply was broke. He signed his contract with the Angels for $13,500 and received an advance of $1000 when he reported to the Riviera Hotel.

Baseball teams do not like to pay salaries in advance. Most of them do it, anyway. Ballplayers are paid on the first and fifteenth of each month during the season. Few can make it through the next winter without an advance if they don't work. Bo Belinsky never worked in the winter. Bo Belinsky always received advances.

"I wanted to hold out for more money," he said, "but I couldn't afford to. I came on, took what they had offered and started to work hard. I wanted to have a good year. I liked the Hollywood life and I wanted to be able to afford it."

An hour before midnight on the reporting date, Belinsky drove his candy apple Eldorado Cadillac into the parking lot of the Riviera Hotel, flipped the doorman two dollars, pointed to his car and announced, "Take care of everything." Then he marched into the lobby of the hotel. A dozen pairs of pretty eyes followed him.

"One thing I always said about the Angels," laughs Bo. "They never trained in a wilderness."

Many ball clubs do. They believe a team can get ready for the rigors of a season only with a spring training routine of incredible abstinence and discipline. The Dodgers have always trained in such a wilderness, the abandoned navy barracks of Vero Beach. Dodger players are famous for climbing out of windows and over fences to make it into town. Even Sandy Koufax fell prey to the great out-doors and was fined for skipping the barracks for a night in town.

Angel players were content to stay close to the team's headquarters. They had no reason to do otherwise. Good things came to them.

"Some friend of mine came down from L.A.," Belinsky says, "and we went out to dinner. I was rooming with Albie Pearson that spring and we took him along, just the three of us, Albie, this other guy, and me. Now we have a great dinner in town and we head back to the hotel. I had set something up for this guy and me and the girls were waiting there as I walked in the door. Albie was as straight and faithful a guy as I had ever met in baseball. Some guys won't take a piece of strange. He wouldn't even think about it. So now the three of us walk through the door. These two girls come over and before I have a chance to introduce my pal, this one girl puts her arms around Albie. She thinks he is her date instead of my pal from L.A. Albie starts getting red in the face and finally I get the situation straightened out. Now Albie breaks away and heads to his room. We're standing there, talking in the lobby, and this girl walks off. She's gone a few minutes and then I hear this loud screaming. I look up and I see Albie running through the halls and out of the lobby of the hotel. The broad had gone crazy over him. You know, he's little and real cute and she wanted him. She had knocked on his hotel door and he had opened it by mistake. She started to chase him and he ran out of the hotel to get away. He jumped in his car and drove all the way home to Riverside where he lived. I think he must have called ten times the next day to find out if she was gone before he would come back for the workout."

While most ballplayers think nothing of having a little friendly entertainment at times, there are those who refuse to get caught up in the whirl.

"One guy on the team, married, with a couple of kids, just wouldn't touch any strange stuff," said Bo. "We used to kid him a lot about it but nobody could move him. He was loyal to his wife and that was it. Great. But he still liked to watch."

One evening Chance had invited a girl up to his room for a little socializing. This fellow had heard about it and asked Chance for a seat in the house.

"He wanted to watch," said Bo, "but he wouldn't touch. Dean told him he could stay in the closet if he was a good boy. Well, Dean gives him the key and he goes up there and gets in the small bedroom closet. Dean comes up a little later with the girl. The guy has been in the closet about a half hour by the time Dean gets upstairs. Now Dean gets moving with the girl. You know Dean, he works slowly. That's the way farmers are. You can't rush him into anything. I guess maybe an hour or an hour and a half passed before Dean let the girl out and went to the door of the bedroom closet. He opens it up and the guy collapses on him. He is as white as a sheet and he starts gasping for breath. Dean puts him on the bed and opens the window. The guy finally starts breathing normally. It was really a hairy scene. Can you imagine a guy so weird he would suffocate himself just to see something like that?"

Chance and Belinsky and the rest of the Angels worked hard getting themselves in shape for the 1963 season. The Angels had finished third the previous season and seriously thought they could challenge the domination of the Yankees. It was a good spring training. True to his style, Belinsky was working as hard on the field as he was off the field. He pitched well by day and night and the lobby of the Riviera was always filled with beautiful girls. The only problem with beautiful girls is the fact that they sometimes become pregnant. One of the major unrecorded expense items of ball clubs throughout baseball is the cost of settling paternity suits out of court or advancing money to players, especially married players, to handle abortions.

"Dean had been pulling a few tricks on me," said Bo, "so I decided to get even with him. I would scare hell out of him."

Bo instructed one of his lady friends on the next move. He waited until Dean was in his room and marched the girl to the house phone. He stood next to her as the young lady asked for Chance's room.

"Hello."

"Dean?"

"Yes, who is this?"

"Jane, Jane Evans, from Sacramento."

The girl made the name up. She could say anything. The reason Chance would accept any name was because ballplayers often date girls without knowing their names, something that prevents involvement and keeps the consciences of all concerned clear.

"Yeah, hi, Jane."

"I'm downstairs and I want to come up. I have something very important to tell you."

"Important? What do you mean?"

"Well, I can't tell you on the house phone, but it's very important."

"Look, who is this and what do you want?"

"Dean Chance," she said in the loudest voice she could summon, "I'm pregnant and you are the father."

The silence was oppressive on the opposite end of the phone. The girl just announced that she was coming up and Dean better acknowledge his dirty deed.

"I just stood there breaking up," said Bo. "All of a sudden, here comes Dean, panting, racing out of the elevator. He's really shook. I make believe I don't see him. 'Bo, Bo, I gotta talk to you. Something awful's just happened.' He's almost screaming at me. I still make believe I don't hear him. 'Calm down, Dean, you're acting like an expectant father.' "

Chance stared at Belinsky and realized he had been had. He told him he would get even with him and didn't want to talk to him again unless he apologized for giving him a heart attack.

"I think it took Dean about a week," said Bo, "before he got his nerves together after that one."

The final days of spring training are the most difficult for ballplayers. The manager allows two or three weeks before he begins making serious decisions. Then each game, each inning pitched, becomes significant to the player's career. It is only when a player has the status of a Mays, a Musial, a Koufax, an Aaron that he can train at his own pace, under his own conditions.

Rigney had cut the squad to a dozen pitchers. Two more had to go before the Angels would open the season April 9 at Chavez Ravine against the Boston Red Sox. Belinsky had not pitched well and he was in the running for a ticket to the minor leagues.

"When you are a fringe player," said Belinsky, "more things come into play at cutdown time than your pitching record. They always held my off-field activities against me. If I was a straight and narrow guy I would have stayed around a lot longer."

It is one thing for ballplayers to discreetly entertain girls in their rooms. This is accepted as the code of the road. It is another thing to entertain them flamboyantly as Belinsky did, parading the beautiful girls through the lobby, past the manager and the coaches, past the other club officials, and past a dozen drooling teammates. It is not good for team morale. So they say. When a manager finds that his club is not going well, outside activities become the first cause. He may immediately forget that his team lived and loved exactly the same when they were winning. But when they lose, that's the cause. Wes Westrum, the successor to Casey Stengel and a kind of gentle man who was a marvelous coach and an overwhelmed leader, once attacked his Mets players in a clubhouse meeting. He shouted at them for their inefficiency. He told them they were not hustling, not thinking, not concentrating on their jobs.

"And what's more," he shouted in a fit of anger, "no more broads in the rooms."

The clubhouse was deathly silent until one veteran player said in a stage whisper, "Hell, I didn't know he allowed broads in the rooms."

Both Chance and Belinsky made the club as the Angels traveled home for the start of the season. But everything started off wrong. Nobody hit. The veterans seemed to have grown old over the winter. The fielding was horrible. Every move Rigney made backfired. Chance couldn't win. And as for Belinsky, he was terrible and unlucky, a very bad combination for any pitcher.

Rigney started Belinsky in rotation simply because his arm was sound. Nobody else was winning and there was no other pitcher on the Angels who could replace Bo. By May 15 the Angels were 17–19 on the season, in seventh place, and five games behind the leading Chicago White Sox. They could draw some solace from the fact that the Yankees, in third place, were struggling along as well, two games out of first place. Ralph Houk didn't panic. He knew he had the players. Rigney wasn't sure. He wondered if 1962, the glorious third-place finish, had been a fluke or was this simply a bad start?

"I was one-six on the season, but I was still smiling," said Bo. "I hadn't been pitching well, but I hadn't been getting any runs, either. In five of my six losses, I got one run or less. That doesn't help break a losing streak."

Belinsky and Chance needed some recreation. It was the only thing that could take their minds off these horrible games. They decided to have a party in Belinsky's penthouse pad. This one would be different. No girls. Just guys for gambling, a little Las Vegas West.

After the drinks, Chance leaned back in his chair and nonchalantly suggested a game.

"Let's shoot a little craps just to kill some time," he said. "Nothing big."

It was near midnight; there was a day game the next afternoon, so everybody knew the game couldn't go more than ten or twelve hours before everybody would have to leave for the ball park.

"Okay," said Bo, "let's go upstairs."

The players marched into the parlor ready for action. The table had been set up surprisingly with dice, chips, and drinks. Everything was ready.

"You know how Dean moves," said Bo. "Real slow, with the big legs just sliding along the ground. Now he moves toward the wall and gets ready to plug in a table light. Everybody is at the table ready to go, their sleeves are rolled up, the chips are counted out. All we need to start the game is Dean. Nobody is really watching him except me. Everybody figured he was just getting a drink or hanging up his coat. He winks and picks up the wire and plugs it into the socket."

Sparks flew, there was a loud flash of flame and smoke and some anxious yelling and screaming.

"Dean," said Bo, "had blown all the lights in the house."

That ended the game. It also ended Dean's electronic career in Belinsky's apartment.

"After that," said Bo, "I wouldn't let him change a light bulb."

The aborted party didn't change conditions in the club very much. Belinsky continued to struggle and Chance was losing games at a rapid rate.

On May 26 Belinsky was called into manager Bill Rigney's office. It wasn't a good sign. Ballplayers are only called into a manager's office to hear bad news; a mistake they made, a violation of curfew, a dressing down for real or imagined offenses, or most unhappily, to be sent to some other club or to the minor leagues.

"Hey, Bo," said trainer Freddie Frederico, a small, bouncy man who administered to the players' aches, real and imagined, "Rig wants to see you."

It was said without any hint of the message that was to come. One look at Rigney's face gave it away. He avoided Bo's eyes as the left-hander walked into his office.

"Bo," he said softly, "we think . . ."

It is interesting that managers suddenly lose all their poise, confidence, and security when they have to tell a player he is being sent to the minors. They remembered how it felt. They try to make the player realize it isn't their own decision. It was a group cabal that was sending Belinsky to Hawaii.

". . . you have to get straightened out, get your stuff back . . . work on your control . . . we have to . . . uhh . . . we think . . . maybe . . . if you worked on your control in Hawaii you could rejoin us. . . ."

"I was smiling the whole time I sat in there," Belinsky said. "I was smiling when I came out of there. They can shoot knives at me but I'll still be smiling. That's my only defense."

Belinsky had a 1–7 record when he was sent on option to Hawaii. He had walked thirteen hitters in his last three starts and had little grounds for defense when Rigney gave him the news. He knew a 1–7 record was hard to defend. Another pitcher might have gotten a couple of more months to straighten out, but Belinsky was not an ordinary pitcher. He proved it when he was interviewed the next day and promised he would return, like MacArthur, to the scene of his greatest triumphs.

Chance arranged hurriedly for a farewell party and Belinsky was wined and wooed before setting out on the final flight of the night from Los Angeles to Hawaii. It had been only four years since Hawaii became a state. It would now undergo the severest test of its desire to stay in the union. Bo was coming to the Island Paradise.

The love affair was immediate. Belinsky took quickly to the bright days and the dark nights. He loved the smooth skin and the elegant beauty of the Hawaiian women. He was received as a conquering hero, wined and dined by the owners of the club, local politicians, business executives, industrialists. He was invited to shoot pool in the homes of millionaires. He was treated like a Hollywood celebrity. He was interviewed almost daily. He was introduced to most of the island's important people.

"Some days I surfed on the beach and swam. Other days I just took in the sun and never moved. Sometimes I went deep into the jungle and to the tiniest of islands to get away from it all. I made friends with a lot of the local people and got tan enough to pass for a native. I even took to wearing a lei around my neck most of the time. I was never happier playing ball in my life."

As had always happened with Belinsky, his reputation had preceded him. He was greeted by his teammates with a mixture of jealousy and curiosity.

"None of that ever bothered me," Bo says. "If a guy likes me he likes me, if he doesn't he doesn't and there isn't anything I can do about it."

One player, a big, strong right-handed pitcher, had been the team's most conspicuous operator until Belinsky came along. Every day he had a different girl—morning, noon, or night. He showed them off and brought them around. He never had the same girl around twice. He was the Bob Shaw of minor league baseball.

Shaw, a handsome, egocentric right-hander for the Chicago White Sox, was a swinging bachelor when he played for the manager of the White Sox, Al Lopez. For a week Lopez observed Shaw in action, a date every night, a different girl at breakfast, a new girl at lunch, a new face almost every time the manager saw him. Finally Lopez couldn't stand it any longer. He turned to one of his coaches as Shaw walked out of the hotel with another beautiful girl.

"I've got to find out," said Lopez, "whether he is the lousiest lay in the world or the cheapest son of a bitch in baseball. Why else wouldn't a girl date him twice?"

Bo's new teammate kept needling Belinsky about his success back in the States, about his love affairs, his dates with Tina Louise, Ann-Margret, other Hollywood beauties, about his reputation with the ladies all across America.

"I do pretty good out here myself," he said.

"I've always thought that a guy's dates were his own business," says Bo. "This guy was just a big pain in the ass. I had to shut him up. I couldn't see spending a season in Hawaii with a guy like this on my ass all the time."

The best way to handle a braggart is to set him up with a cooperative girl, a girl who will do something strange and wonderful to embarrass him.

"The only better way is to set him up with a queen," Belinsky said.

With two other players, Belinsky went down to the Glades, a club on Waikiki Beach, famous as a hangout for drag queens—boys who dress as pretty girls.

"We get down there this one night and pick out the best looking queen we can find. I'll tell you if I didn't know I was in a fag place I would never know. This girl—or guy—was beautiful, big eyelashes, big eyes, real cute face, and a great body. She, it, he really had a pair of tits. I don't know if they grow it that way with silicone or it is all stuffed or what, but there is no way you could tell this drag queen from a pretty girl. We go up to her and tell her our story. We have this guy who's bugging us and we want him to make it with a queen. We tell her we will give her fifty bucks if she will spend the night with him. She grabs at the offer and we set up the date. This pitcher is to meet the queen the next night in the lobby of the hotel.

We arrange for the queen to call us every step of the way. So the pitcher meets him and we are sitting in the lobby of the hotel. He waves to us as he walks by to show off his new broad. We have all we can do to keep from breaking up. Now they go out to dinner. About an hour later he calls us and tells us they are sitting down for dinner, have had a couple of drinks and he doesn't know a thing. The queen is sure the pitcher will invite him back to his room. Sure enough, a couple of hours later, the pitcher and his queen parade through the lobby of the hotel. They march to the elevator. The pitcher's got this sick grin on his face. Now we follow them upstairs in the next elevator. We have the room next to his and we climb up the transom and watch everything. He's loving this queen up, kissing his neck, running his hand against the thigh, maneuvering down to the queen's underpants. The queen lets him go just so far and then pushes him away. Finally, he's getting a little restless and he makes his moves to get the dress off. 'Oh no,' the queen says, 'it's my time of the month.' Well, they soul kiss for a few more minutes after that and he finally sends the queen home."

Belinsky meets the queen in the lobby, pays the fifty bucks, congratulates the queen for a job well done and asks for a favor.

"I've got to have your button with your autograph," Belinsky says.

The queen wears a button saying, 'Hi, I'm a boy,' under the inside collar of his dress. He pulls the button off, signs the back of it to the pitcher and gives Bo a note to deliver thanking the pitcher for a wonderful evening.

"The next day we deliver the note to the pitcher," Bo says, "and he really squirms. He won't believe a word of it. He keeps shaking his head, saying we were making it up, throwing the button down and having us pick it up each time. I'll tell you one thing about that guy. He was quiet as a mouse the rest of that season. I never heard him mention any broads after that. As a matter of fact, I never heard him mention anything after that. I think he lost his tongue that night."

The sun and the surf in Hawaii agreed with Belinsky. "I had a chance to breathe again," said Bo, "and I needed it. The Hollywood scene was great and I enjoyed every minute of it, but sometimes it got too much. It seemed that in Hawaii I could move at my own pace."

The change agreed with Belinsky. In a little less than two months of pitching there, he won four games, lost only one, had an earned run average of 2.50 and regained his confidence as a pitcher. Every pitcher, even a Bo Belinsky, needs to win once in a while to think that he might win again. That was the best thing about Hawaii. The second best thing were the girls.

"I don't think I have ever seen as many beautiful girls per square inch anyplace in the world as there are in Hawaii. I'm sure there were ugly girls there as there must be anyplace, but they were never near me. There's something about their coloring, their skin, the way they look and act and dance that absolutely drove me wild. The country is beautiful, the people are marvelous, and the whole scene was out of this world."

In late August the dream ended. Bo was recalled to the Angels.

"Everybody thinks the major leagues are such a big deal. If you have a good spot in the minors it's not B.A.D. There are a lot worse things you can do than play baseball in Hawaii. When the Angels called me back, I was depressed. For a long while I considered not reporting to them."

Belinsky decided he would give the Angels one more chance to make him happy. He rejoined the club and was immediately back in form with the Hollywood crowd. He went away in shame and returned a conquering hero. All the sportswriters agreed that Belinsky was definitely headed for the Hall of Fame now that he had worked out his problems in Hawaii. Even Belinsky couldn't help the staggering Angels. He could tell the sportswriters some funny stories about his Hawaiian adventures to take their minds off the team but it wouldn't change things very much. The Angels had had a depressing season. On September 29 they ended their season in Boston. It was a trip of thanksgiving back to Los Angeles. They wouldn't have to face the standings of the clubs for another winter. Los Angeles had finished in ninth place with a 70–91 mark, thirty-four games out of first place. The Yankees had won the pennant again.

Belinsky had managed to win another game and lose two more after rejoining the club. He ended his season with a 2–9 record, a

5.73 ERA and only seventy-seven innings pitched. He did have sixty strikeouts to thirty-five walks. That convinced the Angels that Belinsky just had a bad year in 1963 and would make a comeback in 1964. They needed every thread of hope they could find.

"I went back to my pad in the Hollywood Hills when the season ended," said Bo, "and I just rested. No broads. No calls. No newspapermen. No parties. Just rest. In two days I was recovered."

Belinsky had suffered through a bad year on the field but it didn't slow down the publicity output. Hardly a day passed without a story about Bo in the paper—there was something about the prospects of rebuilding in 1964 or something about the off-season activities of the Hollywood set with Belinsky.

One day the phone rang in Belinsky's apartment. It was a booking agent for the Silver Slipper, a swinging lounge along the strip at Las Vegas. They wanted to hire Belinsky for an act they were putting together starring Hank Henry, a standup comic.

"No, I don't think I'm interested."

"Hank is a hell of a guy to work with."

"No, thanks, I just don't think I want to do it."

"We'll pay a thousand dollars for the week and give you an option for a second week."

"When do I have to be in Vegas?"

The next afternoon Belinsky packed his yellow bathing suit, his orange bathing suit, a few wild Hawaiian bathing shirts and took the midnight plane to Las Vegas. He was going into show business. There were some major considerations, outside of the thousand-dollar salary, that forced Belinsky into accepting the deal. Vegas is filled with beautiful girls. Vegas is filled with gambling men. Both were major attractions for Belinsky.

"Vegas is the kind of town you need every so often to rejuvenate yourself," says Bo. "You can't take that scene for more than a couple of weeks at a time but while you are there it's a groovy place. I always managed to hit Vegas all through my career. Even when I lived in Hawaii I would catch a flight back to Los Angeles every so often and jump on the plane for Vegas. I would gamble for a few days, make some of the clubs, make some of the broads, jump on the night plane back to L.A., get the next plane to Hawaii, and be out surfboarding before anyone had missed me. Vegas is a good quick-shot town."

Late in October, just after the Dodgers had swept the World Series from the New York Yankees four games to none, Belinsky's name went up in lights at the Silver Slipper just under the name of the star of the show, Hank Henry. Less than a mile away, another club was being headlined by an act led by Maury Wills of the Los Angeles Dodgers, an accomplished banjo player and singer. Vegas crowds like names. If the names can sing, dance, or tell jokes, so much the better.

Belinsky's act was a success at the Silver Slipper. Henry bounced some funny lines off Bo and the crowd ate it up. Belinsky, half Polish and half Jewish, spent two weeks listening to Polish and Jewish jokes about himself. He didn't care at all. It was an easy way to make two thousand bucks.

"Vegas is a mad scene," Bo says. "You start your day about six o'clock at night with breakfast. Then you lounge around the hotel for a while and casually move over to the club for a couple of drinks. By then it's eight-thirty and you are ready for the first show. You do that one, go out to the tables, or make it with some broadie, and you are all set for the midnight show. On Friday and Saturday nights they make you work a little harder with a show at two thirty A.M. All you get then are the drunks who struck out with the broadies all night long. Those guys are usually too pissed off that they didn't make out or too loaded with booze to laugh. They just sit there and fall off their chairs after a while."

Early in the second week of his stay in Vegas, Belinsky got a tap on the shoulder. He turned around to see the grinning face of Dean Chance.

"I thought I'd come over and say hello," said Chance.

"When did you get in?"

"About an hour ago."

"Did you have dinner yet? I was just going."

Belinsky and Chance went to dinner and Bo caught him up on the doings of the town. Dean picked up the check and with a big flourish paid the bill.

"Dean's a generous guy," Bo says, "but you have to remember

he's a farmer from Ohio. He could pick up a forty- or fifty-dollar dinner check just like that and put two dollars on the table for a tip."

Chance had come to see Belinsky do his standup act, so when they finished eating they prepared to go back to the club for the midnight show.

"Wait a second, Bo. Before you go, I have to go to the bathroom. I'll be right back."

"OK, I'll wait for you right here."

Chance walked off toward the lobby of the hotel, just past the cashier's window and the gambling tables. He never made it to the bathroom. Bo waited. Twenty minutes passed. Chance finally returned.

"It took you a hell of a long time to piss."

"I never made it to the bathroom."

"Where the hell were you?"

"I stopped at the crap tables."

"And . . . ?"

"I lost fifteen hundred bucks."

Chance only stayed one night and one day in Las Vegas before returning to his farm in Wooster, Ohio.

Belinsky finished his stay in Las Vegas and returned to Hollywood. He was ready for a new round of Hollywood parties. He found his way into a couple of television programs and several agents suggested he might have a future as the tall, dark, good-looking villain in the movies. He weighed the idea.

"Lance," he said, "Lance Belinsky starring in *The Last Shootout at Bo's Corral.* I think I could dig that."

Belinsky did several episodes of "77 Sunset Strip," "Dakota," "Surfside Six" and a few other long-forgotten television shows, mostly cowboy epics.

"I was always the guy with the black hat who would walk up to the tough guy in the bar and say, 'Tex wants to see you outside.' They always had to have a lot of takes with me. I would break everybody up on the set. But a lot of the producers and directors said I had a lot of talent and could make good money in acting if I wanted to give up baseball. I thought about it, I really did. But then I heard that actors start work at six o'clock in the morning. That sort of soured me on the whole thing."

Belinsky returned to his Hollywood pad for the rest of the winter. He really looked forward to spring training of 1964 because he believed he had learned enough in Hawaii to be a winning pitcher again. He signed a contract for $15,500, a raise of $2000, despite his horrible season. The Angels were trying to encourage him. They needed a stronger year in 1964 and their two young star pitchers, Chance and Belinsky, had slipped back horribly. They were both young enough for a comeback.

Rigney sat in his California home making plans for the season. Chance sat in his Wooster home thinking about making a strong comeback in 1964. Belinsky sat in his Hollywood pad thinking about that very evening.

Mamie was back in town.

Bo, I don't want you smoking in my bedroom. The cigarette stains get on the canopy.

—MAMIE VAN DOREN

Once in Love with Mamie

Marilyn Monroe had dominated Hollywood in the late fifties with her sensuous open-mouthed beauty, her exquisite form, her gaspy, small-girl voice. Her off-camera life had as much excitement as her movies. She had been married to the greatest baseball player of the era, Joe DiMaggio, and their storybook romance filled the pages of newspapers for months. Then DiMaggio had been portrayed as cold and unappreciative of this great beauty, forcing Marilyn deeper into depressions and eroding what self-confidence she had. Gay Talese, in a brilliant article in *Esquire,* described Marilyn's triumphant tour of Korea when, wearing a tight, sequined dress, she had sung and wiggled for thousands of lovesick soldiers at an airfield in Seoul. When she returned to Japan where she and DiMaggio were honeymooning, she told Joe D. of the reception. "Joe, Joe," she said breathlessly, "you never heard such cheering." Talese wrote that DiMaggio, who had stirred Yankee Stadium crowds just by gliding back for a fly ball, answered, "Yes, I have." DiMaggio had brought Marilyn to spring training when he was a batting coach for the Yankees and the picture of her flowing hair in the Fort Lauderdale,

Florida, breezes had made the front pages of most of the country's newspapers.

Her suicide in 1962 left a huge gap in the Hollywood scene. There were no sex symbols to peddle in Sheboygan on Saturday night. Universal Studios in Hollywood nominated a busty, blonde, vivacious beauty to fill the vacuum. Her name was Mamie Van Doren.

Early in 1931 in Rowena, South Dakota, a town of less than a thousand people, a pretty blonde baby was born and named Joan Olander.

"I had always been a movie fan," Mrs. Olander said, "so I named the baby after my favorite actress, Joan Crawford. I never thought for a moment she would wind up in the movies."

By the time she was twelve years old, Joan Olander had developed into a beautiful young woman with sparkling eyes, fine legs and an angelic figure. She turned heads on Main Street in Rowena every time she ventured downtown. She began thinking of a world beyond the confines of the drug store on Main Street or the one movie show. Her mother began thinking of the same thing. She picked up young Joan and together they moved to Los Angeles, California.

"It wasn't that I didn't like Rowena," said Mamie years later to columnist Earl Wilson. "It was simply a question of going someplace where I could find out just how far I could go. I could never find that out in Rowena, South Dakota."

At fifteen Joan Olander began frequenting the lots of Twentieth Century, Universal, Paramount, and Metro-Goldwyn-Mayer looking for a place in the movies.

At sixteen she met a wealthy, middle-aged Los Angeles shirt manufacturer. After a whirlwind courtship, Joan Olander was a young bride. Ninety days later she was divorced.

At twenty-one she walked onto the lot of Universal Studios in Hollywood. She was walking across the parking area from one studio to another when a man walked by, stopped, looked at her and asked her name.

"Joan Olander," she said.

"Are you with Universal?"

"No, but I'd like to be."

The casting director, Phil Benjamin, took another good look at that lovely face, that marvelous body, and those shapely legs, and said, "Come with me, young lady."

He brought Joan to studio officials. They liked what they saw. She was signed for $250 a week. The only thing they weren't sure about were the legs. They were a little less than perfect after a close inspection.

"I'm slightly bow-legged," she confessed to columnist Wilson. "I have always been like that. I think my legs are shaped that way because I used to play the cello as a young girl."

Joan Olander was told to report to the studio publicity department the next morning. The first thing they had to do for her was give her a name. She reported on time and three heavy-set men, with lighted cigars hanging from their mouths, studied her face and form.

"What's your name, sweetheart?"

"Joan Olander," she said.

"Jesus Christ."

"What's wrong with Joan Olander?"

"Nothing, honey, except it ain't a name for a movie star. You want to be a movie star don't you?"

"Yes, I do, very much."

"They finally settled on Mamie. For the President's wife. Mamie seems like a good name for you. It's going to be a popular name for the next four years. Your last name is Van Doren, after the poet. That's it, Mamie Van Doren."

She went through the Hollywood publicity buildup. Press agents arranged for dates with celebrities. They dropped her name into the gossip columns. They started fan clubs and got the movie magazines to write features stories about her, giving each magazine new and never-before-published information about her, fresh from their fertile minds.

Mamie Van Doren's career dragged along slowly. There were no starring roles, just some small parts in forgotten pictures. Neither Mamie nor the studio were discouraged. It generally takes from eight to ten years for a star to be discovered "overnight," and Mamie was still young and pretty with a solid chance at serious fame.

In 1955 Mamie met bandleader Ray Anthony. On August 29,

1955, they were married in Toledo, Ohio. It was Anthony's second marriage. The publicity release issued by the studio said it was Mamie's first marriage. They were right. Mamie Van Doren had never been married before.

The following year a son, named Perry after their good friend Perry Como, was born to Mr. and Mrs. Ray Anthony. Mamie retired for some time to raise her new son. Anthony toured the country with his band. The marriage was on shaky grounds much of the time.

Mamie never seemed to be able to capture the imagination of the producers, directors, and public like Marilyn Monroe. By 1960 her career had reached a roadblock. She didn't seem to be advancing as fast as she had hoped. Her marriage with Ray Anthony was in trouble. Finally, they were divorced. Still there were no starring roles for the blonde beauty from Rowena.

One night the phone rang in Mamie's apartment in Hollywood.

"Hi, honey. This is Ray."

"Hi."

"What are you doing? I'd like you to come down here and meet some friends."

Mamie would have none of that at the moment. She told her former husband to call her next time at a more reasonable hour, and hung up on him.

The friends that Ray Anthony wanted Mamie to meet were Walter Winchell and his alter ego, Robert Belinsky.

"I was in one of those nice quiet lounges on La Cienega Boulevard," says Bo. "Walter had invited me out for a drink and we were sitting there with a few actor friends of mine and Bill Gazzara of the Hollywood-A-Go-Go. Ray Anthony comes over and we are having a quiet time drinking and talking and laughing. All of a sudden, out of nowhere, Anthony looks at me and says, 'How would you like to meet a beautiful broad?' How the hell did I know the broad he wanted me to meet was Mamie? Later on I figured it out: If I met Mamie and fell in love with her and married her, he would save himself a lot of alimony bread."

Anthony continued talking and Belinsky continued listening. In a few moments Anthony was moving to telephone his ex-wife and introduce Belinsky. The fact that she turned him down didn't discourage Bo. He went to the phone himself after Anthony came back and dialed Mamie's number.

"Hi, this is Bo Belinsky. I'm here with Ray."

"I'm still not coming out tonight."

"No, I don't mean tonight. I'd just like to meet you. Maybe we can do it some other night."

"Maybe we can. Why don't you call me?"

Belinsky called again the next night. This time Mamie accepted a date. Belinsky told her he would take her to the Peppermint West, a swinging lounge celebrated for couples twisting until the first light of morning. He asked if she was free on Thursday. Thursday was celebrity night and Zsa Zsa Gabor would be the celebrity of the night. That meant the place would be jammed with big name Hollywood people who had come to pay homage to Zsa Zsa. If she felt like it, Zsa Zsa might even get up herself and honor the establishment with a twist. Belinsky told Mamie that he would be accompanied by Walter Winchell.

"Fine," said Mamie, "you can pick me up about nine o'clock."

Winchell hired a limousine and arrived at Mamie's apartment as scheduled. Mamie was ready and looked incredibly beautiful.

"She had this sequin dress on," said Bo. "One of these real tight-fitting jobs, I mean she could hardly walk in the damn thing but she looked great. She had no bra on and you could see everything through that dress; no pants on, either, and you could tell where her hips ended and her legs began. She was some beautiful sight. She gets in the back seat of the car between me and Walter and he almost creamed his pants right there. He started talking real fast and putting his hand on her knee and telling her how great she looked and how he thought she certainly had the looks and the talent to be one of Hollywood's biggest stars and how he would see what he could do for her career."

The night was a howling success. Zsa Zsa showed and drew a huge crowd of followers. Winchell held court in the Peppermint West and handsome men asked him who the beautiful chick was. Bo and Mamie twisted and the crowd cheered them as they really bore down hard.

The next day's papers made Bo and Mamie an item in Winchell's column.

Bo and Mamie began making the rounds of Hollywood all through the late summer of 1962 and into 1963. They attended parties together, danced at the Peppermint West, dined at La Scala, got their pictures in the Los Angeles papers.

"I don't know if I loved her," Bo says now, "but I certainly was infatuated with her. I know she was hung up on me."

The romance flourished for all to see, including the California Angels.

"Rigney made a big deal of it," said Bo. "Everybody has bad games and nothing is said. If I had a bad game he would mention Mamie's name and suggest that if I didn't go out with Mamie maybe I would win more games. I felt like telling him if I got more runs and the guys behind me played better, maybe I'd win more games."

Bo and Mamie spent a great deal of time together in the winter of 1962.

"She was great to be with," said Bo. "A lot of fun and we liked the same things. She did have a couple of traits that used to drive me nuts. She was always worried about her place. She had this fantastic white bed with a huge canopy in her bedroom. She was always getting on me about smoking in her bedroom. She couldn't stand the smell from smoking and she always complained about the stains on her canopy."

Mamie became as much a fixture around the Angels as the bats and balls.

"Most of the time Rigney and Autry were telling me to get rid of her, but I think they really liked having her around. She was great to look at, she was a Hollywood personality and she brought them and the club a lot of attention. There was something else. We had a couple of parties with the club—players, wives, officials—and I brought Mamie to them. Every time I look up there's Rigney or Haney or Autry getting her a drink and being real friendly to her and acting like she was with them. Then the next day they would tell me she was bad for me, bad for the club, bad for baseball. If she was so bad for baseball, why didn't they stay the hell away from her?"

With spring training drawing near and Mamie doing a show back east, they drifted apart for a while. Belinsky reported to the Riviera Hotel in Palm Springs late in February of 1963.

"I had almost forgotten about her," said Bo, "when I got this message in my box that Mamie had called. She had gone off to Vancouver for a week to work in a club called The Cave and was returning the second week in March to Palm Springs. She wanted to see me. Bud Furillo kept asking me if I was engaged to Mamie. I told him we were just dear friends. He was writing a lot of stories about me and Mamie and soon all the other papers and the gossip columnists were carrying items about me and Mamie. We had become big news. Mamie came back to Palm Springs, we saw each other a lot, and Furillo kept pressing the engagement thing. Finally, I said, 'Yeah, we're engaged.' I really didn't mean it. I just said it to get him off my back. Now he goes and calls Mamie up to confirm the engagement."

"Are you engaged," Furillo asks Mamie.

"I don't think so," Mamie says.

"Bo says you are engaged."

"If Bo says we are engaged," Mamie answered, "then we are engaged."

The date was April 1, 1963.

Furillo's story led the *Herald-Examiner* the next day and the *Los Angeles Times* bannered it on page one with a picture of Bo and Mamie and headlines eight inches tall. It was a quiet news day.

Congratulations poured in from all over the league. Belinsky received telegrams from many of his friends, males and females, for the wonderful news. The whole world loves a lover and Belinsky was advertising that he had succeeded with this beautiful movie star where only a shirt manufacturer and a bandleader had been able to whirl her to the altar before. Mamie was thirty-one and Bo was twenty-six. He announced that their age difference meant little to him.

"Some people," he said, "mature faster. I'm very mature for my age."

The romance started to sour almost immediately after the engagement announcement.

"Mamie became very possessive after that," said Bo. "All the other girls had been fun girls and Mamie had been a fun girl. All of a sudden she's asking me when I'm going to set the wedding date. I didn't know what she was talking about. She wanted to put a ring in my nose. She said, 'Are we engaged or not?' I said, 'Sure we're engaged but that doesn't mean I have to set the wedding date so fast.' All of a sudden Mamie got the idea that we were going to be married right away. Getting engaged is one thing. Getting married, hell, that's a whole different ball game."

The relationship became stormy but continued on into the first two months of the season. Bo and Mamie fought and made up dozens of times. Mamie continued to press for a wedding date.

"One night she really got angry at me and said if I didn't set a wedding date the whole thing was off and she wouldn't go out with me any more. I just stormed out of her place, went down to the Whiskey-A-Go-Go, picked out some little broadie and had a hell of a night. Mamie was cooled off the next night."

Things improved and Bo decided that the gentlemanly thing to do, since he was going on a road trip and Mamie was doing a club date, was to buy her a ring. He decided only the very best was good enough for his fiancée.

"There's this jeweler in Los Angeles, Marvin Hines, good friend of mine, and I went to see him. I told him I wanted to buy an engagement ring for Mamie. He shows me this big, beautiful engagement ring with a gigantic diamond in it and says because I'm a good friend he will let me have it for two thousand dollars. I nearly choked. He made a deal with me. He said if I made sure that I told the press often enough where I got the ring he would let me pay it out over a long period of time. We didn't even sign a contract or anything. He just took my word that I would get him some publicity and he would get his two thousand dollars before the year was out."

Belinsky slipped the ring on Mamie's finger that night and stuffed the bill deeper into his pocket.

Things were peaceful for a few days. Then Bo and Mamie had another shouting match and Bo decided he would end the engagement once and for all. He went to his attorney, Paul Caruso, and asked him for advice.

"I want to end the engagement," said Bo, "but I like Mamie a lot. I don't want to hurt her feelings."

"I understand. You want out but you want to look like you are the bad guy."

"That's it, something like that."

"I got it," said Caruso. "You were engaged on April 1. Let's put out a statement saying the whole thing was a bad April Fool's joke."

Belinsky couldn't go for that idea.

"I just decided to stick it out for a while and see what happens," he said.

What happened was he got shipped out to Hawaii.

"I am sure my fiancée, Miss Van Doren, will visit me while I'm there," he told reporters.

Mamie came out to Hawaii and under the romantic setting of the blue Hawaiian skies and the clear, clean water, love flourished again. The romance took on new excitement and the engagement carried them along for another year.

In 1964 Belinsky, back in Los Angeles with the Angels, had made the acquaintance of Ricky DuPont, a beautiful blonde widow of a DuPont of Delaware. Mrs. DuPont, older than Bo, older than Mamie, and richer than both, pursued Belinsky with vigor. She introduced Belinsky to new elegance he had never known before.

"She knew all the best people in Hollywood," Bo said, "not only the stars; the behind-the-scenes people, the producers, the money men, the bankers, the angels for shows. She lived in the old Duncan Hines estate and had parties with people like Merle Oberon, who was married to some billionaire and Paulette Goddard and the finest Hollywood people. She was friendly with some Polish royalty and some fabulous designers of clothing. I didn't know people had this kind of money until I met Ricky. She really opened my eyes to things. Here, I thought it was a big deal to be riding around in a Cadillac. Her chauffeurs rode around in Cadillacs when they went for the groceries."

Bo's romance with Mamie was on and off when he met Ricky DuPont and started dating her. Every so often, when Belinsky would make a road trip with the Angels, Mamie would show up in that town and the item would filter back to the Los Angeles papers. Mamie would not take kindly to double-dealing. After all, she was still an engaged lady, had a ring to show for it, and didn't like the idea that her fiancé was running around with some older woman. She let slip to reporters that she and Bo were still engaged and she assumed they would be married soon.

"When Ricky read these items," said Bo, "she really got pissed. I was having a good time with her and when she asked me if I was finished with Mamie, I told her I was. My next job was to get my ring back from her. Especially since I owed two thousand dollars on it."

Belinsky went to his lawyer for advice.

"Write her a letter, tell her the engagement is over and ask for the ring back," said Caruso.

"I don't think she'll like that."

"It's better than announcing in the papers that the engagement is off," said Caruso.

"What if she doesn't send the ring back?"

"If she doesn't send it back we'll think of something else."

The next day Bo dispatched his "Dear Mamie" letter and waited for results. A week went by. No ring. Two weeks. No ring. A month. No ring—and no word from Mamie.

"I think," Bo told Caruso, "we had better think of some other way."

Bo had told Ricky DuPont that the engagement with Mamie was off and that Ricky wouldn't be reading any more in the papers about Bo and Mamie.

"There's only one problem," Bo said, "I can't get my ring back. As long as she has that she can tell everybody we are still engaged."

Mamie was being rather stubborn about the silly ring. Bo wanted it back because he felt he was no longer engaged to Mamie, and he felt that he didn't want to hold up his jeweler any longer. Bo decided to make Mamie give that ring back even if he had to embarrass her to do it.

"Ricky said she would give me the money to take care of everything," Bo said. "I picked up the phone and called some private detective agency. I arranged for them to follow Mamie all around the country. Wherever Mamie goes, the detective won't be far behind. All I had to do was get one little thing on her that she might not like seeing in the papers and I would have the ring back."

Arrangements were made and the detective set out for the East where Mamie was appearing in a show. He carried all the standard equipment with him in his little suitcase, the large black notebook, the tape recorder with sufficient tapes, the long-lens camera, the tripod, and even the silly, squashed hat the detectives wear in the movies.

"Ricky put up all the dough and I never bothered to ask the price. I'm sure it was a bundle but she liked me and she would do anything for me," Bo says modestly.

The detective watched Mamie at night, by day, in the morning, and in the early afternoon. He saw her dressed and undressing by herself. He saw her eating lunch in her room and studying her part in front of her mirror. He saw her going for short walks and he saw her coming back to her hotel, alone, tired after her show. For eight days he watched her every move. He called Bo and reported that he had nothing to report.

On the ninth day he reported that he had something to report.

A young man in the show with Mamie had been invited up to her room for a drink and the tape recorder whirled away with some interesting conversation. The detective smiled. He knew he would earn himself a bonus for his perseverance.

"When I heard the tape," said Bo, "I knew I would get my ring back, get that jeweler off my ass, and get Ricky quieted down. It was just getting too much."

Caruso sent Mamie a legal letter suggesting that if the ring were not returned he would take the case to court. He suggested that since Belinsky had renounced the engagement the ring belonged to him. He further suggested that if Mamie decided to keep the ring he would bring his tape recorder to open court, play the conversation and allow the court to decide if the conversation between Mamie and her friend was the way an engaged lady was supposed to act.

"All this time I'm waiting for the ring to come back," said Bo, "and Ricky keeps telling me she will take Mamie to court for me to get it back. I didn't want anything like that. Mamie was a good kid. I really liked her. I just wanted to get the whole thing finished. It wasn't that I was mad at Mamie or was going to run off with Ricky. It was just that I didn't like the idea of being obligated to any woman. I had to be free like a bird to fly my own way. Since I was engaged to Mamie and Ricky was with me all the time, I just didn't feel free. Things were closing in. It was getting to be time to split. I wanted to make it to Hawaii that winter but I wanted the thing with Mamie and the ring over with."

Three days later, Belinsky received an envelope. The only writing on the envelope was Bo's address on La Pressa Drive. No message. No return address. Nothing but an envelope with an address, and inside: a two-thousand-dollar ring.

Bo and Mamie again became good and great friends after they stopped being engaged. Mamie showed up every so often and Bo took her out to dinner. They went to several Hollywood parties after the engagement ended. They danced at the Peppermint West.

"We were free and loose," said Bo. "She could go her way and I could go mine. It was a damn good arrangement. Neither of us had a hold on the other. That's the way it has got to be. Nobody wants to walk around the street with a chain around his neck or a ring in his nose."

In the spring of 1965, after he had been traded to the Philadelphia Phillies from the Los Angeles Angels, Belinsky received a call from Mamie. She was in Clearwater where the Phillies trained. Belinsky was delighted to see her. She looked lovely as always and was very good company.

"I had learned from my experiences with the Angels," said Bo. "I didn't want anybody to give me any heat over the fact that Mamie was in town. I decided to tell the press that I brought her to Clearwater to help me with spring training. Mamie was there to serve as my physical fitness director."

Bo and Mamie had a delightful spring in Clearwater as Bo hit some of his old familiar spots from his days as an Oriole farmhand in the winter league. He made the Phillies ball club, had a good spring, and seemed on his way to a new start in a new league. Mamie still gained more than she lost by the association. She played parts in a few movies, starred in some summer stock productions, did especially well in *Gentlemen Prefer Blondes,* and seemed to be recovering nobly from the broken romance with Bo.

"Ahh," says Bo, "I don't think she ever really got over me. Why else would she go and do a silly thing like she did?"

Several years after Bo and Mamie ended their engagement in a battle of headlines, Miss Van Doren announced that she was engaged to another baseball player, one Lee Meyers, a skinny left-handed pitcher from Huntington Park, California. Meyers was nineteen years old when Mamie announced the engagement to the press, and she was thirty-five. Meyers had been signed by the Cubs in 1964 and had pitched in Wenatchee in 1965 with a 7–11 record and a 5.08 ERA. He wasn't considered one of the Cubs' better prospects. There was something else about Meyers that caused excitement when the engagement was announced.

The left-handed pitcher was reported to be worth several million dollars.

"I never believed it," said Bo. "It was just Mamie's way of getting back at me for dropping her for Ricky. She was saying that she could marry a young guy, younger than me, and he would be a hell of a lot richer than me and Ricky. I don't count anybody else's money, but if the guy was worth a million dollars what the hell would he be playing baseball for? Tell me that? Do you think anybody with a million dollars would get a sore arm and take bullshit from a manager and stand out there on the mound and let those line drives whistle by your ears? I don't. I know I wouldn't."

Miss Van Doren did marry Meyers and there was no public statement as to their combined or individual wealth. The marriage didn't have much staying power and Mamie and her boy-wonder pitcher were soon divorced. Mamie liked left-handed pitchers but she just couldn't make relationships with them last.

"We had our laughs," Bo says of Mamie. "She was a good broadie. If it wasn't for that whole damn engagement thing we would have stayed together a lot longer. Mamie was fun to be with and had a lot of class. She was great to look at and took real good care of that body of hers. Mamie and I were a lot alike. We were independent and liked to go our own ways. That's probably why we never could have gotten married."

For several years after Mamie and Bo broke up, Miss Van Doren would stop off in Trenton to visit Bo's mother. It was an exciting evening for Mrs. Belinsky, and it was a good chance for Mamie to get a thing or two off her lovely chest about Bo.

"I always told her," Mrs. Belinsky said, "that I wasn't reponsible for what Bo did. She is a lovely lady and always treated us nice when she came and with respect. She can visit any time she likes but when she cried on my shoulder about Bo, I told her I just couldn't do anything about it. Nobody tells Bo what to do, not even me."

Like a true lady, Mamie came to visit Mrs. Belinsky a few years back and was told that Bo had married Jo Collins. She said good-bye to Mr. and Mrs. Belinsky that night. They knew they would never see her again. They would miss her visits.

"We are plain people," Mrs. Belinsky says. "It was glamorous to entertain a movie actress."

Bo feels the same way about Mamie.

"We had a lot of fun with no regrets," says Bo. "She gained some things from being with me and I gained some things from being with her. Isn't that the way it's supposed to be when you are going with a girl?"

He's snoring, Bo, so at least he isn't dead.

**—DEAN CHANCE TO BO BELINSKY AFTER THE VISIT FROM REPORTER
BRAVEN DYER.**

*So You Want To Be
a Sportswriter*

In the spring of 1964, the Los Angeles writers decided it was time
for the "New Bo" stories, that annual ritual of sportswriting that
comes with the robins each spring. Every baseball team has a player
or two who does not advance as rapidly in his profession as the
scouts, the manager, and the coaches believe he should. The player
is disappointed. The fans are disappointed. The general manager
is disappointed. They decide their opinions can not be wrong. Instead of accepting the idea that the man they have touted as the
second coming of Koufax is merely an average baseball pitcher, they
indicate his off-field activities have kept him from achieving instant
stardom. The sportswriters then convince the player that if he indi-
cates to them he will mend his ways, they will write the annual "new
man in town" stories, convincing one and all that serious efforts in
the spring will be rewarded with twenty-game winning seasons in
the summer.

Bo went along with the gag. The 1964 spring training season of
the Angels in the Riviera Hotel in Palm Springs was filled with
indications of the "new Bo." He was respectful to his manager, paid

homage to his pitching coach, indicated that the stay in Hawaii was horribly unpleasant and convinced everyone he would work hard, be a good boy and win the pennant for the Angels with his pitching.

Bo did work hard on the field.

Bo did work hard off the field.

"I had this one chick with me one night," Bo says, "and she was a doll. We had dined in luxury in my room, steak, wine, Caesar salad, the whole bit. The table was piled high with the glasses, the drained bottles, the dirty dishes. Now we decide it's time for a little loving, so we push the table back a little and jump into bed. Everything's going great and I'm down to the short strokes and my legs are hanging off the end of the bed and then it happens. Wham."

In his enthusiastic ardor, Belinsky had caught his right leg under the dining table, had tipped the table over backwards and had sent dishes, glasses, bottles, napkins, knives, forks, spoons, and a table-cloth crashing to the floor.

"Bo," the girl said, "what do we do now?"

"What do you always do after you fuck, doll? You go to sleep."

"But, I mean, the broken glass, the broken dishes, the spoons, all over the place."

"Just make sure," said Belinsky, "you don't have to get up in the middle of the night to piss."

Convinced that this was protocol in such situations, the girl retired for the night. Belinsky lay awake for a few minutes. He had an uncomfortable thought.

"I just don't want to be in the room when the maid comes in to clean up," he decided.

He left an early call for the room, got up promptly, dressed, stepped over the broken glass and was out of the room with his girl friend shortly before eight o'clock. The maid knocked on the door shortly after nine o'clock, heard no answer and opened the room with her passkey. She shrieked when she saw the mess. She immediately ran to get the supervisor who took one look at the mess and called the manager of the hotel. This was a situation she wanted out of her hands and into his.

The hotel manager immediately called general manager Fred Haney and explained the problem.

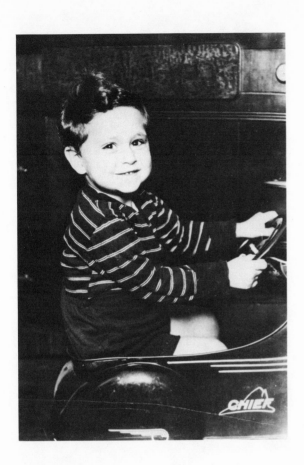

LITTLE BOY BO
First candyapple convertible, age two.

ANGEL FACE
A precocious 13, Bo already had a
couple of pets and a couple of scores.

THE FAMOUS NO-HITTER
After the Game, May 5, 1962.

THE BELINSKYS' BO
The family's one and only studio portrait.

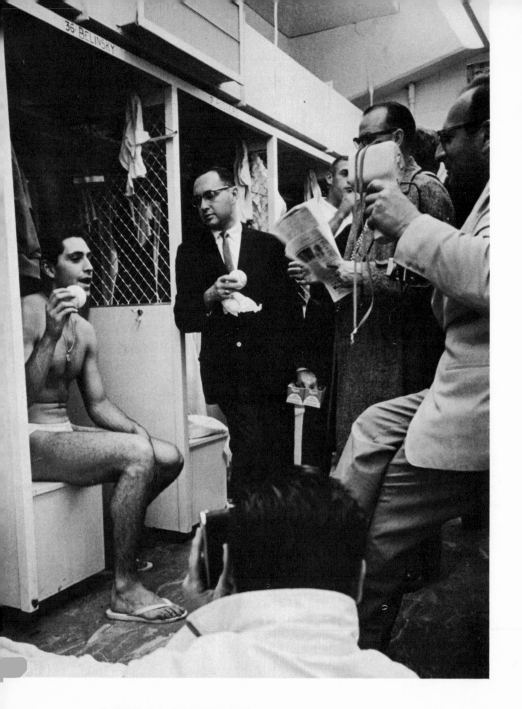

EARLY BO CHEESECAKE
Reporters loved to interview, photographers loved to shoot, girls loved to dream about Belinsky.

LONG DAY'S JOURNEY INTO NIGHT
Pitching and wooing puts a hell of a dent in a man's sleeping time.

PAUSE THAT REFRESHES
While others study the game, Bo grabs a few drags. It's forbidden here but that makes it more of a challenge.

→
CARNAL KNOWLEDGE
(overleaf) Bo romanced Ann-Margret before her fame was spread by the successful film.

NO BIZ LIKE IT
Doris Day and Cary Grant toast the great Angel in the dugout after his no-hitter.

ONCE IN LOVE WITH MAMIE
Swinging at the Peppermint West with Mamie Van Doren. A great friendship never spoiled by marriage.

THE CONTINENTAL, TINA LOUISE
The actress taught Bo some French. He instructed her, too.

← *"LET'S GO TO PRESS"* (opposite) Bo wasn't as much fun for Walter Winchell as racketeers like "Lepke," but not as dangerous either.

OUT OF MY LEAGUE
Mrs. Ricky DuPont of the
Delaware DuPonts and
Bo enjoy an evening out with
the Hollywood set.

THE SOUNDS OF MUSIC
Lionel Hampton explains the fine points of jazz.

LOVE IS PART OF THE GAME
*Dinah Shore, famed Hollywood tennis player, follows the bouncing
ball with* **Bo Belinsky.**

COPS AND ROBBERS
FBI Chief J. Edgar Hoover escorts two of his favorite young men, Dean Chance and Bo, through Headquarters. No arrests were made.

MY WORLD—AND I'M WELCOME TO IT
Bo's got it all, cruising around the Hollywood Hills in his candyapple convertible.

BEACH PARTY

Girls at the beach always stopped to ask Bo for the right time. They always had the right place.

HOLLYWOOD HAIRDRESSER
Nobody steps out into the Hollywood lights without each strand of hair being just right.

HEAVEN FOR A HEDONIST
Bo relaxes in his satin dressing gown in his penthouse apartment high above Hollywood. It's 3 P.M. as he awaits breakfast.

LAS VEGAS
Bo dances with some show business lovelies in a brief career.

BUNNY HOP
Playmate Jo Collins Belinsky was graduated
with honors to Bunny Mother. Bo didn't
like being Bunny Daddy.

**AMERICA'S SWEETHEARTS,
JO AND BO**
Under the Hawaii sky where they were
happiest together.

SURFBOARD HAWAII
*In search of new adventures following
the sun to fun.*

"Don't tell me whose room it was," said Haney, "let me guess."

"Yes," said the hotel manager, "it's them again."

Haney had been visiting with John Ford, the famed Hollywood director and Los Angeles Angels fan. Haney decided to show Ford how a general manager directs a baseball team. Ford joined Haney and then both of them went to the hotel room shared by Bo Belinsky and Dean Chance.

The floor supervisor showed them the damage. Haney decided to sit in the room and wait for Belinsky to return.

After an hour there was a gentle knocking on the door. Haney was ready for Belinsky and nodded to Ford that this was the supreme moment in the drama. Another small knock on the door.

"Hey, Bo, it's me, Dean. Are you finished in there? Can I get back into the room?"

Haney whipped open the door and stared at Chance. Chance stared back at Haney. Ford stared at both of them. Chance recovered first.

"What the hell's going on in here?"

"You tell me," said Haney, "and you tell me where Belinsky is."

"Bo? I haven't seen Bo since yesterday."

Belinsky had taken his date home. While Haney, Ford, and a surprised Chance stood in the corner of the room examining broken glass for evidence, Belinsky was driving casually to the ball park for the workout.

"Haney was really mad when he came to the park," says Bo. "I think he was embarrassed because he had John Ford with him and he didn't get to put on an act in front of him. The next day I was in his office promptly. I didn't want to fool around. I wanted to make the club and have a good year."

Belinsky went into Haney's office smiling. He came out smiling. He also came out five hundred dollars poorer.

"They called it a fine for disciplinary reasons," said Bo, "but I guess it went to the hotel for the broken glass."

Belinsky recovered rapidly from his crashing night and had a good spring training. Mamie showed up for a few days, a few other friends came down from Los Angeles, and a few local villagers all helped Bo relax that spring. Belinsky had thrown well all spring and

Rigney was counting on him as one of his regular four starters. Chance had been marvelous. At twenty-two years old, he had suddenly matured as a pitcher. His fast ball was explosive, his curve was sharp, his changeup was effective, and his control was uncanny. Chance was the best the Angels had and Belinsky wasn't far behind. Chance opened the season with a win in Washington.

The Angels, unfortunately, had a slow start in 1964 and were languishing in the second division in the middle of May. They were to finish in fifth place in 1964, but were one of the best teams in the league in the second half of the season as the Yankees came from behind under Yogi Berra to win the pennant. The big Yankee move came after a utility infielder named Phil Linz, famed for his witty lines ("Play me or keep me"; and when stopped by a cop for a traffic violation, and asked why he wasn't wearing his glasses, said, "I got contacts," the cop said, "I don't care who you know, you still have to wear your glasses when you drive."), made the big play. It was on a harmonica while riding the team bus. Linz played "Mary Had a Little Lamb," and Berra complained about the music after a doubleheader loss to the White Sox on a steaming Chicago day. When the bus got stuck in traffic getting to the airport, Linz's harmonica playing really irritated the manager. He told Linz, "Shove that harmonica up your ass," Linz then flipped it to Berra. The manager fired it back at Linz, missed, and hit Joe Pepitone in the knee. Pepitone limped for a week. (Berra was fired later despite winning the pennant because he couldn't control his players and Linz wound up owning three New York restaurants.) The Yankees immediately reacted by going on a long winning streak with Linz playing the best ball of his life. Yankee teams reacted that way to adversity. Los Angeles Angel teams just laughed and lost anyway.

In late May the Angels were trying to shake their early season slump. They arrived in Boston with an off day. They stayed at the Somerset Hotel, a staid, quiet, conservative Boston establishment. It gave Belinsky a bad case of the nerves. As soon as he put his bags down in his room he would head for more interesting surroundings.

The team arrived in the early evening and Belinsky was the scheduled pitcher for the next night in Fenway Park. A left-handed pitcher had to fortify himself to face the Green Monster—the left field wall so named because it was only 315 feet away from home plate—and the tough right-handed Boston batters. Belinsky called one of his friends and made a date with her for dinner. After dinner, he made it clear, it had to be her pad. He just didn't like the Somerset.

"I was out with a doll, a real China doll," said Bo. "She looked a lot like Zenida. Fantastic broad and when she greeted me with that tight Chinese dress on, I knew I would have one of my better nights in Boston."

While Belinsky dined peacefully with his Chinese girl and adjourned afterward for entertainment at her pad, the rest of the Angels were not letting the hotel get them down, either. Chance had organized a party to pass the time away. There were two or three other players in attendance and a half dozen sportswriters. The drinks and the laughter went well into the morning.

"I had had it by about four o'clock in the morning," said Chance, "So I just took off and went to bed. Those other guys were still going good when I left."

Chance crashed into bed shortly before five o'clock and an hour later, as the first hint of sunlight could be seen sneaking into his window, his telephone rang. He almost knocked the night table over as he reached for the phone.

"Dean, get up, get out of the hotel, there's a fire."

"Who is this?"

"Bud Furillo. No bullshit. There really is a fire. Just get up and get out. You'll smell the smoke in the halls. Just get on out of there."

"If you are shitting me I am going to have your ass, Mr. Furillo. I'm so goddamn tired I can't breathe."

"No, no, this is real. Get on out. I have to call some other guys."

Chance struggled out of bed, put a pair of pants on and walked out of his room. He smelled smoke and saw confusion as guests hurried for the fire exits. He made it to the street. It was almost light. He walked up to Bill Rigney and several of the coaches, all dressed in their pajamas, and asked how serious the fire was. Nobody knew. Rigney was too busy counting heads.

They were one short.

"Dean, where's Bo?" Rigney asked.

"Bo, why Bo is here, isn't he? I mean I'm sure I saw Bo here a moment ago."

"Is he in the goddamn hotel?"

At that very instant, a taxi cab pulled up at the corner of the Somerset Hotel. Out stepped Mr. Robert Belinsky.

"I pay the driver," said Bo, "and I looked up. I see smoke and a lot of haze. Then I see a lot of people standing on the street, a lot of my people, players, coaches, newspapermen, all looking idiotic in their pajamas. I could't figure why in hell anybody would want to have a pajama party in the streets of Boston. I figured I'd better join the pajama party so I take off my jacket, put it over a trash can and loosen my tie. Now I figure I can just slide over to the group and never be noticed."

Rigney was still uncertain as to Belinsky's whereabouts.

"Is Bo in that hotel or not?"

"Why, Skip," said Chance. "Here's Bo. I told you he was around somewhere."

Rigney took one look at Belinsky and it was all over.

"Goddamnit," he said, "I'll see you in my office at the park."

That adventure set Belinsky back another five hundred dollars.

"The funniest part of the whole thing," said Chance, "was what happened with Furillo. He appointed himself team fireman and was calling everybody else on the club about the fire. Did a terrific job. Really got a lot of guys out of bed and into the street. He called everybody, he sure did. He only forgot to make one call. He forgot to call his newspaper back in Los Angeles. He got scooped on the big fire story."

Ever since the Dodgers moved to Los Angeles in 1958, the newspapermen in that town had waged war on each other, the stories getting wilder and less honest as the competition grew more severe. There is less accuracy in sports journalism than in any other form of writing, simply because few people get hurt if the truth is bent and a story entertains. A misquote from a ball-player can only anger a ball club or a player or a general manager. It can't start a war. Players use writers as much as writers use them. A player will often criticize the club through a writer and then deny it. What's more, they will feel no guilt over it. Some class players will criticize the club or even the fans and stand behind their quote if reported accurately. Duke Snider, while still playing in Brooklyn, called Brooklyn fans "front-runners." They booed him for the rest of his Dodger career, but he never denied it.

On August 13, 1964, Bo Belinsky was to get a lesson in journalism he would never forget.

Belinsky had pitched at home, had been hit hard, and was the victim of some poor defense by the Angels. Many reporters will avoid a player when he has a bad game. They don't like taking abuse. The good reporters know that the most dramatic stories often come from the loser. *New York Post* photographer Barney Stein won a prize for his photo of Ralph Branca crying on the clubhouse steps of the Polo Grounds after giving up his famous 1951 home run to Bobby Thomson. The other photographers were all trying to shoot Thomson in a crowd scene in the other locker room.

After Belinsky's tough loss, only Charlie Maher, a good reporter, questioned him. Belinsky was distraught and said he was discouraged by his performance, unhappy with the team defense, and considering retiring from baseball. Maher, who worked for the Associated Press, wrote a fine story citing Belinsky's attitude and pointing out correctly that all this was spoken in deep depression after a hard loss. He mentioned that Belinsky talked of quitting, but he also mentioned that he probably didn't mean it.

While Maher sat in the press box in Chavez Ravine writing his story, the Los Angeles Angels and the group of writers who traveled with the club boarded a bus for the airport. They had a cross-country trip ahead of them to Washington to open a series against the Senators on August 14.

The Angels flew in the plane owned by the Los Angeles Dodgers. The flight took nearly nine hours. All of the regular writers, including Braven Dyer, the sixty-year-old reporter for the *Los Angeles Times,* could eat and drink as much as they wished. The players had a two-drink limit.

At 1:30 A.M. the group arrived at the Shoreham Hotel in Washington. They were tired, restless, uncomfortable and edgy from the long trip, the dull bus ride to the hotel, the time difference and the late hour. Few people can go to sleep immediately after a long plane ride. Many of the writers, including Dyer, were fighting the lingering effects of too much drink and too much jet lag. The players and press had to wait about half an hour before their suitcases would arrive from the airport. Belinsky and Chance went out to a late dinner at the Black Steer.

They arrived back at the Shoreham Hotel shortly before 3 A.M. A couple of players and a couple of sportswriters, who had all gone out for a late snack before retiring, stood in the hotel lobby as Chance and Belinsky arrived back at the Shoreham.

Jimmy Piersall, who had fought back from a mental breakdown to save his baseball career, spotted Belinsky coming through the door.

"Bo," Piersall said, "Dyer's looking for you."

"What the hell for?"

"I think it has to do with some story in the paper."

"Fuck him," said Bo, "I'm going to bed."

"I think he's really after your ass."

Belinsky and Chance walked past Piersall and took the elevator to their room on the sixth floor of the Shoreham Hotel.

"I'm going to take a bath," said Chance. "I'm sore all over from that trip."

Just then the phone rang in Belinsky's ear with a jolt. He looked at his watch, saw that it was nearly three-thirty and tried to ignore it. Chance urged him to answer the call.

"Yeah," said Bo.

"This is Dyer. I want to talk to you."

"What the fuck about."

"About that fucking story you gave Maher, about quitting."

"I didn't tell him I was quitting. Who are you to tell me what I can tell him and what I can't. Just get off my ass."

"I want to write a story for my paper. I want to know if you're quitting."

"Oh, shut the fuck up, you old bastard, and stay out of my way."

"Don't you curse me."

"Look, Dyer, I've had enough of your shit for three years. You've never liked me and you've been ripping me ever since I got here. Now I don't want to put up with any more of your bullshit again. Just stay the fuck away from me. If you ever come within two feet of me again I'll put your face in the toilet bowl and flush it."

"You gutless son of a bitch. Let's see you do it. I'll be right up."

"Yeah, you do that. You come up here and I flush your goddamn head in the toilet bowl."

Belinsky hung up the phone. Chance asked him about the conversation.

"He says he's coming up here. Can you imagine that?"

Chance and Belinsky sat on their beds and talked for the next ten minutes. Nobody came to their room. Chance started the water running for his bath. Belinsky called the front desk, ordered all calls stopped until noon of the next day, asked for a wake-up call at that hour, put the "Do Not Disturb" sign outside his door, and hung his clothes in a closet.

Twenty minutes later Braven Dyer got into the hotel elevator with Dick Miller, another of the traveling newspapermen.

"Where are you going?" Miller asked.

"I'm going upstairs to straighten Belinsky out."

Dyer was wearing a jacket and tie. He took off his jacket and hung it on the doorknob of the room next to the one shared by Belinsky and Chance. He opened his tie. Inside, Chance sat in the hot tub and Belinsky was brushing his teeth. He held a cup full of water in his right hand and his toothbrush in his left hand. There was a knock on the door. Belinsky walked to the door to answer it. He carried the cup of water with him. He opened the door and Dyer stepped into the room. According to Belinsky, this is what happened:

"Now, you gutless son of a bitch, let's see you put my head in the toilet bowl."

"For crissakes, Braven, go back to your room and sober up."

"Go ahead, tough guy, let's see you put me on my ass, let's see you."

Dyer had moved Belinsky back into the room. His chest was almost against Bo's. Chance got out of the tub, put a towel around his middle and peeked out from the bathroom to observe the action. Belinsky then made his move.

"I threw the glass of water in his face," said Bo. "He was getting close to me and I didn't want to have to hit him. I thought that might sober him up and make him leave."

According to Bo, Dyer jerked his head as the water hit him, reached down into Belinsky's attache case, pulled out a bottle of hair tonic and swung it at Bo. Belinsky moved back and the bottle grazed the side of his face.

"Then," said Belinsky, "I flattened him with my left hand."

According to Dyer, now working in semi-retirement on a small newspaper in Palm Springs, this is what happened:

"Bo called me about the story. I had already written that he was quitting and he wanted me to change it. I told him it was too late to change it. He told me he was going to stick my head in the toilet and called me a dirty name. I wasn't going to take that. I went to his room, opened the door and walked toward him. We argued for about a minute and I looked for Dean. When I turned my head to look for Dean, Bo hit me. I never reached for any bottle of hair tonic. I never held a grudge against him. If he had been man enough to apologize I would have forgotten about the whole thing."

Belinsky had swung his left hand, opened, and caught Dyer on the side of his head, hard against his right ear. The reporter slipped backwards, banged the back of his head against the wall, caught the light switch with his skull as he was going down, and collapsed at Belinsky's feet. Blood was gushing from his ear and the side of his head.

Dyer lay on his back, his head propped up slightly at the wall, his eyes tightly closed, his mouth open, his arms spread out wide. Blood covered his face.

"Bo," said Chance, "this is bad. Let's get the doc, quick. Maybe you killed him."

"Get a towel. Let's wipe the blood up."

Chance went into the bathroom and came back with a wet towel. He began wiping Dyer's face, wiping away some of the blood. Then he heard the happy sound of Dyer snoring.

"He's snoring, Bo, so at least he isn't dead."

"Maybe he's only got a fractured skull."

"Bo, this is bad, you better call your lawyer, quick. This is going to be big trouble. I wouldn't wait."

"Let's get the doc up here."

Chance went to the phone and asked for the room of the Angels' trainer, Freddie Frederico. He was still awake watching the late, late show on television.

"This is Dean, get up here quick; Braven Dyer's had an accident. He's hurt."

"What happened, what happened? Did you call Rig?"

"No, I'll call him, just get up here quick."

Chance hung up the phone. Frederico immediately picked it up and asked for manager Bill Rigney's room. He was asleep. Frederico told him what Chance had said. Rigney told him to get up there and he would be there as soon as he got dressed.

Frederico walked into the open room and took one look at Dyer, one look at the blood coming off the side of his face and announced, "Oh my God, he's got a punctured eardrum. He might die. We have to get him to a hospital, quick."

"How do you know he's got a punctured eardrum? He's bleeding because he's cut," Chance said.

"It's a punctured eardrum. I can tell. I can see the blood."

"Don't panic. Let's just get him up."

Frederico put a coagulant on the side of Dyer's head. He then put some smelling salts under the reporter's nose and Dyer responded with some painful grunts. He was coming to now, just as the manager walked into the room.

"What happened?" Rigney asked.

"I told him everything the way it was," said Belinsky. "I don't think he believed a word I said. I think he was looking for something to get me on. This was the perfect spot. All the time he's questioning me, never, not once, did he ask me what the hell Dyer was doing in my room at four o'clock in the morning. Wasn't that part of the whole story?"

Rigney arranged to have Dyer sent immediately to the nearest hospital where he was examined thoroughly, X-rayed, treated, and released in the morning. He had suffered a severe gash to the right ear, cuts and bruises on the side and the back of his head, but no serious damage. He posed for pictures in the morning with his ear heavily bandaged. He looked like an old man who had walked down a dark street in New York and been mugged.

Rigney called Haney and Belinsky was immediately suspended. Arrangements were made to put him on the next plane to Los Angeles.

"Nobody wanted to hear my side of the story," says Bo. "All they were interested in was the fact that I had flattened Dyer. Nobody cared that he had come to my room. I didn't go to his. Nobody cared that he had been drinking on the plane and I hadn't. Nobody cared that Dean saw the whole thing and could have told them what happened. Nobody asked him. All anybody seemed interested in was getting me suspended and out of town as fast as possible. Even in a court of law, I'm supposed to be innocent until I'm proven guilty. Why doesn't baseball operate that way? They assumed I was guilty without giving me a chance."

Rigney told Belinsky he was suspended without pay. He said he would be hearing more from the club after he returned home to Los Angeles. He advised him not to go popping off to the press about the incident.

"The White Rat wanted to make sure I didn't get my side of the story across," said Bo. "That's the way things always are when there's a dispute between a player and the club. It's impossible to get the player's side of the story to anybody."

Belinsky was a subdued young man when he boarded the plane at Washington's National Airport for the flight back to Los Angeles. He knew that his career hung limply in the balance. He knew that ballplayers can get away with being drunk, with infidelity, with paternity suits, with social diseases, with clubhouse fights among themselves, and disrespect toward the manager. He knew, also, that he probably could not get away with hitting a sportswriter, especially an elderly sportswriter, especially an elderly sportswriter for the *Los Angeles Times,* the biggest paper in town and one of the biggest in the country. Robert Belinsky might actually have to go to work for a living.

"It was a sickening thought," said Bo. "I felt like I was just about to get into the big money. I felt like I was just learning how to pitch and win in the major leagues. I was on the threshold of becoming a star and making fifty thousand dollars for the next ten years."

Belinsky landed at Los Angeles International Airport and his attorney, Paul Caruso, picked him up and drove him home. The discussion centered mainly on what Belinsky could do to appeal the decision of the Angels to suspend him without pay and without a hearing. Caruso said he would investigate the legal machinery for challenging such a decision.

When Belinsky left the club he had a 9–8 record, 91 strikeouts in 135 innings and a very impressive earned run averqge of 2.87.

"I was pitching about as well as Dean was at that time," says Bo, "and he went on to win the Cy Young Award. I'm sure if I had stayed with the Angels all season I would have won fifteen or eighteen games for them. I know they hurt me when they sent me home, but I think they hurt themselves even more."

Belinsky recovered almost immediately from the depression of the suspension. He arrived home in Los Angeles to find that he was a bigger celebrity than he had ever been. Reporters hounded him for his exclusive story of the event and the doings of the Dodgers were almost lost in the confusion of Belinsky's suspension. Bo relaxed by day in his penthouse pad on La Pressa Drive and swung wildly at night. Walter Winchell had come up with some new names and Belinsky had a full date book. He had some old numbers he hadn't favored for a while so he entertained them at Peppermint West, twisting and cavorting until breakfast.

Then there was Mrs. Ricky DuPont.

She welcomed Bo home with open arms and introduced him to some very exciting Hollywood people.

"She really helped me out of my depression," said Bo. "I realized I could still go on having fun even if I wasn't playing baseball for the Los Angeles Angels. I didn't have a job but most of Ricky's friends didn't seem to have jobs, either. It wasn't any handicap."

While Belinsky pushed his after-hours life, Caruso attempted to get him reinstated. He talked by phone to Haney and to Rigney and both seemed determined to keep Belinsky off the club. There were rumors of a big lawsuit against Belinsky and against the Angels by Dyer and his paper, so the Angels did what they could to hush up the entire matter. They assumed the very best thing they could do would be to keep Belinsky out of everybody's sight.

A week passed and Belinsky was still a suspended ballplayer. According to baseball rules, a suspended ballplayer must have a chance for an appeal before the Commissioner of Baseball. Belinsky and Caruso considered their next move. Then came the bombshell.

The Los Angeles Angels sent Bo Belinsky to Hawaii on twenty-four-hour recall.

"They can't do that," fumed Belinsky when he received a telegram from the club ordering him to report to the Hawaii club. "How can they ship me out? I'm the best pitcher they have."

The Angels had decided to send Belinsky to Hawaii instead of allowing him to remain suspended and thereby possibly cause unwanted litigation.

Caruso decided there would be only one way to handle the suspension. He would call Commissioner of Baseball Ford Frick and ask for a hearing. He placed his call to Frick's office and reached a secretary. She said the commissioner was not in. Caruso left his number and waited for the commissioner to call back. He did not receive a call. The next day Belinsky told the Los Angeles Angels he would not report to Hawaii. Haney immediately dispatched a telegram to Frick's New York office requesting that pitcher Bo Belinsky be placed on the disqualified list. Frick immediately agreed and ordered Charles Segar, the secretary-treasurer of baseball, to prepare the necessary papers for all clubs concerned and for Belinsky. A player on the disqualified list receives no pay, cannot work out with any other club, cannot sign with any other club in baseball, and is ineligible to play for the club that puts him on the list until request for reinstatement is granted. Bo Belinsky, as far as baseball was concerned, was a nonperson.

Caruso placed another call to Frick and waited again. Still no answer.

"We have only one choice, Bo, and we'd better take it. We have to go to New York and see Frick," Caruso said.

The next morning Belinsky and Caruso boarded a plane for New York. They paid their own fare and checked into the Roosevelt Hotel in New York. The next morning they appeared at Frick's office. They were told he was out.

"Let me tell you something," Bo says, "I know I got the good runaround from Elmer Fudd Frick. He just wouldn't see me and he just wouldn't face up to making any kind of a decision. He's the guy you have to see and it doesn't pay to see him. He's talking about one thing and you're talking about another. I don't know how he ever found his way around New York. If you let him out of his office, he would never find his way back. They put a guy in that job just to have a body there. Frick was a body, all right, that's all he was."

Frick says the question of Belinsky's reinstatement by the Angels was completely out of his hands. It is not the job of the Commissioner to tell a team who they can send to the minor leagues and who they can't.

"Belinsky was optioned to the Angels' club in Hawaii," said Frick. "As far as the Commissioner was concerned that was all there was to it."

Caruso and Belinsky, upset that they couldn't get to see Frick and get a legitimate hearing, flew back to Los Angeles.

"I didn't care anymore," said Bo. "I figured I was never going to play baseball again anyway. I was having fun with Ricky DuPont, I was having a good time on the Hollywood scene, I had a lot of good friends, I had all the money I needed to get by. What the hell did I need baseball for?"

When Belinsky failed to report to Hawaii, the Angels decided they would try to trade him to another big league club in hopes of receiving something on their investment. Nothing hurts a ball club worse than losing a player, by retirement or disqualification, before they can turn him into money or another serviceable player. Curt Flood, in his challenge to baseball's reserve clause, called himself a "ninety thousand dollar slave, but a slave, nevertheless." Belinsky was only a $15,500 slave, but he was a piece of property that the Angels were unwilling to lose without compensation.

Toward the end of the season of 1964 the Angels began putting out feelers to those clubs interested in Belinsky's services. They made discreet inquiries to most of the clubs in the National League. They wanted to trade Belinsky, but they didn't want to be embarrassed by trading him to a club in their own league. He just might come back and win some big games in the American League and he just might come back and beat the Angels enough times to force them to lose face with their fans. Baseball teams will sink to the bottom of the league before they will admit they have made a mistake on a trade, misjudged a prospect, or hired the wrong manager for the wrong club. Baseball annals are filled with names of super-prospects, who were paid large bonuses on the say-so of some scout, who stayed around the majors longer than they should have because nobody wanted the responsibility of admitting a mistake. A face saved is a face that lives to take home a baseball paycheck again.

Saving face in a trade is sometimes even more important. Untried prospects are generally gambles. Proven pitchers are generally known qualities. The Angels had to trade Belinsky out of the American League.

In a very exciting World Series the St. Louis Cardinals defeated the New York Yankees in 1964 by four games to three. Johnny Keane, saving face because he was insulted by owner Gussie Busch's attempt at hiring Leo Durocher to manage the Cardinals, resigned after winning the Series. Rumors persisted that his move was one of baseball's most eloquent grandstand plays since Keane had already been approached by the Yankees as to his availability for managing that team. Mayo Smith, a Yankee superscout, was supposed to have made the approach. Keane strongly denied the rumor. He took the secret to his grave when he died less than a year after being fired by the Yankees.

While all these tricky maneuvers were going on, Bo Belinsky sat comfortably vacationing on the beach at Waikiki in Hawaii. He had friends and enough money, had accepted the fact that he wouldn't play baseball anymore, and decided he would live the good life of a beach bum.

But the Los Angeles Angels still didn't take kindly to the idea that they would get no value for a twenty seven-year-old left-handed pitcher, at the prime of his pitching life, without any injury, who had won twenty one games in a little more than two seasons. At the winter meetings in December of 1964 they approached most of the National League clubs seeking a trade for the pitcher they had drafted two years earlier from the Baltimore Orioles for twenty-five thousand dollars.

On the last day of the week of baseball meetings, the Los Angeles Angels and the Philadelphia Phillies announced jointly that they had completed a trade. The Phillies were to send first baseman Costen Shockley, a home-run hitting prospect, and pitcher Rudy May, a relief pitcher of little note, to the Angels in exchange for Bo Belinsky.

Belinsky was deep into the brush when the news hit the wires. It was two days before he would return to the main part of the island to receive news that he was now a member of the Philadelphia Phillies.

His stay in Philadelphia would be memorable. He would be forever enshrined as the man who coined the elegant phrase about the fans in Philadelphia, "They would even boo a funeral."

The Boo Birds of Happiness

On a beautiful December day in 1964 Bo Belinsky sat in the Honolulu sun contemplating his future. He was now assigned to the Philadelphia Phillies by the laws of baseball and he knew he just wouldn't dig that scene. He just couldn't see giving up Waikiki for Market Street in Philadelphia.

He had become close to an Hawaiian entrepreneur named J. J. Morgan, who introduced Belinsky to Hawaii's social set, arranged for Bo to meet and later dine with Doris Duke, established a relationship with Conrad Hilton, and brought Bo together with some of Hawaii's most successful and interesting citizens, restaurateur Don the Beachcomber, entertainer Don Ho, and dozens of other Hawaiian celebrities. Philadelphia just couldn't compete.

"Hawaii is a very romantic place," says Bo. "It can make you horny just getting up in the morning and looking out of the window at the surf and sand. One guy I knew bought himself the highest-priced, most powerful telescope so he could get on the high roof of his home and shoot beaver across the water to one of the smaller islands where the girls bathed in the nude. He kept writing to lens companies back in the States for more powerful telescopes. He was always disappointed when they would write him that the most powerful lens in the world was their model number so and so, and that was always the one he was already using."

Since Belinsky was unemployed for the moment, people came to him with magnificent business deals. Ricky DuPont wanted Bo to operate a movie production company for her. J. J. Morgan wanted to set Belinsky up in land development. Several Hollywood people suggested Bo could make a full-time career of the movies. Then came the dude-ranch deal.

"I had met a guy through J. J. who had a fabulous career. He was a retired doctor. He had practiced all over the world and had worked with some wild diseases, jungle rot, and all that. For years he had been the private physician of the rulers of the kingdom of Kuwait. That's supposed to be one of the richest places in the world, and he really had it made. I guess he was rich enough and tired of living in Kuwait so one day he just got up and left. He came to Hawaii and settled down."

Belinsky's doctor friend had a great deal of money to invest. He still liked the idea of making money but he didn't feel like working for it. He decided a dude ranch would go over big in Hawaii and a slow-moving, long-legged, handsome cowpoke like Robert Belinsky would be just the perfect man to run his ranch.

"We had several meetings and the deal was just about set," Bo says. "He had transferred some stocks into cash and now we had been able to pick the spot and get ready to build. I was really happy with the deal. It would give me something to do but it wouldn't be too strenuous. J. J. decided to throw a big party to celebrate the final terms of the deal. We would be at the bank the next day to settle everything. I was going to work for him, but be a part owner at the same time. If things worked out, I would have become full owner of the place within five years."

The party was organized and J. J. invited a dozen people over for dinner. Cocktails were set for six o'clock with dinner scheduled for eight. Things were going well until one of the waiters brought around a tray full of snacks.

"Somebody had mixed up a batch of cookies," said Bo, "and

dropped acid in them for a joke. Nobody knew a thing and we just gobbled everything down. It was like a Mickey shot. All of a sudden my head started spinning and I thought I would die. Everybody's flying and screaming and carrying on and falling on their asses. It was a mad scene. Somebody pulls out a joint and everybody starts taking some puffs of that. Now we are all on the acid and the marijuana and we are stoned. Then the doctor arrives."

The doctor had been traveling that day and arrived in his own car, a brand new yellow Oldsmobile, while his wife arrived a few minutes later in her own blue Thunderbird. They stepped inside and saw the party in high gear.

"Now you have to remember that these were very fancy, elegant, rich people," says Bo, "who had mingled with sheikhs in Africa, kings, princes, dukes, the whole thing. This wasn't some guy off the street."

The doctor and his wife did not bother to inquire why everybody was acting so mysteriously. They merely assumed that the party had been raging long before they got there and that everyone was flying high from the booze. They had a drink and then they reached for the tray of snacks.

"Uhh," said Bo, "I wouldn't have that stuff if I were you, doc, I think something's in it. I think everybody bombed out from those snacks."

"Nonsense," said the doctor. "My boy, I have been all over the world, lived everywhere, did everything, eating and drinking every food known to man."

"I don't think you've had this stuff, doc."

"Ahh, let me try it. Here, my dear, have one of these little tidbits."

The doctor and his wife dined heartily. They tried each of the delicacies. In a few moments they were swinging with the rest of the party.

"His old lady was really a beaut," says Bo. "She takes off her dress right away, rolls down the stockings and starts dancing in the buckets of ice. It was the wildest thing I had seen all night. Now the doctor goes wild and he's throwing things in the air and screaming and dancing and carrying on something awful. It was like the first time kids get drunk. They do the wildest things because they just don't know how to handle anything like that."

About an hour later the house was in marvelous disarray and people were sprawled out on the floor. Several people started coming down hard from their trip. The doctor and his lady began arguing about everything and anything.

"You're a goddamn whore," the doctor said, "and you just came here because you hope somebody makes a pass at you."

"Who are you calling a whore, you goddamn eunuch?"

"That's some shit. Your pussy is like an icebox."

That went on back and forth, with serves and counterserves for ten minutes. Finally the doctor stood up and announced, "I'm leaving this place. Let's go the fuck home."

"You go," the wife said, "I'm staying because I'm having too much fun."

"I'm going and I'm taking your car. You'll have to walk home."

The doctor stormed out of the front door and staggered to the Oldsmobile. He starts the engine. He gets out of the car. He leaves the motor running. He fumbles for another set of keys in his pocket. He walks to the Thunderbird parked next to the Oldsmobile. He gets in. He starts the engine. He drives it out of the driveway and on to the road. He puts the car in park and gets out. He gets into the Oldsmobile. He drives it down the driveway and stops behind the Thunderbird. He gets out and goes back into the Thunderbird. He drives five hundred yards. Now he gets out and walks back to the Oldsmobile. He drives that five hundred yards, bumps into the rear of the Thunderbird, stops and gets out. Then back into the Thunderbird.

The doctor had decided to drive both cars home by himself.

"All of a sudden," said Bo, "we hear this loud honking of horns and yelling and carrying on outside. We get out of the house, pile into a car and drive down the road about two miles. The doctor is standing on the hood of the Thunderbird yelling and screaming at a bunch of guys. Both cars have been turned sideways across the highway and nobody can pass. It was a hell of a traffic mess."

With a little assist from the local police, everybody made it home safe and sound and hardly worse for the experience.

"I know one thing," said Bo, "I had a head you wouldn't believe after that night. Anybody taking acid has to be out of his mind. What the hell good is taking acid when you don't remember whether you had any fun or not? I like having fun. I also like thinking about yesterday in the light of the next morning. The only thing you think about when you trip acid is whether or not you will live. You hope you don't because then you won't have to go through such pain again."

In the confusion, the dude ranch deal fell through.

Belinsky continued his sunny life through January and early February. He let his hair grow long and grew a beard. He slept in grass shacks in Hawaiian villages. He spent most of the days learning to surfboard with the natives. He walked the beaches and partied with the fancy set. He sunned himself in the patios of the elegant hotels. He made friends with all the beach boys, especially one young man named Fat, who scouted guests for Bo.

"Fat tried to make it with everybody himself but he just couldn't cut it. When he struck out he would tout me on some good-looking girl. I must say he had a hell of an eye," Bo said.

Once or twice during the winter Belinsky would tire of the native scene and hop a plane back to Los Angeles. There were some girls there waiting to offer him love and affection in his moments of need.

"I was getting on great with Mamie then," Bo said. "We had broken off our engagement so now we were better friends than we had ever been. One time I flew back to Los Angeles and my friend Andy Spagnola picked me up at the airport. He had Mamie with him. She had heard I was coming back so she came out to the airport to greet me. Mamie can really greet you when she wants to. Andy was sitting in the front seat of the car and Mamie and I were in the back seat. Mamie and I really went at it pretty good and it was a wonder that Andy didn't lose control of that car and drive us off the road. He spent more time staring into the mirror at us than he did watching the other cars on the road. I can't say that I blamed him. Mamie was really looking super then."

A few days of rest and recuperation in Los Angeles and Bo was back in Hawaii. It was February 15 and the Phillies were opening spring training in a week. Belinsky would soon have to make the decision to go or stay.

The decision was easy. He was broke again. He would go.

No team in baseball had ever looked forward less to opening a spring training season than did the Philadelphia Phillies of 1965. They had just come off the biggest pennant choke in baseball history. Ten days before the 1964 season ended, the Phillies had an almost insurmountable lead. In those ten days they blew the pennant with an incredible ten-game losing streak and a six-game loss in the standings. The manager, Gene Mauch, an intense, good-looking, gray-haired man, who had been an unsuccessful baseball player, had brought the Phillies back to respectability, after taking over in the 1960 season.

By 1964, he had rebuilt the club completely. He had some fine young players in rookie Richie Allen, a slugging third baseman from Wampum, Pennsylvania, Johnny Callison, Tony Taylor, Danny Cater, and, late in the season, Frank Thomas, affectionately called by his teammates, The Big Donkey. Thomas had never been on a pennant winner and never would be. Much of the reason was his style of play, a one-for-one and all-for-Frank attitude. He had been a solid home-run hitter, an aggressive outfielder, and a hustling ballplayer.

"Thomas has the kind of personality," one writer suggested, "that makes you want to punch him in the nose when he says good morning."

He added his unique brand of confusion to the team late in the season by getting into a race discussion with Allen and punches were exchanged.

The two best pitchers on the team were Jim Bunning, as fierce a competitor as ever put on a baseball suit, and Chris Short, a big, hulking left-hander with a great deal of stuff and an equal amount of indifference. They were to play the deciding parts in the Philadelphia drama of 1964.

Philadelphia began slumping in early September and the lead began disappearing. With each passing day, Mauch grew more tense as the pennant seemed to be slipping away. The Cardinals were making an incredible drive. Cincinnati and San Francisco were still in contention. The National League was doing it again, exciting the country with one of its hairiest races. The Phillies would see to that.

The Phillies went into Houston and lost a doubleheader. Mauch responded to that defeat by turning over a table filled with greasy spare ribs in the clubhouse. He apologized for his misconduct and bought new suits for several of his players. This really hurt because Mauch had a tight fist wrapped around his money. Now the lead began to shrivel away. Ten games, eight games, seven games, six games, five games. Mauch had decided the only way to guarantee the pennant was by pitching Bunning and Short on two days of rest. Bunning had nineteen wins when he started going on short rest. Short had seventeen. Neither would win another game. The Phillies would go the last ten days of the season blowing the pennant, losing all their games except the final one, and cringing uncomfortably as the baseball world agreed they had choked under the pressure of the race. The Cardinals won it on the last day of the season by beating the Mets after the Cardinals had blown two games to New York, including a memorable Friday night 1–0 win by Al Jackson of the Mets over Bob Gibson of the Cardinals. Gibson would redeem himself for the loss by winning the final game of the season in relief. Short rest sometimes works with the right pitcher.

Philadelphia sportswriters, a talented group including Larry Merchant, Stan Hochman, Frank Dolson, Sandy Grady, Allen Lewis, and Ray Kelly, would spend the winter of 1964 describing the anatomy of the defeat in columns and analytical and critical stories. The blame was spread around to the players, to the front office, to the manager, and even to the fans, who responded to the losing as they always have in Philadelphia, with strong doses of booing.

Besides booing funerals in Philadelphia, as Belinsky was quick to point out, Philadelphia fans would boo an Easter egg hunt, a parade of armless war vets, and the Liberty Bell.

Into the den of the boo birds would march Bo Belinsky.

Ever since he was lionized by the Los Angeles press at poolside in 1962, the arrival of Bo Belinsky at a spring training camp was an event. Reporters waited for his appearance at the Harrison Hotel in downtown Clearwater. They knew he would not fail them. A Bo Belinsky press conference would be an easy day of work for any reporter. One needed only to keep one's ears open and one's pencil moving. Belinsky would provide the rest.

The hotel press conference wasn't quite as extravagant as Belinsky's Los Angeles arrival. He looked beautiful, as he always did for reporters, his hair long, dark, and slick, his sport shirt a gaudy green, his pants yellow, his shoes a highly polished set of alligator loafers. He wore dark glasses and carried an attache case like some visiting executive.

"I don't know if I can win the pennant for this team," confessed Bo. "You guys have to remember I didn't pitch the last two months of the season. I don't know what kind of shape I'm in."

"What kind of shape is Mamie in?"

Belinsky laughed and knew he was on his way.

"Mamie? Oh, you mean my physical fitness director. Oh, she's fine. I think she'll be down here in a few days. I'll give you guys a shot at interviewing her."

"When will she be here?"

"Oh, probably in a week or so. It depends how my conditioning down here goes and when I'm ready for her."

"Are you still engaged?"

"No, no, we're not engaged anymore. Just write that we are still in love. That's a lot better than being engaged."

"Is she engaged?"

"No. She doesn't like being engaged anymore either. It's much too confining."

The reporters spent almost an hour with Belinsky and finally allowed him to leave. He had entertained them, informed them, and given them something more invigorating to write than some tired old ballplayer's sore winter muscles. Bo would be a hit in Philadelphia with the sportswriters as he had been every place he went. It wasn't writers who gave him trouble. It was managers and hitters. He would do well in Philadelphia every place but on the field. The hitters would hit him, the manager would hate him, and the fans would boo him. The feeling would be mutual.

"Some day," Belinsky said, "I would like to go up in the stands and boo some fans."

Belinsky's reputation always helped him with the ladies. But Gene

Mauch wasn't as charmed by Belinsky as most of the young and old ladies around Clearwater were. Mauch is a rather dashing figure, a fine dresser, just the proper amount of gray in his hair and syrup in his voice. Like Rigney, he allowed for only one star on his team. That star would not be Belinsky.

Mauch was under extreme pressure in the spring of 1965. His team had blown the 1964 pennant in horrible fashion and that was all anybody wanted to talk about. That was the one thing Mauch didn't want to talk about. He tried hard to create a new season, a new atmosphere around the Phillies; but with the same team in a new season, it was nearly impossible.

"I don't think it took me three weeks to realize why this team didn't win," said Belinsky. "They were a bunch of hypochondriacs. Every time you turned around, somebody on this team was on the training table, complaining about this ailment or that one. It was a joke. It was as if they were all afraid to play baseball. There was also their fear of the manager. Mauch could really ream a guy out if he went bad. So they played cautiously. They were afraid to do anything at all that would get them in trouble with the manager. If he got mad at you, he would really let you have it. You really knew he was mad when he cursed you with his favorite word, 'cunt.' He just loved that word. If he called you cunt you knew you were on his shit list and it would be a long time before you ever got off. I used to laugh when he called me a cunt. I don't know why, I really can't explain it. It just struck me as very funny."

Chris Short and Jim Bunning got off well, Richie Allen was hitting. But the Phillies had lost that drive and ambition they had throughout most of the 1964 season. They never really recovered from that defeat. They would slip to sixth place in 1965, fourth in 1966, fifth in 1967, and seventh in 1968 as the Gene Mauch era in Philadelphia ended. He was fired in midseason and returned in 1969 to lead the new expansion club in Canada, the Montreal Expos.

Much of Mauch's trouble after the loss of the 1964 season revolved around the talented but temperamental third baseman, Richie Allen. No ballplayer was ever maligned as much in his time as Allen was in Philadelphia. He refused to pay homage or be

courtly to the press. For his surliness and moodiness, he was criti-
cized unmercifully. Much of the criticism was racial. He was an
"uppity nigger" and sportswriters didn't like "uppity niggers" any
more than the rest of the population did. Few Northern towns in
America have as much deeply rooted hate for blacks as Philadelphia
does. The Philadelphia ghettos rate with the country's ugliest and
the Philadelphia ball park was on the edge of the ghetto. Visiting
teams had to ride through the ghetto on the team bus to reach the
park from downtown. It was a depressing sight.

"I got along great with Richie," says Belinsky. "He was the kind
of guy you couldn't push. He goes his way and I go mine. He talks
when he feels like it. The writers didn't like him because he wouldn't
sit around the clubhouse and bullshit with them all day. They didn't
like that. Some of the players resented that too. The guy did his job.
Nobody played baseball harder on the field. Once in a while he was
late to the park, so what. Once in a while he took a nip in the
clubhouse, so what. I know a hell of a lot of guys who took nips in
the clubhouse. I know a lot of managers who kept the bottle in the
bottom drawer of their office desks. Nobody got excited about that.
I can say that I never saw Richie miss a game because he was drunk.
Well, maybe once in a while his eyes would be a little bloodshot, but
whose weren't?"

Allen's supposed drinking problem was one of baseball's most
recurring rumors. It also was part of the way baseball people tend
to downgrade black players. When the Dodgers first signed Jackie
Robinson to a professional contract with Montreal in 1946, they
knew he could play baseball. They were worried about his off-field
activities.

"They scouted me," Roy Campanella once said, "and were about
to sign me. I went into Mr. [Branch] Rickey's office and sat across
the table from him. He told me he had scouts watching me for
months. There was no question I could play. What he couldn't tell
was my habits. Did I drink? Did I run around with women? Would
I embarrass the club with my conduct? That's what they had to be
sure of before they signed any Negro player."

No man lived a more exemplary life than Jackie Robinson. On and off the field, he opened the door dramatically for blacks. Still, into the 1960s and 1970s, a double standard existed. There were no black managers and few black front office people. Though baseball had become totally integrated on the field, one could still hear players referred to as "niggers." Few teams integrated black players and white players as roommates. Double standards existed in salaries and management-player relations. Richie Allen suffered more abuse because he was black than he would have if he were a white player. Any baseball official or writer who denies that simply does not understand the machinations of a ball club—or he lies.

White players nip from bottles, are surly to the press, and are never maligned as Allen was. And sometimes they have a lot less talent. One white pitcher was actually drunk when he took the mound in 1969 during the championship playoff. He was excused because he was nervous. One black player was traded while still a star and fans wondered why. After reporters could not pin management down to a legitimate reason for this obviously poor trade, the club owner took the press into his confidence and off-the-record revealed that the player had contracted a social disease after he had been warned not to let it happen again. No figures are available, but because there are three white players to every black player in baseball, it is a fair guess that there are three white players who suffer from social diseases to every black player.

It was a white player, not a black player, who infected his entire team one season, by passing along the name of a girl who was an easy lay. It turned out she was a typhoid Mary and a fine team passed quietly and quickly out of the pennant race in July.

The abusive treatment to Allen finally ended in Philadelphia when he was traded to the St. Louis Cardinals in 1970. He finished off his stay in Philadelphia by scratching out huge letters B . . . O . . . O . . . in the dirt around first base as a farewell address for the Philadelphia fans. He was then traded to the Los Angeles Dodgers and on to the Chicago White Sox. The White Sox at least made one concession to him. Allen wanted to be called Dick Allen. Every club and every sportswriter always called him Richie, a name he considered childish and demeaning. Chicago finally put out a press brochure and called for all their writers to describe him as Dick Allen.

Rather a minor concession to one of the most talented players the game has ever seen.

The Phillies did not do well in the season of 1965. They suffered from the 1964 hangover and were merely playing out the year for their salaries.

The team was terribly fragmented, some blaming Mauch for the horrible 1964 loss, others defending him. Belinsky never really took sides because he hadn't been with the club in 1964 when the trouble developed.

"My major problem was with the way Gene used me," Belinsky said. "He got me because I was supposed to be his fourth starting pitcher. Then he used me starting, in long relief, and in short relief. My arm just couldn't take it. I never really was a very good pitcher after the 1965 season. I would have to say Gene Mauch had an awful lot to do with that."

Belinsky tried unsuccessfully to pitch in relief. He had neither the talent nor the temperament. Relief pitchers are baseball's nervy firemen and only a limited number of pitchers can handle the task.

"The fans in Philadelphia didn't help much, either," said Bo. "Every time I walked on the field they greeted me with some lusty booing. Sometimes they booed me even though I hadn't pitched in a week or ten days. I think most of those people just sit home at night, stare into a mirror and practice their booing. It's the major activity of the fans in Philadelphia."

One day Belinsky was warming up in the bullpen. He was about to enter the game and let loose with a sharp curve ball to see if he was ready. He felt severe pain along the side and down into his lower back.

"I was hurting but there was nothing I could do about it," said Bo. "I just couldn't go to the trainer because Mauch didn't allow anybody to get hurt. He knew most of them were faking. The shortstop, Bobby Wine, was suffering with a bad back. You could see it, day after day, he could hardly move. He's a mild kid and he isn't about to complain, so he keeps going along like that. Finally he tells Mauch he can't play. Mauch tells him he isn't going into the trainer. He tells him that if he is that badly off, he should be in a hospital. Sure enough, they put him in a hospital and operate on his back."

Belinsky's pain lingered for several weeks. He continued to pitch in relief, most of it quite ineffectively. Finally he could stand it no longer and visited a doctor in Philadelphia. The doctor gave him an extensive examination, including X-rays, and told Belinsky, "You have a cracked rib. I'll treat it but you have to be sure you don't pitch for several weeks."

Belinsky was uncertain about telling Mauch. The next day was an off day and Belinsky drove up to New York to have dinner with Dean Chance. The Angels were in town playing the Yankees.

"I can't pitch," Belinsky said, "I have a cracked rib."

"Why don't they put you on the disabled list?"

"I haven't told Mauch."

"Why not?"

"He'll tell me I'm making it up."

"Bring a note from your doctor."

"He'll call me a cunt."

Mauch didn't use Belinsky the next night. By the following morning the secret was out. Chance told a sportswriter at Yankee Stadium about Belinsky's cracked rib. The story was played big in Philadelphia and annoyed Philadelphia sportswriters who, like sportswriters in any city, hate to be scooped on something pertaining to one of their own players by an out-of-town newspaper, especially an out-of-town newspaper from New York.

Mauch called Belinsky into his office and questioned him about the cracked rib.

"Why didn't you tell me about it?"

"I thought I would be able to pitch it out."

"How long has it been bothering you?"

"About three of four weeks now."

"Has it gotten worse during that time?"

"Yes, I think it did."

"Now you're no good at all to the ball club."

"I'm sorry, Skip. I thought it would come around."

"How did you get it?"

"I think I pulled something in a game a few weeks ago and then I hurt it again when I was warming up the other day and tried to throw my curve ball."

"Do you know what I think?"

"No, Skip, what do you think?"

"I think you hurt it while you were surfboarding in Hawaii, that's what I think. You didn't hurt it playing baseball, you hurt it falling off one of those boards."

Mauch ended the discussion and stormed out on the field. Belinsky walked slowly out to the bullpen that evening for a game against the Mets. He knew that he would not have as long and memorable a stay in Philadelphia as Benjamin Franklin.

Methinks I should lie down and bleed awhile and rise to fight again.

—BO BELINSKY

Down, Down, Down, Never Out

In November of 1965, after a trying year in Philadelphia (aren't all years in Philadelphia trying?), Belinsky returned to Hollywood by way of Trenton—two days, Chicago—a week, Little Rock—eight days, and Las Vegas—two weeks. He was, as always, broke. But he could, as always, make a few bucks shooting pool.

"I have an attachment to my pool cue the way Linus has an attachment for his blanket," Bo said.

The secret of Belinsky's pool shooting was not so much whom he played and hustled, it was more with whom he did not play.

In 1959 Belinsky had lived in the Wolf Hotel in Stockton, California, He roomed with a young infielder named Pete Ward, who was to go on to a fine major league career.

"We lived together about a week," said Ward. "Then Bo moved out. I was too tame for him. One thing I learned about him, though. He wouldn't shoot pool with just anybody. He spent a lot of time scouting and studying a guy before he would get in a match with him. I don't know if he was the best pool shooter in the world. I do know that I never saw him lose and that is a talent all by itself."

What Ward and all the world would know about Bo was that no matter how far down he was, he came up again.

In November of 1965 he was way, way down.

He hustled some pool shooters in Vegas and flew on to Los Angeles. Then he got some bad news. He had to move out of his luxurious Hollywood pad in the hills. The owners of his pad had produced a movie and Bo had a cameo part as the proprietor of a beach establishment called Bo Bo's A Go Go's. This was during his Lance, Lance Belinsky stage. Now the movie had been released, bombed as generally expected and a great deal of money went into the ocean. The first thing the bank that held the mortgage on the house did was demand its money. The house had to go and Bo had to go, too. He moved into an undistinguished motel on the beach.

"A terrible blow," Belinsky said. "My aces are going, one by one, slowly but surely. God, I may have to go out and work for a living if my arm doesn't come back."

That horrible thought lingered only until the following evening. Belinsky had a date with a starlet.

"I was going downhill," he said. "The big timers weren't around anymore. I wasn't seeing Mamie now, or Ann-Margret, or Tina Louise, or the stars. I was down to starlets. But they weren't dogs. I was still doing pretty good. I wasn't depressed."

The Phillies were kind enough to give Belinsky a small pay raise to eighteen thousand dollars for the 1966 season despite a poor year in 1965. He had won only four games, lost nine and compiled a horrible earned run average of 4.83. Bo didn't have much hope for the 1966 season.

"Uncle Gene just about ruined my arm," Bo said. "My side still hurt every so often, and I just don't seem to have any juice on the ball. I was going to spring training for the first time with serious doubts about myself."

Despite the uncomfortable relationship with Mauch in 1965, Belinsky tried to start clean. He arrived on time, this time Mamie was nowhere in sight, and he vowed that he would pitch his way onto the ball club.

"Bo always was a good-time guy, even when I knew him as a kid," said Pete Ward, "and he always had broads around even then. But

I never doubted that he was serious about his pitching. He would walk out on that mound and he would be as tough a competitor as you would ever want to see in a baseball game."

Other than his opening streak in 1962 with the Angels when he zoomed into the Hollywood sun on the strength of his 5–0 record and his no-hitter, Belinsky probably pitched more effectively in the spring of 1966 than at any other time. He had to impress Mauch that he could come back from the rib injury and pitch well again. He also had another incentive that spring. He had bet Dean Chance that he would have a better spring than Dean. The prize was a Hollywood champagne party at the season's end. Belinsky was going up against tough odds. Chance had been the best pitcher in baseball in 1964 and had come back from a slow start in 1965 to win fifteen more games. But Bo did it. He had a fine spring, won his bet, and won a spot on the Philadelphia pitching staff.

At twenty-nine years old, Belinsky could still fool the most astute of baseball people. At twenty-nine, after some twelve years of pitching winter and summer, Belinsky was still considered a prospect.

Bob Carpenter, the millionaire owner of the Phillies and a member of the DuPonts of Delaware, always liked Belinsky. He also admired Belinsky's taste in women, especially Ricky DuPont, a member in good standing of Bob Carpenter's own distinguished set. Carpenter sat at the bar one day in the Harrison Hotel and mused about Belinsky. He still thought Belinsky could be the pitcher who could change the Phillies overnight into winners, the pitcher who would undo all the damage of 1964 and lead the Phillies to the pennant that got away.

"If he just walked into this camp today," said Carpenter, "and you didn't know who he was and you just watched him warm up, you would have to say to yourself that he was one fine pitcher, a great prospect and the kind of golden arm that you would be forced to bid for. I know that if I saw Bo as a kid with that arm of his, I would start bidding for him at one hundred thousand dollars."

Belinsky reported to the Phillies in excellent shape. He had actually worked out a little on the beach in California before coming to camp. He seemed more serious about baseball than he had been in years. He impressed Mauch with his determination to make the club.

"I've been shut out on the field and off the field," said Belinsky, "and now I want to come back."

In the last week of March Belinsky pitched impressively against the Mets and the Cardinals and solidified his hold on the ball club. He had started throwing the spitter with much effectiveness. It was the difference in making the club. Lew Burdette, who had been with the Phillies all of 1965 but was gone now to the Angels, of all places, in 1966, had left his legacy with Bo.

"When I was young and could throw hard I wouldn't fool with a pitch like that. I just leaned back and threw the ball by people. Now I couldn't throw hard and I needed all the help I could get. The spitter was a lot of help. It kept me in the big leagues when all else failed."

The Phillies broke camp in Clearwater and headed north. Belinsky had made it again, this time with diligent efforts and good fortune to see several of his pitching teammates suffer with sore arms. But the early season weather was horrible, as it often is in April, and Belinsky's tired old arm just didn't respond to the cold and dampness of Philadelphia. Mauch used him sparingly and Belinsky pitched in long relief in lost games. His major league career was ebbing and everyone knew it. The Phillies had several young pitchers in the farm system they wanted to bring up to the big club. First they had to clear a space on the roster. Speculation began in the press that the next song around Philadelphia would be, "Bye, Bye, Bo, Baby."

"I was trying to fight off the inevitable," said Bo. "I thought maybe if I could squeeze it through to the summer months my arm would respond in the heat. It got warmer and still it didn't come around. Then I had another great idea. Why not silicone?"

Silicone had rescued the careers of dozens of showgirls, strippers, and waitresses, and Belinsky thought it could rescue his. He wanted to give himself a silicone injection in the left arm and see if it would bring back any life in the dying member.

"At least," he said, "it might impress some of the hitters with its size."

Surprising everyone, including himself, Belinsky survived the May 15 cutdown date. Now he had to make it through the June 15 trading deadline. The Phillies were talking trades with almost every club in a vain attempt to get into the pennant race. Nothing worked out and the club stumbled along for the next month. Every week or so, Belinsky would get an inning or two, strike out a hitter and be rescued again from the garbage heap. He had to last a week more at least. His friend had planned a day for him.

"It was a very exciting thing," said Bo's mother. "We all went down to Philadelphia to honor him. I think everybody in Trenton turned out for the event. The politicians were all there and his high school teachers were there and all of his friends. It's funny how people will jump on Bo's bandwagon when he's on top. But when he's down, nobody wants to know him. That's when the only thing that matters is your family. We love him and we care for him, not just when he wins. A lot of those friends, especially those Hollywood friends, they didn't want to have anything to do with him after he stopped winning a lot of games."

Belinsky stood at home plate and was honored and extolled by his Trenton friends. He was presented with a plaque and a large, animated portrait of himself. Some of the joy of the day was taken away as he stood at the microphone to thank his friends. The booing increased in intensity and the applause of his friends was almost drowned out.

"I didn't think they were really booing," Bo says. "You see, it was one of those very chilly Philadelphia nights and there wasn't any heat in the ball park so they had to rub their hands together like that just to keep warm. You don't think the fine fans in Philadelphia would boo a man on his day, do you?"

A week later it all ended in Philadelphia.

Gene Mauch had sent his emissary out to fetch Belinsky. The ritual would be short and sweet without any of the amenities.

"We've outrighted you to San Diego," Mauch said. "Good luck."

The operation was painless. Mauch studied his lineup card as he sent Bo away. It didn't take more than a minute. Belinsky didn't have much to say to Mauch.

"We probably should have liked each other more," said Bo, "but we didn't. We were a lot alike. He was a hustler just like me. He tried to make it on his wits and so did I. That's probably because neither of us had much talent. He did a better job fooling people than I did. We both were famous for things we didn't do instead of things we did do. I was famous because I didn't win very much after the 1962 no-hitter. Mauch was famous because he didn't win very much the last week of the 1964 season. Can you imagine how a guy could blow a pennant like that and have the nerve to tell other people they weren't tough enough for the game? Gene was an experience. Every manager in baseball usually is."

Belinsky would now be faced with the usual decision. What would he do with his future? If he went to San Diego, as assigned, he would be paid the rest of his contract at the same rate he was being paid in Philadelphia. It is one of the few positive things about baseball contractual rules. Ball clubs cannot cut a player's salary once he has signed for that season, whether or not he stays with that club. Of course, they could always release him. But that is quite rare. They would still want to turn the player over for another player or an equivalent amount of cash. It would be impossible to come up with any other meaningful employment at this stage of the summer so Belinsky decided to go on to San Diego.

"The location of the town had an awful lot to do with the decision," says Bo. "I just didn't want to play in a cold climate any more. I had finally realized I couldn't stand cold weather. San Diego would be nice and sunny. Just right and just down the road from L.A. and across the street from Mexico. I had always done well with the señoritas.

Once when he was a rising young teenager, Belinsky had picked up a girl in his battered, old convertible. The car was not quite airtight. Belinsky drove his girl out into the woods someplace on a cold and snowy night. They began necking and the car began steaming up. Belinsky rolled the window down a little for some air. Then he went ahead with his possible mission.

"I finally got the broadie's clothes off and I'm balling her. The car engine was on and the heater was working okay, so I knew I would survive. I'm going at it pretty good when a big blast of wind somes along and blows some snow into the car and right on to my crotch. I nearly died when that snow hit my bare body. I vowed then and there I would get rich and never have to do that again in the snow.

I didn't like making it in the car and I didn't like making it in the snow. There had to be a better way to live. I found out there was."

Belinsky left Philadelphia and flew out to San Diego by way of Los Angeles. This time there were no welcoming parades for him when he got into town. In fact he couldn't even get anybody to pick him up at the airport.

"You know you are going downhill," Bo says, "when you have to pay a cabdriver to take you to your pad. You also know you are going downhill when you enjoy telling him your troubles."

Belinsky spent three days in Los Angeles and drove down to San Diego to join the Phillies Triple-A farm club. He had one goal in mind: to pitch well enough to get another chance with another club.

"I still thought I could pitch," he said. "I was fooling myself because I didn't want to face up to any alternatives. I was twenty-nine, had no dough, a bad arm, and no future. It looked pretty sour for a while. But I figured I could get myself together in a place like San Diego. There would be no pressure and maybe I would do well enough to get another job with another club."

For the first time since he was in Hawaii in 1963, Belinsky was back in the minor leagues. He didn't mind it one bit. He was making a major league salary, he was living in a beachside motel, he was an instant celebrity with the newsmen in town, and soon he was getting all the attention in the Pacific Coast League that any Indian potentate or head of state would earn.

"If I had to live my life over," Belinsky says, "I wouldn't mind pitching in the minor leagues for twenty years. There are a hell of a lot worse ways to make a living. There are some swinging towns in this country and you can pretty much call your own shot down there. There's no pressure in the minor leagues, not much competition, and nobody is trying to use you to get ahead with somebody or something."

The warm California sun did wonders for Belinsky's arm. He suddenly felt strong again and was able to go nine innings several times. He was only 2–4 at San Diego with a 4.83 earned run average, but he had gotten back his strikeout pitch. He had struck out fifty-four batters in fifty-four innings, a successful season under the Rickey ratio of strikeouts compared to innings pitched. Late in

September he left the San Diego club for the season. He believed there was still life left in the old left arm.

Belinsky spent a few days in Los Angeles when the season ended and then took off for Hawaii. He sunned and surfed like a man without a care in the world. He rested his arm and rested his tired body. He forgot about baseball and lived off his charm.

On November 28, 1966, nine days before his thirtieth birthday, his name came up again at baseball's winter meetings.

Spec Richardson, the vice-president of the Houston club, stood up at the annual convention of baseball people, pulled a sheet of paper from his pocket and announced, "The Houston club drafts pitcher Bo Belinsky from the San Diego roster."

Belinsky was on his way to Texas.

The Houston Astros (formed as the Houston Colt .45s in 1962), along with the New York Mets, had been one of baseball's worst teams in some of baseball's most plush surroundings. Judge Roy C. Hofheinz, who had once been the mayor of Houston, owned the club. Despite all sorts of local political opposition, he had produced a building he gleefully described as the "ninth wonder of the world." Hofheinz had built baseball's first covered, air-conditioned, domed stadium, a magnificent structure eight stories high, deep into Texas oil country. He had done it all for a modest cost of some $40 million. Shea Stadium in New York had cost nearly thirty million as an old-fashioned, uncovered, open-air ball park. A half dozen years later, New Orleans contemplated a domed stadium in that city and early estimates said it would cost the builders some $200 million.

Hofheinz's Astrodome was opulent with skybox seats, an animated scoreboard with electric lights and fireworks, cushioned chairs, an elegant stadium club and restaurant, a full apartment for Hofheinz overlooking his production and Astroturf, a green carpet of "grass" developed by the Monsanto Company. Hofheinz added miniskirted usherettes, some of the best snack counters in any ball park, and accessible rest rooms and water fountains.

He had everything in the Astrodome but a good team.

The Astros had selected younger players in the first expansion draft as the Mets had selected older players. The Mets felt they needed established names to compete with the Yankees, while the Astros would be content with an improving young team and a chance to display their wares against the best teams in the National League. For four straight seasons the Mets had finished last under Casey Stengel with their used-up old men. Houston had finished eighth in their first season, then ninth three years in a row. In 1966 they had finished eighth under new manager Grady Hatton and seemed on their way to respectability as a competitive team in 1967, their sixth year in the National League. They had some fine young players, including a right-handed pitcher headed for stardom named Larry Dierker and the strongest little man in baseball, Jimmy Wynn, a home-run-hitting 165-pounder.

Hatton felt that one of the major weaknesses of the team was in left-handed pitching. He urged the club to trade or draft a left-handed pitcher. He thought the answer to his prayers came when Richardson stood up and announced, "The Houston club drafts pitcher Bo Belinsky."

The *Houston Post* and the *Houston Chronicle* loved the deal. Each of the papers assigned a man to track Belinsky down and interview him on his promotion from San Diego to Houston. Bo was supposed to be thrilled to be back in the big leagues. The first thing Bo did was hold out.

"They wanted to cut my salary," said Bo, "just because I had been sent out to San Diego. I finally convinced Spec Richardson I had to have more money. He gave me a two thousand dollar advance on my 1967 salary and we settled on eighteen thousand dollars. The money didn't mean anything to me. I was just interested in seeing what the Texas cowgirls were like."

Across America, when his new teammates on the Houston club read about the acquisition of Bo Belinsky, they were filled with curiosity. Belinsky was as much an element of interest for the players as he was for the press. He had done very little of note with his baseball career, except for a no-hitter now five years behind him, but he still received more press coverage than almost any other player in baseball, save for Mickey Mantle and his sore legs, Willie Mays, Hank Aaron, and the recently retired Sandy Koufax. Koufax had decided to quite after pitching against Baltimore in the 1966

World Series, swept four games to none by the Orioles and their splendid young pitching staff. Koufax had been bothered for several years by a sore elbow, diagnosed as arthritic, and to save his arm, he ended his career.

"There are a lot more things in life I want to do," said Koufax. "I don't want to do them as a sore-armed person."

"I knew I'd make him quit," said Belinsky. "Los Angeles just wasn't big enough for both of us."

Mickey Herskowitz, a fine Houston sportswriter, tracked Belinsky down in Honolulu and did an excellent reporting job on Bo's career. As always, Mamie was a significant part of that story. Ever since the first day Bo and Mamie's names were linked, reporters asked about her. Sometimes players did, too.

"I remember when we heard she was coming to the Phillies camp in 1965," said Johnny Callison, a teammate of Belinsky's then. "We were curious. Hell, you had to be. It isn't every day that you get a chance to see a glamorous movie actress in a baseball camp. I was real disappointed. I never saw her."

Callison, recalling Bo's Philadelphia career some years later, said the players on the Phillies were quite curious about Belinsky when he reported to them in Clearwater.

"You hear a lot about a guy," said Callison, "and you want to meet him and make up your own mind. I think Bo was a good guy to have on the club. I know he didn't get along all that well with Gene but most of the players liked him. He went his own way a lot but he was fun to be around. I'll say one thing for Bo. He had this big reputation with the broads, Hollywood, and all. But I really don't ever remember seeing him with any broads. I think he did his moving in private. I never saw him try and hustle any girl around the hotel or anyplace else. He did get a lot of phone calls and was always getting paged in the lobby. He had been around baseball a long time. I guess he had a lot of friends. There's nothing wrong with that. And when he pitched, he concentrated on the game. Bo was a good pitcher, a good competitor."

After Herkowitz tracked Belinsky down in Hawaii, the club was able to reach him. Richardson agreed to the advance, Belinsky was wired money and sent an airplane ticket and told to report to Cocoa

Beach, Florida, for the opening of spring training. He was allowed to cash in the airplane ticket and drive his Cadillac from Los Angeles to Cocoa Beach. Like all Belinsky trips, it would be eventful.

"Things went pretty smoothly until I got to Texas," Bo said. "I was just driving along casually enjoying the countryside, listening to the radio, looking out at the cactus, and figuring what a place like Cocoa Beach would be like. I guess I forgot to look at the speedometer."

The speedometer raced up to 90 miles and hour, then to 100, then to the end of the scale at 110 miles and hour. Then came the music that generally accompanies a 110-mile-an-hour automobile ride—the mad, whirling sound of a police siren. Bo scanned his rear mirror, saw the police car, considered a chase for a fleeting instant just for fun and then decided against it. He pulled over.

The police car stopped in front of Belinsky's car. The officer, looking like the good guy in all the cowboy movies, with a huge cowboy hat, polished boots, starched shirt, a huge, glistening badge, and a shiny six-gun, walked slowly to Bo's car.

"All right, Buddy, let me see your license."

"I'm sorry, officer, I was just getting a little to carried away because——"

"Just your license."

"I'm on my way——"

"Just your license."

Belinsky pulled out his California driving license. The police officer studied it carefully.

"Belinsky. Robert Belinsky. Your name is familiar."

"Bo Belinsky. I'm a baseball player."

"Bo Belinsky, sure. You're the guy who has been making it with Mamie. I know you. I read about you in the papers. Hey, I read this story about you in *Confidential.* It was about you and this Chinese broad and how she chased you all over the country and then you dropped her like a hot potato. Yeah, that was a funny goddamn story, how you like to screw and smoke at the same time, yeah, that was it."

"Yeah, that's me."

Zenida, Belinsky's old Oriental cupcake, had sold her life with Bo
to *Confidential* and now Belinsky was reaping the first dividend.

"Hey, look, you're going to be with the Astros, right?"

"Right, that's where I'm headed right now."

Belinsky got off with a warning and a few stories about Mamie. He
stayed under a hundred miles an hour as he roared through Louisiana, Mississippi, Alabama, and on into northern Florida. He was
running out of money so he decided to drive hard and make it to
Cocoa Beach that night so he could get some money from the club
and get something to eat.

"I guess I was just thirty, forty miles from Cocoa Beach, when I
saw this old jalopy on the side of the road. A old black guy was
standing next to the car waving a handkerchief. It was pretty dark
and the roads were pretty deserted. I figured he ran out of gas and
I could give him a ride to the nearest station. Then the station could
give him some gas, drive him back to the car, and everybody could
live happily ever after."

Belinsky pulled his car to a screeching halt, backed up and spoke
to the old man from his car.

"What seems to be the trouble, pop?"

"Our car broke down."

"I'll drive you on to a service station if you like. Hop on in."

"Oh, God bless you, my son, God bless you. Let's go, everybody."

They came at Belinsky in waves, small children, large children,
girls, boys, mother, grandmother, grandfather, every size and
shape, coming at him from every door, piling into the back and the
front and squeezing next to him. Then the father clapped his hands
and all of them, eleven people in all, began singing, "Give Me That
Oldtime Religion."

"They were very religious people," said Bo, "and they had just
come back from some revival meeting in Virginia and they had been
in the car together for a couple of days and now they were all laying
all over me. And they stunk like hell. I almost passed out. They
started singing as loud as they could and I couldn't hear myself
think. It was one wild scene. I just kept driving as fast as I could.
I kept hoping I would see a gas station."

The singing and the handclapping and the praying (Belinsky was moving at a hundred miles an hour now) went on for some five miles. Finally, Belinsky spotted a small service station.

"When I turned out of that garage," said Bo, "I could hear them singing for a long time and I could also hear a lot of them saying, 'God bless you, God bless you.' They were good people and I was sorry to leave them. I just wish they hadn't stunk so much."

Belinsky drove on to Cocoa Beach. He owned a new Cadillac now and his former manager at Los Angeles, Bill Rigney, remembers when he got it.

"Bo had that candy apple Cadillac the first couple of years he was out there and everybody knew the car. Bud Furillo had written about it enough. Bo had been stopped by the cops a dozen times and the fans all sat on his car outside the ball park. So one day Belinsky decided he had to have a new car. He was a marked man in the candy apple Cadillac. He comes into the clubhouse one day, all smiles, like a kid with a new toy. 'Skip,' he said, 'I decided to get a new car. I think my candy apple Cadiallac is too pretentious.' Bo always liked to use those big words and sound very educated. Of course, most of the time he misused them and sounded ridiculous.

"Well, anyway, I was happy that the kid had decided to get a new car. That other thing was really too big and it was too pretentious and everybody could spot him and it really would be easier for him if he drove a car that every fan and every cop on the highway didn't recognize. So I was happy when he told me he had traded in his candy apple Cadillac and had bought something else. 'What did you buy, Bo?' I figured he would tell me a small Chevy or a small Ford or something like that. 'Skip, I got the most beautiful new car you ever saw, a gold, Eldorado Cadillac. It's a gas, really.' I almost cracked up. Here, he's getting a new car so that nobody can spot him and he changes from a candy apple Cadillac to a gold Cadillac. I'm telling you there was only one Bo Belinsky."

That one Bo Belinsky drove his gold Cadillac through the orange groves and the grapefruit country, through the warm winds of Florida toward Cocoa Beach. The Astros were quartered in an army-style barracks complex that just wouldn't be big enough for Bo. For now, he was tired from the trip, dusty, worn out from his driving adventures and broke. It was enough for him to settle peacefully into the barracks.

"Tomorrow," he said, "I've got to go someplace else in the light of day."

Bo was on the threshold of a new dimension in his life as he joined the Houston Astros in their training camp at Cocoa Beach, Florida.

He was about to fall in love twice in the same year.

First it would be with a cute little dog named Alfie.

Then it would be with a gorgeous stack of womanhood named Jo.

As long as Bo pitches good, Alfie can stay in his own locker.

—GRADY HATTON

What's It All About, Alfie?

Grady Hatton was one of Bo Belinsky's good-guy managers. Hatton had been a fine left-handed hitting third baseman for Cincinnati for nine seasons before moving on to the Chicago White Sox, Boston Red Sox, Baltimore Orioles, St. Louis Cardinals, San Francisco Giants, and Chicago Cubs. He had become a coach for the Cubs after managing in the minor leagues at San Antonio, then became the director of player personnel for the new Houston team in 1961, went to Oklahoma City to manage their Triple-A club in 1963, and was named manager of the Astros in 1966. A native of Beaumont, Texas, Hatton had been a big favorite of Houston fans when he got the job. The team had moved to eighth place in his first season and now, in the spring of 1967, he seemed determined to make a pennant contender out of the improving Astros.

Hatton had enjoyed his major league career as a player and he saw no reason why any other player shouldn't have fun during his time in the big leagues. He expected discipline from his players, but he wasn't suspicious of their absences like Rigney or a tyrant like Mauch. Hatton had a mature approach to managing.

"I think the only thing that really matters, he said, "is how they perform on the field."

That was music to Belinsky's ears. Bo had always thought there was absolutely no relationship between his performance on the field and his performance off.

"We have certain rules," said Hatton. "For example I have a midnight curfew. All our players have to adhere to it. One time Belinsky asked if he could stay out in town until one thirty A.M. He said he had some important business to take care of. He asked for permission and I gave it to him."

Early in spring training Hatton was asked if he treated Bo any differently from any of his other players or if he had a fatherly talk with Bo about the last chance as a pitcher.

"Hell, no," said Hatton. "I treat every player alike, I treat them like men. I told him he could do whatever he wanted to do off the field as long as he followed our rules. He had to make curfew and he had to be ready to pitch when it was his turn. He seems like a hard worker when he gets on the field. He knows what he has to do to make the ball club."

Belinsky was, of course, a celebrity, as always, in the Astros camp. Writers crowded around his locker almost daily to catch the latest witticisms and philosophizings from Chairman Bo. *New York Post* columnist Milton Gross, the father of the psychological in-depth probing of athletes in American journalism, addressed himself to Belinsky's psyche one day at Cocoa Beach.

"Do you think you have wasted your pitching potential?" Gross asked.

"I've done a lot of crazy things in my life," said Bo. "But I'm a single man and my responsibility is to myself. I probably will never get married because I wouldn't make a good husband anyway. Baseball hasn't been my whole life. I don't even like to put on a uniform."

Bob Rodgers, Bo's catcher with the Angels, said that he never saw a ballplayer get into uniform as carelessly as Bo.

"Belinsky would consider himself ready when he put on a shirt, trousers, belt, pants, socks, and shoes. No undershirt, no cup, no jockstrap, no underwear, no sanitary socks. Once I asked him about it. 'Buck,' he says, 'clothes bind me.' "

Gross probed deeper into Belinsky's psyche when he asked him a leading question on March 15, 1967.

"What would you consider a good year?"

"Just to last the entire season," Bo said, "would be slightly sensational."

It was a typical Belinsky response. He never reached for the stars because there were too many disappointments if one were to reach and fail. Belinsky was the reincarnation of Billy Loes, a pitcher with the Brooklyn Dodgers in the early 1950s. The skinny right-hander for the Dodgers had exceptional ability and baseball scouts were always dismayed that he didn't win more than the thirteen or fourteen games he was accustomed to each season. One day a sportswriter asked him why he didn't win twenty games.

"Oh, hell," said Loes, "if you win twenty games they want you to do it every year."

"To win," Bill Rigney once said of Belinsky, "you have to pay the price. Bo just won't."

Satisfied that his goal of survival was well within his reach, Belinsky worked hard in the Astros camp. He did his running and his throwing on schedule. He got his legs, his arms, and his body in shape. He was ready to pitch when the exhibition games began. What's more, his conduct was beyond reproach.

Nelson Fox, a fine hitter for many years, was a coach with the Astros that spring. One of his main duties was to make the bed check each midnight to see if the players were in their barracks beds.

"The barracks were closed at midnight," said Fox. "If a guy came in a minute past midnight he had to ring a night bell to get in the building. Then he had to walk in through the front office, past all the club officials and sign his name and the time in a book. Nobody wanted to go through that. Each bed had a number and a few minutes past midnight I would make the rounds with a flashlight, check the numer on the bed and check the body in the bed. If it wasn't the right body I'd know that in a second. Not once that whole spring training did Belinsky miss bed check."

Belinsky had pitched creditably his first two times on the mound. Hatton was pleased with his performance. His teammates were pleased. The fawning press, thrilled to have such a live body with such a dull team, was pleased. The general manager and the owner,

certain that Belinsky's fame would sell some tickets in the Astrodome, were pleased. Even Alfie was pleased.

"Ahh, Alfie," says Bo, with fond memories. "I did love him so."

The Astros had defeated the Braves in an exhibition game one
afternoon. After dinner that night, Belinsky went for a walk around
the grounds. His mind was filled with thoughts of the past, of the
night life in L.A., the sun on the California beach, the tight dresses
Mamie wore, and dozens of other pleasant things. Then he heard
a yapping at his feet as he approached the barracks door. It was love
at first sight.

A small dog was barking at Bo's feet. The animal bounced back
and forth as Bo walked, barked a little, and then leaned against him
as he walked to the door.

"I bent down to play with him a little and the thing was so excited
he almost pissed on my hand. I knew then he was emotional about
me. He was my kind of dog," said Bo.

Belinsky opened the door of the barracks and the dog followed
him in. Belinsky went to the kitchen of the compound, got a dish,
filled it with some hamburger meat and made a friend for life.

Alfie and Bo became a Texas entry.

The dog was a black and grey cocker spaniel and poodle, about
a year old, very lively and bouncy, with a sad little face and scrawny
legs.

"I couldn't let a thing like that make it in the world," said Bo, "all
by himself. I had to adopt him. I decided I would keep him and then
I had to come up with a name for him."

The hottest movie of the time was *Alfie*, a British picture starring
Michael Caine, who loved and seduced his woman with much poise
and charm. Caine was the archetype antihero, not magnificently
dressed, no fantastic cars, a dour look and a small unpretentious
apartment. His loving seemed almost accidental, rather than absolutely essential as it was to Bo.

"I called him Alfie," said Bo, "but in formal company, when Judge
Hofheinz was around, or somebody important, I referred to him by
his Christian name, Alfred."

Alfie was outfitted with an Astros T-shirt, size one around his
middle. He was presented with an orange ball to work out with. He

was set up in the clubhouse with a locker, given a gray water bucket and a red bowl for food. He was immediately accepted as part of the team.

Grady Hatton, a dog fancier, allowed Alfie all the privileges of any member of the team.

"Remember, Bo," he said, "Alfie has to be in by midnight, same as anybody else."

The Astros didn't have many stars that spring so Belinsky and Alfie dominated the Houston papers.

Most newspaper men knew that two stories always sell, a good juicy, sex-murder-rape story and a dog story. Since sex-murder-rape stories were hard to come by in Cocoa Beach that spring, Mickey Herskowitz, John Wilson, Dick Peebles, and the rest of the Houston writers played the hell out of Alfie.

"One day I'm sitting there in the clubhouse reading the papers about Alfie's latest exploits and somebody tells me there is an important phone call for Alfie and could I take it for him. I go to the phone and it's some guy who tells me he is from the Alpo Company and he wants to see that Alfie is well fed. He has been reading a lot about Alfie and he thinks now that Alfie is famous he should be eating good. So he tells me that he will send me a case of Alpo to start Alfie off right, and then for every inning I pitch in Florida and during the season and shut out the other side Alfie will get a case of Alpo. I thought it was a joke but I said okay and all of a sudden those trucks started backing up with the Alpo."

By now, Alfie and Bo were getting more attention in the Houston press than Jimmy Wynn, Larry Dierker, Grady Hatton, and the rest of the Houston assemblage combined. The green monster of jealousy began rearing its ugly head. Some player drafted a petition for Alfie's removal from the premises and attempted to gain signatures. Only a few of the players signed. Most of them liked Alfie. Most of the players also liked Bo. Few players wanted to be labeled as antidog. It just isn't good for a player's image to be against dogs, mom, or apple pie. Hatton heard about the petition.

"As song as I am the manager," Hatton announced, "Alfie can stay."

"That really made Alfie a big dog," said Bo. "It isn't often a manager sticks up for a dog like that, especially a dog that hasn't even shown if he can hit or not."

Late in March the Alfie case had its first crisis. The Astros were preparing to break camp and head home to Houston for the season. What about Bo? What about Alfie?

On March 29 Hatton cut the squad. Bo made it. On March 30 Alfie made it.

"He's pretty popular in Houston now," said Bill Giles, the bright and creative publicity director of the Astros. "Alfie has been selling a lot of tickets for us. When we go home, he goes with us."

The Astros were to fly home. Belinsky wasn't sure how Alfie would take to the plane. He asked Jimmy Lake, the clubhouse man of the Astros, to drive Alfie home in his truck with the luggage and the baseball equipment.

"Alfie's made the club," Hatton announced one day. "He's in real good shape. He's up to five laps now. Sometimes he gets a little weary but we all do. At least he has sense enough to collapse in front of his own locker."

The Astros were opening their home exhibition schedule on a Friday night in the Houston Astrodome against the Yankees. It would be the debut in Texas for Alfie and Bo.

Just a short while before the club was to play its final Florida game before the Houston exhibition, Jimmy Lake answered a knock at the clubhouse door. A man stood at the door, announced his name, and said, "You people have my dog. His name isn't Alfie, it's Brownie."

Jimmy Lake brought the man over to Belinsky for a confrontation.

"That's my dog," he said, pointing to Alfie as he snoozed in his Atros T-shirt after a hard workout.

"How can you say that's your dog, man? He hasn't even moved."

"That's because he isn't used to seeing me without my kids. He really is my kids' dog, you know."

"How can you prove it's your dog?"

"He's got a spot right on the inside of his neck, a brown spot."

"Come on over here, Alfie, let me examine you."

The dog leaped up on Belinsky's lap, growled a bit as he spotted the other man, and allowed Belinsky to check his neck.

"Well, you're right. Doggone it, you must be Alfie's master. What will you take for him?"

"I don't want to sell him. I just want my dog back."

"Gee, mister, we've had him here a month and he really has become part of the team. Are you an Astros fan?"

"Yes, I am, but I still don't want to sell the dog."

"Look, he's only a mongrel, you can get another one in five minutes. We just sort of got fond of him and if we don't get him back to Houston we have no chance to win the pennant."

"Well, I don't know . . . I might be interested."

"I'll give you twenty-five bucks."

"I don't know. I think he's worth a lot more than that."

". . . and an autographed ball."

"I don't know if I want to sell him."

". . . and a team picture."

"Well, maybe."

"I'll make it thirty bucks and that's the best I can do."

"How about two balls instead of one?"

The deal was finalized. Belinsky paid thirty bucks for Alfie, two autographed Houston baseballs, a set of autographed pictures of every Houston player, and a team picture of the club. The man signed a slip of paper saying Alfie (né Brownie) now belonged to Bo Belinsky.

Alfie and Bo were on their way to the bigs.

Alfie left by truck with Jimmy Lake and Bo left by plane with the rest of the Astros for a three-game weekend series against the New York Yankees at the Astrodome.

Belinsky was assigned a locker in the Houston clubhouse just off the manager's office. Alfie got the next locker, a full-sized stall with an orange shelf, metal rack for clothing and a bar stool for dressing. Alfie's extra Astros T-shirt, size one, was hung from his rack and his bucket, bowl, and ball were all piled neatly into his locker.

Hatton announced that Alfie could have his own locker as long as Belinsky pitched winning baseball. Alfie also had a large part of the Astros storage closet, just off the clubhouse door. Baseball equipment and cans of Alpo filled the small room.

"It was really a beautiful scene for Alfie," said Bo. "No dog ever had lived in a lap of luxury like Alfie."

On a Friday night, in air-conditioned splendor, with more than forty thousand people in the stands at the Astrodome, Alfie and Bo

were ready to make their Houston debut against the Yankees. Bo
was dressed in his uniform and Alfie was in his.

"Good evening, ladies and gentlemen," intoned the public address announcer, "and welcome to the Astrodome."

He then introduced the Yankees as they gathered on the foul line
in order. The introduction of Mickey Mantle, who lived in Dallas,
drew a huge hand. The rest of the Yankees were introduced in turn
and now stood quietly as the hometown favorite Astros were introduced to the crowd. There was a moderate amount of cheers for all
of the local players and a large, warm welcome as Belinsky was
introduced. Trailing behind him, head held high, trotting slowly
behind his master, came Alfie. The applause was almost deafening.
Lassie had never been greeted more warmly even after his best
performance.

". . . and now ladies and gentlemen, our national anthem."

Fifty men and a dog stood at attention as the band played the
national anthem.

The Astros took their places on the field and Alfie raced over to
inspect the Yankee bench. He stood in front of their dugout. He
examined the Yankee players. He ran up and down in front of the
bench. Then he stopped. Then he crapped on the Astroturf.

"I think he was a little nervous seeing all those great Yankee
stars," Belinsky said. "He just couldn't control himself with all that
excitement."

Alfie would spend the early afternoon before a game fooling with
the early arrivals, Nelson Fox, Jim Busby, Grady Hatton, and a few
players. But he'd drop everyone and everything when Bo showed
up.

"Fox wrestles with him," Jimmy Lake said, "Busby gives him gum,
Grady plays with him, but Bo gives him lots of loving."

"I've always had a thing about dogs," Bo said. "They are better
than broads. They can give you a lot of love without ever giving you
any bullshit. And no dog ever asked me to marry her."

Belinsky also says a trained dog can also be a woman's best friend.

"Some broads just like to do it all," said Bo. "I knew this one
broad who actually trained a big dog to go down on her. It was
unbelievable. That dog would leap on her, start licking at the

snatch, and that woman would go out of her mind. One time we had a wild party and now she decides to let the dog go into his act. She takes off all her clothes and the dog leaps up on her and does it all. It was fantastic. Then I went over to the broad to give her a little peck on the cheek just to show her I appreciated the entertainment. That goddamn dog almost bit my fucking head off. He was one jealous son of a bitch, I'll tell you."

Alfie wasn't quite that talented. He was jovial and entertaining, but he confined his activities to generally accepted dog behavior. By mid-June, Alfie was doing better than Bo. Belinsky had been in only seven games for the Astros and had pitched only seventeen innings. Then came his big chance. He was going to make his first start of the season.

Belinsky was rooming on the road with Ron Brand, a small, stocky, young catcher. Brand was a nondrinking, nonsmoking Mormon whose most foul word was "shoot." In spring training Brand and Belinsky had adjacent lockers. The high-living Belinsky and the quite-living Brand were naturally paired together by the Astros.

"Everybody thought it was funny that we would get together," said Brand, "but Bo was really a good roommate, very considerate and very understanding. He paid his share and more. He was first class in everything he did."

Cutdown date was nearing and Brand and Belinsky were both sweating it out. Grady Hatton called them into his office together one night and announced, "Bo is starting tomorrow and, Ron, you will catch him."

They went to their room after the game and thought about the following night.

"This is a big game for us," said Brand.

"Yeah, if we both do lousy we could be in Oklahoma City by morning."

"Have you ever been there?"

"Yeah," said Bo, "it's not bad if you take along enough Alka-Seltzer."

"I'd hate to wind up there."

"Don't worry, kid. I just might pitch another no-hitter and make us both look great."

It was nearly four o'clock in the morning before Brand and Belinsky finally dozed off. Belinsky awoke refreshed at one o'clock that afternoon.

Brand and Belinsky ordered room service.

"I'll have a bowl of cereal with cream, a glass of milk, and two doughnuts," said Brand.

"And I'll have chopped, chipped beef on toast," said Belinsky, "and a pot of coffee."

Brand remembers Belinsky's dining style.

"Most of the time he would eat in those greasy spoons—two or three hamburgers, a cup of coffee and that was it. But when he went into the fine restaurants, he could really put it on."

The game was played and Belinsky was splendid. He pitched seven strong innings, left with a 3–2 lead and watched his Astro mates tear up the Phillies for twelve runs in the next two innings for a 15–3 win. It was Bo's first victory of the year.

"In New York," he said, "we celebrate."

The Astros bused up to New York from Philadelphia and settled into the Roosevelt Hotel on New York's East Side. The phone began ringing almost immediately. Brand always answered.

"Some of the girls claimed they knew Bo," said Brand, "but most of them didn't. They were just offering themselves to him because they had heard of him. He turned most of them down."

The Mets and the Astros were rained out on Friday night. Bo had a date before the umpires had waved their arms that the game was off. Brand settled for a midtown Manhattan movie house.

"Tomorrow," Belinsky said, as he took off on his date, "we dine out."

The Astros beat the Mets in a day game at Shea Stadium before 28,000 people. The Astros almost always beat the Mets in Shea Stadium. The Astros almost always beat the Mets in the Astrodome. The Astros almost always beat the Mets in the old Polo Grounds. The Astros almost always beat the Mets in the old Colts Stadium. The Mets, at least, had an excuse in Colts Stadium. They were chewed up by bugs that collected in the ball park from the water in the holes being dug across the way as ground was being broken for Judge Hofheinz's magnificent dome. Bugs, bugs, bugs, everywhere, upsetting the Mets. Of course, they never bit a Houston player.

"This is the only town," Mets outfielder Richie Ashburn once said, "where women wear insect repellant instead of perfume."

On this Saturday night Belinsky was feeling and smelling beautiful.

"He always cared about his appearance," Ron Brand said. "He would never leave the room until he looked just right. He could be wearing a fancy suit or a pair of dungarees but it had to look right. Bo had style. He knew how to carry himself, be it a hamburger joint or Voisin."

There are a half dozen restaurants in this country of such elegance and magnificence that the very sound of their names conjured up pictures of enormous wealth and style. Most of them were either in New York, San Francisco, or Los Angeles. Belinsky was on a first-name basis with headwaiters in all of them, La Scala and Chasen's in Los Angeles, the Blue Fox and Ernie's in San Francisco, 21 and Voisin in New York.

"I don't think I had ever heard of the place," Brand said, "before Bo took me to Voisin. I really didn't go much for fancy restaurants. I ate most of my meals in the hotel. In some towns I'd walk down the street for a malted milk or something. This one night Bo said we were going out in style, so I put on my best suit, shined my shoes, and prepared for the evening."

"You look great, kid," said Bo. "You look like one of those millionaire Hollywood producers."

"You look pretty good yourself, Bo."

"All right, my man, let's move."

Belinsky and Brand went down in the hotel elevator, walked out to the front, and waited for a cab. Belinsky pressed a dollar in the doorman's hand as he opened the door of the cab.

"First class," said Brand. "Everything he did was first class."

They climbed into the back seat of the cab, Belinsky quickly read the name of the driver on the license and said, in cultured British tones, "Voisin, please, Mister Marshall."

Mister Marshall, surprised to be so addressed, turned quickly toward Bo and said, "Did you say Voisin, buddy?"

"Yes, my good man, I trust you know where the establishment is."

"Yeah, I been there before."

The cabdriver shook his head and drove off. He wasn't sure about the gentleman in the back seat.

Belinsky paid the driver, tipped him a buck, and waited for the doorman at Voisin to open the door.

"Good evening, Mr. Belinsky," he said.

Brand just followed Belinsky into the restaurant, his eyes opened wide to such munificence.

"Ahh, Mr. Belinsky," said the maître d', "a table for two, sir, right this way."

A small corner table, dimly lit, a gentle candle as a centerpiece, and a glistening glass at each setting, awaited Belinsky's arrival.

"I trust you are having a good season, Mr. Belinsky."

"Splendid," Bo said, "I owe it all to Mr. Brand, here, my marvelous young catcher."

"Good evening, Mister Brand," said the head waiter.

"Good evening."

The waiter placed their napkins in their laps gently and offered Belinsky and Brand huge menus.

"And the wine list," Bo said.

"Yes, sir."

"I wonder how the chopped chipped beef is in a place like this," Brand whispered.

Belinsky was in familiar territory. He had dined with Mamie in Voisin, with Winchell and with several other show business friends in the salad days of 1962 to 1963. He had stopped by at least once every season since just to keep his hand in the franchise.

"You must keep contact with your associates in places like that," Bo said. "It's unreal how often they change headwaiters."

Belinsky ordered escargots while Brand settled for a shrimp cocktail as an appetizer. They decided to share a Caesar salad. Now it was time for the wine.

Belinsky made his selection, a twenty-dollar bottle of fine French wine.

"I know you won't believe this," Brand said to the wine steward, "but I'd like some water."

The wine steward's eyes almost popped out of his head.

"Water, monsieur?"

"Yes, plain water, please."

"I'm glad," Belinsky said, "you didn't order a malted milk. He would have really blown his mind."

"I don't think he had ever poured water before," said Brand. "Some of it spilled over the side of the glass."

Belinsky ended the meal in style by ordering a huge chocolate souffle for desert. Brand ate more than his share of that and Belinsky leaned back in his chair to finish a cigarette.

"There was an incredible look of contentment on his face," Brand said. "I think he really enjoyed the idea of eating in places like that more than he really enjoyed the food. It was all part of living up to his own self-image."

Now for the *pièce de résistance.* The check came to sixty-seven dollars. Belinsky pulled four twenty-dollar bills out of his pocket, dropped them on a silver plate, nodded to the waiter and waved him off. He dropped five dollars into the hand of the maître d' and another buck into the doorman's hand.

"I always was a guy who lived like I made a hundred thousand dollars a year," Belinsky says, "when I was struggling along on fifteen."

Belinsky and Brand got into a cab. Belinsky ordered the driver to take them downtown to Greenwich Village. They walked the streets for a while, checking the local gentry, before Belinsky announced, let's go into this joint for a nightcap."

They marched into a small Village bar filled with pimps, whores, homosexuals, lesbians, thieves, and straights. Belinsky was just as comfortable as he had been in Voisin.

"Gin and tonic," he said.

"A Coke," said Brand.

The evening ended with a cab ride back uptown to the Roosevelt Hotel. The two players walked through the hotel lobby as the huge clock on the wall read eleven fifty-five. It had been a full and rich evening for Bo Belinsky and Ron Brand.

"I think of those days with Bo," Brand said several years later, "and I can only think how insecure he was, how much he did for show, how much he had to live up to what people expected of him. He would always say, 'I never did half of what guys write about me, but it doesn't hurt so I let it go on.' In a way, it was sad, very sad."

Brand said Belinsky was a unique man, someone who will never come along again in his lifetime.

"The more I got to know him," he said, "the more I liked him. Bo is good people. But he's different. I remember one game we were playing against the Cardinals. Bo says to me before the game that he thinks he can win if he pitches around Cepeda. He hit him three times in the game. That was his idea of pitching around somebody."

It was, in a way, a beautiful marriage of interesting souls, that Bo Belinsky-Ron Brand team, that partnership of Errol Flynn and Huckleberry Finn. It was a strange and wonderful marriage.

It was nothing compared to the marriage Bo Belinsky was about to undertake.

A playboy? This guy was a pussycat.

—*JO COLLINS*

Love, Belinsky Style: Jo and Bo

Alfie was living with Jimmy Lake in Houston during the early winter of 1968 and Bo was living on the beach at Waikiki. He had thought about playing winter ball in Venezuela again, had thought about playing in the Dominican, had thought about playing in Puerto Rico. While he thought about all this, he surfed and sunned himself in Hawaii, took up skindiving, worked hard on getting his skin to a luxurious deep tan, and wondered if the three games he won for Houston in 1967 would allow him to ask for a huge raise. Belinsky was commuting between the small islands across from Waikiki and the small beach cottages along the surf. On December 7, 1967, Belinsky celebrated his thirty-second birthday. A friend, J. J. Morgan, threw a magnificent party for him. It was the most strenuous day of work Bo was to spend all winter.

By the middle of January, he had decided to give the Astros one more chance to appreciate him. He would return to Cocoa Beach in late February and maybe this time around, Grady Hatton would know enough to start him every four days and make him a big winner again.

"I'll think about that tomorrow," Belinsky told J. J. "Tonight I have a date with a beautiful girl."

Bo had a dinner date but decided to drop in on J. J. before driving down the coast for his date and dinner. One thing led to another and a few strange girls showed up at J. J.'s place and Belinsky forgot all about his date. The evening became morning and Belinsky bedded down at six o'clock. After a breakfast of coffee and two cigarettes at three o'clock, Belinsky got dressed for a walk on the beach. He put on his orange bathing suit with the huge, blue letters on the side, his orange beach jacket, his floppy orange hat, and his sandals. He strolled down the beach. He walked toward a cabana where several of his friends had gathered for an afternoon drink.

Fat, the beach boy in Hawaii, sat at a table with a lovely blonde girl named June. She had been Belinsky's supposed date the night before.

"Fat, how goes it, my man?"

"Bo, baby. You look rested."

"Never been better. June, sweetheart, I want to explain why I never made it out to your place last night. I started out to get you, stopped at J. J.'s for a drink——"

"Oh, Bo, don't give me any of your bullshit. The least you can do is call me so I don't have to sit around all goddamn night figuring you got killed in an accident on the highway."

"Never happen again, sweetheart. My word."

"Your word isn't worth a bottle of warm piss."

"Oh, honey, now you are being mean."

Fat turned from Belinsky and addressed a remark to a girl at the next table. She was a gorgeous, dark-eyed, dark-haired girl, with the cheeks and looks of Sophia Loren, a suntanned beauty among all these beasts of the beach. She wore a yellow bikini with a white T-shirt over the top of the outfit. The white T-shirt could do nothing to hide the magnificent structural accomplishment underneath it.

The girl's name was Jo Collins.

"Bo sat there ignoring me," says Jo. "There were two or three guys in the group trying to hustle me. You know how it is on the beach with a group of guys and girls. Some of them are always operating. Bo was cool, just sat there, talking to this other girl, looking off into the sun and the sand, peeking over every so often to see if I was watching him. I must admit he was incredibly handsome, that dark, tanned face, the handsome smile, the black hair, that strong, young, firm body of his. He was some sight."

"Hey, let's go over to the Queen's Surf," one of the boys suggested. "They have some sounds over there that are great."

"Yeah, that sounds great," said Fat. "I dig that place. C'mon, Bo, why don't you join us? It will be laughs."

"Thanks, Fat, I think I'm just going to cool it here awhile."

"C'mon, Jo, why don't you come along with us. It's really a groovy place."

"If you go, Fat, I'll go."

"Sure, I'm going."

"Well, maybe I might go along, too," said Bo.

"Oh, by the way, Bo, this is Jo Collins, from *Playboy*, she's down here on a promotion. Jo, this is Bo Belinsky, you know, the baseball player."

"I don't know anything about baseball," said Jo. "I'm a football fan."

"That's all right," said Bo. "I don't know much about baseball myself."

The group gathered at the Queen's Surf, a barefoot bar just down the road, for some music and dance. Belinsky stayed near Jo but didn't push. Other guys in the group worked hard at gaining her attention. A lot of them were coming on real strong. Jo felt crowded in. The afternoon wore on into evening and people began to split. Jo had to get back to her hotel for a date that night. Now she and Belinsky were almost alone at the bar for the last drink together of the day.

"There's something I've wanted to do ever since I met you," Belinsky said.

"What's that?"

"This," said Bo. Then he leaned over and kissed Jo lightly on the mouth.

Jo smiled and left the bar. She felt warm walking back to her hotel. She kept seeing that handsome face in her mind and thinking about those silly orange bathing shorts with the BB on them. She remembered now that she knew the name Bo Belinsky. She knew that was the ballplayer from Los Angeles, yes, the one who had gone out with Mamie Van Doren, the playboy of baseball.

"A playboy?" she thought. "This guy was a pussycat."

Jo couldn't keep her mind on her date's conversation that night. She kept thinking about that tall, thin, handsome face on the beach. She urged her date to take her back to her hotel quickly, complaining about a sudden headache, thinking about that boy Bo. It took a long time to fall asleep that night. She awoke late, ordered breakfast in the room and was surprised by a sudden knock on her door.

"Who is it?"

"The bellboy, ma'am. I have a delivery for you."

Jo opened the door and the bellboy stood in front of her.

"He was holding the largest, most beautiful bouquet of red roses I had ever seen," said Jo.

She accepted them, pulled out a card, and read the message quickly. "Would you have dinner with me tonight?" The card was signed, "Bo."

"We went out, had a very pleasant, very quiet, very romantic dinner that night," said Jo. "He was so kind, so considerate, so gentle and amusing. When he took me home I knew that I had fallen in love with Bo Belinsky."

The path to the sands and sun of Hawaii and the life and love of Bo Belinsky had been a long, winding, difficult, and exciting journey for Jo Collins.

It began in a place called Lebanon, Oregon, a small town some two hundred miles from Eugene, with a population of some three thousand people. On August 5, 1945, Janet Lorraine Lockhart was born to William and Lorraine Lockhart. Her father worked as a superintendent of warehousing.

"My parents never really got along," she says. "They were always fighting over money and a dozen other things. My mother is a very strong woman. She ruled the house. When I was a year old, my parents were divorced. I never really knew my father. My mother remarried a man named Laws and I grew up most of my early life known as Janet Laws. My mother has had three husbands. It sometimes gets very confusing."

By the time she was twelve years old, Janet Lorraine Lockhart, now known as Janet Laws, and later to be known as Jo Collins, had already been noticed often in Lebanon for her rapid maturity and impressive beauty. She was an average student in grade school and managed to pass her work at North Eugene High School. By the time she was fifteen, the football players and the town heroes were paying more and more attention to Janet. She had grown to marvelous womanhood, with dimensions later to be immortalized by *Playboy* magazine as a Playmate at 36–24–36. At sixteen she married a high school classmate named Bob Anderson, a marriage she refuses to discuss nowadays in any detail. They were soon separated.

Janet was winning all the local beauty contests. She was elected Christmas Queen at North Eugene High and she was elected May Day Queen of her hometown.

"In those days," she said, "all I could ever think about was cheerleading. I loved cheerleading. I wanted to be the world's greatest cheerleader. That's as far as my interest went. I wanted to go on to the University of Oregon to major in cheerleading. I wasn't that interested in school, but I knew I had to go on to the university if I wanted to continue my cheerleading practice."

Beautifully put together at five feet four and 118 pounds, Janet had one other major interest in the summer of 1964, after her graduation from high school, and that was, surprisingly, softball.

"I was actually quite athletic," she says, "and I played shortstop on the Lumber Jilles, a girls' softball team out of Roseburg, Oregon. We had a pretty good team and I was a pretty good player, if I say so myself."

It figured that when Bo Belinsky finally got married he would marry a shortstop.

Janet matriculated in the University of Oregon in the fall of 1964. She knew she was interested in cheerleading. She didn't know if she was interested in anything else.

"I knew I was a pretty girl, but I had no ambitions along a show business career or anything like that. I never really thought past my cheerleading days. I figured something would come along. I guess I figured I would wind up being a housewife in Oregon like my mother," she said.

After a short stay at the University of Oregon, Janet realized the academic halls weren't for her.

"I decided to strike out on my own," she said. "I had never been away from Oregon and I thought I would like to see California. I went down to Malibu with a couple of girl friends of mine, rented a place on the beach and settled in. I figured it would be nice to look at all those handsome blond surfers I had seen in all those beach movies. It was fun. One night I got invited to a party in Malibu. One of the other girls had heard that there were show business people expected at the party. It didn't mean anything to me. I never wanted anything like that. Somebody else said there would be agents at the party. I didn't even know what an agent was. They don't have any agents up in Oregon."

One of the guests at the party was Maxine Reeves, who was in charge of casting and hiring the models used on the television program "Queen For a Day," one of the longest, most successful shows on the air. It had run for years on radio and now was in its tenth season on television. Miss Reeves asked Janet if she had an agent and was interested in working in television.

"No, I don't have an agent. Can I get one? I might be interested in a job."

"I'll tell you what. You go get yourself a nice bathing suit and I'll make an appointment at the American Broadcasting Company studio on Prospect Avenue in Hollywood for you to be screen-tested."

Janet showed up the next day, put on a fetching bikini, carried a can of Johnson's spray wax across a stage and was hired by "Queen For a Day" for $450 a week for three days of work a week. She was nineteen years old.

"That was the end of my dreams about being a cheerleader or helping the world. I had decided just before my money ran out and I took that job that I would go back to college, major in sociology, and help the poor people in Harlem."

Harlem's loss was show business's gain.

A beautiful young thing, Janet was an instant hit on "Queen For a Day" as one of those girls who carries out the products, pushes the sewing machines across stages, demonstrates where the door handles of cars are, and keeps that happy smile pasted on all through the show.

"The program had been on the air on radio and television for about thirty years," she said, "and six months after I joined it the show was cancelled. I really don't think I had anything to do with it."

Janet was broke and out of work. She had lived up to every penny of that $450 a week for those six months. Assuming that show would run forever, she had extended herself financially.

"One thing I learned how to do in Hollywood," she says, "is spend money."

Behind in her bills and unhappy with unemployment after a taste of the good life, Janet decided to make a career out of show business. She studied in actor's school and earned small parts in several beach movies and in several television shows including "My Three Sons," "The Farmer's Daughter," the "Phyllis Diller Show," and other shows. There always seems to be room on an entertainment show for a well-built, beautiful girl.

Several months later, Janet read about an art show of Liberace's work that was being held in a downtown Los Angeles office building. With some time before an acting class, she went over to see Liberace's show.

A photographer approached her as she examined some of the work.

"Hi, my name is Mario Cassilli. I'm a photographer for *Playboy*. Would you like to pose for me?"

"I would not, thank you."

"Well, if you change you mind, here's my card."

Janet was a smalltown girl from Oregon. Even with some time in Hollywood, a broken, youthful marriage, and the awareness of her own beauty, the idea of posing for *Playboy*—she certainly was aware enough to know it had to be in the nude—was just too much for her.

"Here, I am, from Oregon, with all my square relatives and the life I came from. The whole idea just seemed too ridiculous for words."

Several months went by. The picture business was in decline and Janet found those bit part jobs harder to come by. One day she discovered the business card from Mario Cassilli. She called him and arranged for an appointment.

"I went to his studio. He was the only person there. He had all those cameras and lights. It was really frightening. The idea of taking off my clothes to be photographed was even more frightening. After eight sessions with Mario I finally was able to do it."

Cassilli's picture of Janet, her long black hair flowing over her shoulders, a man's white silk shirt, dripping wet, clinging tightly to her full and wonderful bosom, her thighs and legs perfectly smooth, was shipped to the *Playboy* offices in Chicago in July.

The emperor of *Playboy*, Hugh Hefner, picked the picture out of the hundreds offered to him each month for selection as *Playboy*'s Playmate of the Month and announced, "This girl is for the Christmas issue."

The best looking girls are selected for the Christmas issue of *Playboy*, their biggest and best issue each year. In the December issue of *Playboy* magazine in 1964, the centerfold was filled with the lusciousness of a girl named Jo Collins.

"They had paid me three thousand dollars for the picture," Jo said, "and changed my name for free."

In Oregon, several relatives of Janet's got the word that she was staring out at the world in a wet, tight shirt and nothing else. They examined the centerfold and showed it to Janet's mother. One day the phone rang in her apartment in Malibu.

"Janet, I have just seen the centerfold of *Playboy*. Is that you?"

"Yes, mother it is. They paid me three thousand dollars for it. Isn't that wonderful?"

Janet's mother didn't think it was wonderful. All the uncles and aunts, cousins and friends were aghast that their little Janet would do such a thing.

"I was the black sheep of the family," Jo said. "They couldn't go shopping or go to business without people in town asking about it. I was the topic of conversation everywhere. That's all anybody wanted to talk about on those local radio talk shows. There was one good thing about it. *Playboy* sold more magazines in Oregon that month than it had ever done before."

As almost always happens to *Playboy* Playmates, Jo Collins' career boomed. She did a dozen movies in the next year, mostly beach party movies, and several television shows.

Immediately after the *Playboy* layout hit the stands, Jo Collins was

offered a contract by American International Pictures. Their spe-
ciality was beach party movies, those casual surf and sand things of
the 1950s and 1960s that made a lot of money for a lot of people,
but did little for anybody's serious acting career. Jo's parts were
always the same, a pretty girl, well stuffed into a bikini, smiling,
running in the sand, her long, black hair flowing in the breezes. Jo's
forgettable epics included, *How To Stuff a Wild Bikini, Sergeant Dead-
head, Ski Party,* and *Beach Party Bingo.*

Her career was on dead center, but back in Chicago a decision was
being made that would change Jo's life forever. It was time to select
Playboy's Playmate of the Year for 1965.

This is one of Hugh Hefner's most magnificent promotions.
Readers of *Playboy* are asked to submit their votes each year for
Playmate of the Year among the twelve girls whose charms filled the
centerfolds in the previous year. Miss December, Jo Collins, was
gathering votes by the millions from college boys and advertising
executives, from dirty old men and adolescents, from doctors, lawyers, and engineers, from salesmen and school teachers.

"They never really say the Playmate that gets the most votes is the
winner," Jo says. "That just helps them make their decision. The
votes influence but the decision really is made by the editors, photographers, and Hefner. They must look through some twenty thousand pictures before they decide."

A phone call came to Jo's apartment in Malibu and she was told
that Hefner wanted to interview her in Chicago. She was a candidate
for Playmate of the Year.

"It's a tremendous opportunity," Jo said. "The girl who wins gets
twenty thousand in cash for the layout. She gets a pink Sunbeam,
a white mink coat, pink accessories, and cases of pink champagne.
There are other benefits such as contracts for appearances and
promotional possibilities."

The man behind all this largess is a soft-spoken, pipe-smoking,
thin-faced intellectual, who has made girl-watching a dignified, cul-
tural, and admirable sport in America. He had been an *Esquire* editor
who refused to go with the magazine when it moved from Chicago
to New York, opening his own magazine instead, with borrowed
financing. His empire is now valued in the millions, with several

mansions, his publishing enterprises, his private planes, his high-powered cars, every electrical gadget known to man, his swirling bed and ceiling mirrors, his potpourri of gorgeous girls joining him for dinner and movies in his pad with hundreds of escorts.

"Hefner and I are good friends," Jo says. "We respect each other. We have both a close personal and professional relationship. He never pushes you into anything. He has a party in the mansion, tells you about it, if you want to go, fine, if you don't that's okay, too. He's a brilliant man, very decisive in business, very sure of himself. I admire him a great deal."

Through Jo, Bo has met Hefner several times. He says he digs him.

"He's not a bad guy," said Bo. "He's a gracious host. But he has some wild ideas about women. With all his money, all his fame, his mansions and his cars, he's really a lonely guy. No kidding. I caught him once in a place in L.A., The Candy Store; he was just sitting around the bar. He invited me and my friends up to his castle. It didn't mean anything to me. But my friends thought it was a score. It would be something they could talk about for a week. Me? Who needs it. I got bored at the party. So did Hefner. He got up and walked out of his own party."

After more pictures, more interviews with Hefner and his staff, and a background check worthy of the C.I.A., Jo Collins was named *Playboy*'s Playmate of the Year for 1965.

"They announced the selection at a luncheon in Chicago. Don Adams was the emcee. It was a fine party. Agents and writers were there by the dozens. I asked one of the editors out of curiosity how I had been selected over so many other beautiful girls. He said it was because I had come to the interview at eight-thirty in the morning wearing a demure white linen suit. He said they had never seen anybody look that good in that kind of outfit at eight-thirty in the morning."

Jo's Hollywood career improved some after she moved up from Playmate of the Month to Playmate of the Year. She was signed by the William Morris Agency and made several more movies including one with the intriguing title of *Lord Love a Duck,* starring Tuesday Weld and Roddy McDowell. She also played a small part in *What Did You Do in the War, Daddy?*

William Morris was able to get Jo a contract with Universal Studios. They decided to send her to acting school, work over her image, and create a star.

"They were trying to build me up as a new Raquel Welch," said Jo. "I didn't like that part of it. If I'm sexy, I'm sexy. I have to be myself. I couldn't change myself just for the sake of the studio. I had to be just the way I was. On screen was one thing, but off screen I had to be my own woman."

Jo's career, despite her beauty and obvious sexy skills, never quite got out of the starlet class.

"To make it as a big star you have to pay a terrible price," she says. "I just wasn't willing to pay it. I didn't want to sleep around with producers and agents. I didn't want to go out with guys just to get my name in the papers. I thought I could become a good actress just by hard work. But there's a hell of a lot more to Hollywood success than that."

While her movie career floundered, her picture was being studied across the country and around the world, wherever red-blooded American men gathered. She was being hung up on the walls of college dorms, in army barracks across the country, in schools, and in homes where bachelors thought her charms would bring them inspiration in their own passionate pursuits. In most cases, it brought them the same inspiration Alexander Portnoy gained from fondling a Duke Snider model baseball glove.

The Vietnam war had suddenly erupted into a major conflict in 1965. Once again, American GI's were being studied and written about while they risked their lives in the stupidity of an American exercise in futility. The war stank but the kids who fought and died in it were still the same spirited kids who had gone over the top at command in the Argonne, at Iwo Jima, at Bastogne, and at Pork Chop Hill. With new names and new reasons in Vietnam, they still were turned on by the same things. Nothing turned them on more than pretty girls, especially pretty girls almost undressed.

In Vietnam, the 173rd Airborne Division held a contest asking its men what they wanted most for Christmas. There were votes for good food, a clean bed, a trip back home, and a two-week leave in Tokyo. But what they really wanted most was for the Playmate of the Year to come to Vietnam to visit them. One of their officers duly noted the results of the poll and dispatched a note to Hugh Hefner in Chicago notifying him that his Playmate had been elected by the boys of the 173rd and if he could spare her for a few weeks they would love to have her in Vietnam with them.

"One day I'm sitting home in Malibu and I get this call from one of the Bunny Mothers in Chicago. 'How would you like to go to Vietnam?' I thought she was out of her mind. I really didn't know what in the world she was talking about," Jo said.

Hefner, always one step ahead of the opposition, realized he had a fantastic promotion if he could swing the deal. He called some friends in Washington who called some other friends and the details were worked out. The Playmate of the Year would invade Saigon.

"The whole thing was just beautiful," says Jo. "I was to fly to Vietnam to personally deliver a lifetime subscription to *Playboy* to the 173rd Airborne."

With a complete press crew, several photographers, a chaperone, a Bunny Mother, several *Playboy* press agents and a new wardrobe, Jo Collins flew out of San Francisco for Vietnam.

"I was greeted by dozens of officers at the airport, and a lot of the GIs who were supposed to be guarding me and the plane forgot all about that and moved closer. They were all so cute and wonderful to me. They took me to a fine hotel and sent a tailor around to measure me. Then he came back with a beautiful pair of army fatigues with colonel's bars on them. I was going to travel in style. The 173rd was stationed on a hill called Black Virgin Mountain. Naturally. They flew me up there to see them. They had three helicopters for our group and they had covered the front of them with huge bunny heads. There were more than ten thousand soldiers waiting for me when I arrived. They screamed and whistled and yelled. It almost brought tears to my eyes. The mascot of the outfit was a water buffalo and the first thing they did was present me with this huge water buffalo skull. That's got to freak me out right there. Then they brought me over to a set of microphones. I was supposed to make my welcoming address to the troops. I was being filmed by NBC, ABC and CBS. There were hundreds of army photographers and the *Playboy* photographers. There were generals and colonels and GIs all around. I had this nice little speech all written out. I was supposed to say thanks for being selected and to show my appreciation I'm hear to present this lifetime subscription to *Playboy*. Well, I was nervous as you can expect, the only girl, in front of thousands of men. I got to the microphone and I said, 'I'm here to present this lifetime *prescription* to *Playboy*.' Well, they just began roaring. I guess I was about to cry, I was so humiliated. Then somebody yelled out, 'You sure are just what the doctor ordered.' Everybody broke up at that and after that it was easy."

Jo spent the next several days touring the front in Vietnam, wherever it could be found, talking to soldiers and airmen, bringing them beauty from home, wishing them well and giving them some reminder that there were some things worth fighting for.

"One day they took me up a hill and let me shoot a motar. That really struck me as ridiculous. Here I am, a Playmate, visiting these guys and the army wastes money by letting me shoot some motar rounds just for fun."

The trip to Vietnam ended with great success. *Playboy* received worldwide attention for it. Jo Collins' picture was in almost every paper in the country. She was rewarded for her good work with a vacation trip to Hong Kong, Manila, and Honolulu on the way home.

Jo stayed several weeks in Hawaii. She met singer Don Ho, who introduced her to almost all of the important show business people in Hawaii. She did his show several times before returning home, tired and happy.

Several days later, Jo was asked by *Playboy* to do another promotion for them. The town of Appleton, Wisconsin, was opening a new shopping center. They had decided to mark the opening of their beautiful new shopping area with as much beauty as they could get. They had signed Miss America, Miss Wisconsin, and Miss Appleton to appear at the opening. The chamber of commerce decided the topper for the day would be an appearance of the *Playboy* Playmate of the Year fresh from her triumph in Vietnam.

"The office called me and asked if I wanted to go," Jo said, "and I really didn't feel like it. I had just about had it with traveling and I figured it wouldn't be too awful to rest on the beach in the sun for a few weeks before I took anything else on. I told the office I would let them know. A day later they called back and said a big fuss had been raised in Appleton and I wouldn't be going anyway. The mayor of the town told the press he didn't want me. 'No stripper will be allowed to come to Appleton.' That really teed me off. Now I really wanted to go. I called the office back and said if they could arrange the trip I would go. They said the chamber of commerce still wanted me even if the mayor didn't. I decided to go."

Jo flew to Chicago, got a wardrobe for the occasion, and flew up to Appleton, Wisconsin. There, she got a great surprise. A huge Air Force band greeted her. A banner spread across the airport proclaimed, IF SHE'S GOOD ENOUGH TO GO TO VIETNAM, SHE'S GOOD ENOUGH FOR APPLETON.

"They had a parade and I was put at the head of the parade. It was a ball. There were banners all around proclaiming 'Jo Collins for Mayor' and things like that. It was a marvelous day and the funniest part of the whole story was what happened to the mayor. Six months later they kicked him out."

That evening Jo was escorted to nearby Green Bay, Wisconsin, for a party with many members of the Green Bay Packers football team. The party was held at the Right Guard, the bar and restaurant owned by Fuzzy Thurston, the other guard on the Packer championship football teams, along with Jerry Kramer, the well-known writer and former football player.

"I was with Fuzzy Thurston and his wife and several other players and their wives. Then I was introduced to a big, cute, blond hunk of man, Donny Anderson; I think I fell in love with him just looking at him."

Anderson was easy to fall in love with. He had been signed by the Packers for $600,000, the largest amount ever paid in bonus to a football player at the time, by the late Vince Lombardi, who hated paying big bonuses as much as he hated losing football games. Anderson, an All-American running back at Texas Tech, had broken Joe Namath's record for a bonus and was supposed to replace Golden Boy Paul Hornung in the Green Bay lineup. But he never quite made it as big as Lombardi had hoped and in 1972, after an undistinguished career at Green Bay, was traded to the St. Louis Cardinals.

"He is a very handsome fellow," said Jo, "and we hit it off right away. He invited me out several times, I saw a lot of him, and on New Year's Eve, I sat in the stands at Green Bay for the championship game. I had never before been romanced by someone who wasn't there as I watched him from the stands and nearly froze to death. I was getting the feeling he might not be the boy for me. He was awful nice, though, and he had a reputation around Green Bay as sort of a swinger. In fact a lot of people referred to him as football's Bo Belinsky. I really didn't know what they meant. I hadn't met Bo yet and I never heard of him."

In January of 1968 Jo Collins went back to Malibu, bought herself a red Lincoln Continental, purchased a home on the beach, purchased thousands of dollars' worth of clothes, and settled down for some rest.

"I was twenty-two years old, had all that, and the most handsome, richest football player in the world was getting pretty serious about me. Not bad for a little girl from Oregon," Jo said.

The Ford dealers in Hawaii, pushing their new Lincoln and Mercury models, signed a deal for a promotional campaign with *Playboy*. They wanted the Playmate of the Year to kick off their new ad campaign in Waikiki.

"After being in Green Bay, Wisconsin, that sounded like the most beautiful deal in the world," said Jo. "I jumped at the chance. I went out and bought myself all kinds of bathing suits and sun dresses. It was really fun after being bundled up with fur coats in Wisconsin."

Jo made her appearance in Waikiki a week later. She walked into Michel's Restaurant in Honolulu for the kickoff of the ad campaign wearing a white, backless minidress. The general manager and business manager of Lincoln-Mercury almost passed out. The ad guys almost collapsed. The people in the restaurant just turned their chairs and stared at this suntanned beauty with the shocking white dress. She was something to behold.

"I didn't find out until a few days later, but one of the people in the restaurant that night was Bo," Jo said. "He was cool as always. He never turned his head. Bo never would. Nobody can steal Bo's thunder."

The Ford promotion went off handsomely. The picture of Jo in her white mini was spread all over the papers and Ford sales took an enormous upward turn as people came rushing to the auto dealers in hopes of getting a glimpse of Jo as they purchased their new cars. Jo was supposed to stay in Hawaii one week. When the campaign went so well, Jo was asked to stay a second week by the local dealers.

"Are you kidding? You don't have to ask anybody to stay on a second week in Hawaii with all expenses paid. The place is just out of this world. I'd like to settle there when it's time. I think it's the only place in the world Bo and I have ever really been truly happy," she said.

During the second week of her stay in Hawaii, Jo walked out to the beach, sat down with some friends at a cabana and waited for destiny to come calling. In some few moments, there he came, the handsome, dark-haired boy with the BB on his trunks.

"All the other people there made a big fuss over him. I didn't care. I was introduced to him but I didn't know who he was. I was a football fan, right? Well, finally we got together and then he sent me those beautiful flowers. I think that's what did it. He was so thoughtful. Flowers always get to a woman. When he asked me out, I checked around and found out that he was the playboy of the western world. Everybody knew Bo by reputation. He was just the wildest swinger in the history of the world. I had seen that type before so I was ready. I didn't have to be ready. He wasn't a swinger at all. He was just a quiet little homebody. He didn't even want to go out to a nightclub. All he wanted to do was sit home and listen to music. We went out anyway that first night and when I got back home all I could think of was his reputation. This is the playboy I have heard so much about? This guy is just a little pussycat. But he was handsome with that dark hair, those eyes, that long thin face. I fell in love with him that very first date. I decided I would stay on in Hawaii if he asked me."

"Did I ask her? That's all I thought of that first night," said Bo. "For the first time in my life I just wanted to be with a girl I love every minute of every day. If she didn't stay on in Hawaii, I would have killed myself."

Ah'll do what I can for you, sugar.

Marriage, Belinsky Style

By day and night for two weeks, Bo and Jo dined and danced, laughed and loved, walked and talked together under the blue skies and on the sandy surf of Hawaii. They grooved; this gorgeous, sexy, dark-haired *Playboy* Playmate and this handsome, sexy, dark-haired playboy ballplayer. They had both come up through the ranks, living and loving hard, and now the animal attraction pulled them closer and closer together.

"We have great rapport," says Jo. "We struggle to exert our egos on each other and that is half the fun of it. We are probably both selfish and possessive. We are also insanely jealous of each other. It is the thing that angers us the most and at the same time attracts us to each other. We go everywhere, do everything together, we don't want to be separated for a minute."

One morning Belinsky received a phone call from Mickey Hersko-witz, the hardworking, humorous columnist of the *Houston Post.* Herskowitz had gotten wind of the romance of the century between Bo and Jo and had called to confirm the details. Spring training for the Astros was only a couple of days away and Belinsky would be a major attraction in their camp. He would be even more of an attraction if he brought *Playboy*'s Playmate to training camp with him as he had done with Mamie.

"I'm not sure I'm coming to camp," Bo told Herskowitz. "I might retire here with Jo. I'm in love."

Herskowitz spread the news around. Bo and Jo were famous even before the Houston camp opened.

"When the newspapers heard Bo was dating the Playmate of the Year," said Jo, "they went all out with their publicity. I didn't mind it. It's always fun to read about yourself and see your picture in the papers."

General Manager Spec Richardson, who always found himself attracted to Bo, as most baseball people did, despite Bo's wanderings, called Belinsky and told him he wanted him to report to Cocoa Beach. He agreed to Bo's traditional advance, wired him plane fare and awaited the arrival of his left-hander.

"When Bo decided to go to Florida," Jo said, "J. J. decided to throw him the biggest going-away party ever seen in Hawaii. It was incredible. Everybody was there. They had music and drink and endless girls and guys. Just a mad scene. Somebody got drunk and knocked off some glass ashtrays. Nobody bothered to sweep the glass up. I was running around in my bare feet by then and I stepped on the glass. I was rushed to Kaiser Hospital and Bo held my hand all the way and waited while the doctor took the glass out of my foot. Then we went back to the party and finished up at seven o'clock in the morning. Then we rushed Bo to the airport for the last flight out that would get him to training camp on time. It was a tearful scene. I told Bo I would stay on in Hawaii and wait until I heard from him before I did anything."

Jo was sitting in her hotel room the next morning and there was a knock on the door. The bellboy held a telegram from Bo: "I LOVE YOU. I NEED YOU. YOU MUST COME TO FLORIDA RIGHT AWAY."

Belinsky had gone into Richardson's office as soon as he arrived in camp and asked for permission to room with Jo instead of with one of his teammates. Bo told Richardson he had never felt this way about a girl before. He loved her and was going to marry her as soon as she was divorced. He told Richardson Jo couldn't find her former husband to serve him with divorce papers. Richardson told Bo that rules were rules.

"If you show me a marriage certificate you can live out of camp like any other married player," Richardson said.

Jo didn't know quite what to do. She did not answer the request.

"I wasn't divorced," she said. "I knew I couldn't live with him off the base. I didn't know if I wanted to sit around a baseball camp with all those other baseball wives."

Belinsky used his trump card. He called his friend J. J. Morgan and asked him to urge Jo to take the next plane to Florida. Bo said he would handle all the living complications from his end.

"J. J. wasn't too helpful to Bo. He told Bo that he loved me more than I loved him. I think J. J. was working his own scene. J. J. never even told me Bo had called him. The houseboy told me. When I heard that Bo had begged J. J. to send me to Florida to be with Bo, I was convinced he was sincere."

Jo decided to fly to Florida to be with Bo. She asked J. J.'s houseboy to help her pack her bags.

"The houseboy was a twenty-year-old fag who worked the beach going from one home to the next. He really didn't like working for J. J. because J. J. liked to treat him lousy. He thought that was fun. When Greg started packing my bags, he started crying. He begged me to take him with me. At first I wouldn't think of it. Then I decided it wouldn't be such a bad idea. He would help along the way and when I got there he would be company for me while Bo trained with the ball club. That night we flew on to Florida together."

After the next day's workout, Belinsky hurried over to Jo at her motel. They embraced with passion, made love for hours, and decided to marry as soon as they could. Then they had their first fight of the night.

"We were still fighting about midnight," said Jo, "when Bo decided he had to settle things before he could get back to the team. He called Richardson and asked for permission to stay out past the curfew. Richardson said if Bo didn't return to the camp within the hour, he would be suspended. He stayed with me until three o'clock in the morning. By then we had made up again. He returned to the barracks for the rest of the night. Richardson was waiting for him. He immediately suspended Bo."

Belinsky reacted predictably. He picked up his bags, moved out of the barracks, moved in with Jo, moved Greg out, and settled down to await the next move by the Astros.

"The next day the press invaded the motel," Jo said. "They were all after the big scoop. They all wanted to interview and photograph us. Everybody wanted to see this *Playboy* Playmate who made Belinsky jump his team. It was really hilarious. These writers were coming in from all over. Some of the stories were very funny. One headline said, 'Jo Throws Bo Sex Curves.' We didn't care. Bo said if we couldn't be together he didn't care about playing baseball anyway."

A couple of days passed and the Astros made no move to dispose of Bo. Belinsky decided to ask for his unconditional release. He went to see Richardson. The general manager was less than cooperative.

"We're trying to get waivers on you and send you to Oklahoma City," Richardson said.

"I won't report," said Bo. "The only place I'll play again is in Hawaii."

"Our Triple-A club is in Oklahoma City. That's where you are going if you play."

"I won't report."

"Then you won't play."

Belinsky went back to the motel and waited again. The news stories about Bo and Jo were across the country and they were America's sweethearts.

"We gotta get back to Hawaii," Bo said.

"Let me talk to Richardson," Jo said.

The next morning Jo called Richardson at his office. She said she wanted to plead Bo's case. She hoped Richardson would see her.

"Well, sugar, sure I'll see you and talk about Bo. I'll talk to you tomorrow. Why don't you drive over here and I'll meet you at ten o'clock."

Jo drove to the ball park and Richardson came out to see her. She was wearing one of her tight pants outfits and looked smashing.

"Why, Mr. Richardson, it's so nice to meet you," said Jo.

"Well, sugar, it's sure nice to meet you, too."

"Mr. Richardson, I do wish you would send Bo back to Hawaii."

"Well, sugar, those things are complicated in baseball. You just can't send a man where he wants to go. You have to send him to where you have a team."

"I bet you could send him back to Hawaii if you really wanted to now, couldn't you?"

"Well, ahh suppose we could look into it."

"I know you could do it, Mr. Richardson, and I think you will. You know just how grateful I'll be to you for this."

Jo moved a little closer to Richardson in the car, let him smell the fragrance of her perfume, tossed her head back with a smile, tugged on her sweater a little and knew she was close to victory.

"Well, sugar, I'll tell you what. I'll call Jack Quinn and see what we could work out. I'll get back to you later."

When Jo drove off she knew she had won her case.

"He'll do it, Bo, I'm sure of it."

"How did you convince him?"

"He's a man, isn't he?"

In a few hours, Richardson called Belinsky at the motel.

"I'm calling to tell you that we have just traded you to the Hawaii club. I told Jack Quinn you would report in seventy-two hours. Good luck."

The next morning Bo and Jo were on a plane for Hawaii. Jo had charmed the Astros out of two first-class seats to Honolulu, a trade to the town they wanted, a chance to be together again, and a fresh start.

"Bo said he had never heard of a ballplayer traveling first class with his girl friend. We got away with murder. But we were both used to the finer things in life. Hawaii was really our home now and we were happy going home."

Bo and Jo were met at the airport like some visiting foreign dignitaries. The press gathered around them to interview and photograph the happy couple. It was the biggest event in Hawaii since statehood.

Jack Quinn, the son of John Quinn, general manager of the Philadelphia Phillies, had built an exciting franchise in Hawaii. Many of the players were former major leaguers, many with some good years left. Quinn paid good salaries and was a successful operator with a good team and pleasant conditions. He believed in promotion and publicity and was happy to have Belinsky back with the ball club.

"We probably never lived better in our lives," said Jo. "Through Jack Quinn we got settled down in a magnificent cottage on the estate of Henry J. Kaiser. It was completely furnished with the most incredible things. There was a sunken kitchen with gold accessories. The bedroom was huge and beautiful with red velvet furnishings. Everything in the place was operated by remote control. It was right on the ocean. We could get up in the morning, fall out of bed, and land on the surf. Unbelievable. The rest of the players on the team hated us for it. We didn't care. We were friendly with Jack Quinn and his wife and they loved to come over our place for parties. Most of the players were unfriendly to Bo anyway. They were just jealous. It's always been that way since Bo and I got together. You could feel it. What the hell did we care? We were happy. We had each other and Bo was doing good with Hawaii. Only one bad thing happened to us. We had to give up our home on the estate. President Johnson came to Hawaii and the government took it over and moved us into the Kahala Hilton."

By midsummer of 1968, Belinsky was winning regularly for Hawaii, enjoying the sun and the surf with Jo, and thinking of spending the rest of his days in Hawaii. Then he did a terrible thing. He pitched a no-hitter again.

"That was the worst mistake I made," said Bo. "That got all the scouts looking at me again. I would have to go back to the big leagues. I didn't want to go. I was too happy in Hawaii."

Al Michaels, who now broadcasts the games of the Cincinnati Reds, was the play-by-play announcer for KGU in Honolulu the day Bo pitched his no-hitter.

"Bo was really happy in Hawaii," Michaels said. "He seemed very much in love with Jo. Nobody had any trouble with him. Nobody ever heard about Bo staying out late except with Jo. He was a model husband."

The only catch to that was the fact that Bo and Jo hadn't bothered to go through the formality of marriage yet. They were still looking for Jo's husband.

Michaels remembers Bo's finest hour on the field in Hawaii. He really thinks Bo never pitched a better game.

"This is the minor leagues, remember. Not every player on the field can field," Michael said.

Belinsky had gone to the ninth inning against Tacoma without allowing a hit. With one out and one man on first, a grounder was hit to third baseman Rich Morales. It looked like a double play and the end of the game.

"Morales got in front of it," said Michaels, "picked it up and dropped it. Now there were two on, one out, and Bo had a no-hitter and a one-run lead."

Belinsky retired the next batter on a popup but walked another man. Bases loaded, two out, one batter away from losing the game or pitching a no-hitter.

"John Boccabella was the hitter," said Michaels. "He was a strong right-handed hitter who had been with the Cubs. The count went to 3–2 and Bo threw a fast ball, knee high, and Boccabella caught it at the end of the bat, sent it slicing to right and it looked like it would hit the fence. Joe Gaines, who had bounced around the Houston organization for a while, was in right field. He never was considered much of a fielder. He went back as hard as he could, jumped and got the ball in the top of his glove. Then he banged against the fence and the ball floated up in the air. He stuck out his bare hand and caught it as it was about to hit the ground. It was the most amazing thing I had ever seen."

Belinsky walked off the field in triumph as the fans raced on to the field to congratulate him. Jo was sitting in the stands and was in tears.

"I knew how much he wanted it," said Jo. "He wanted to prove to everybody he could still pitch. It gave him a tremendous lift. It really restored his confidence, not only in his pitching ability but in himself. He was a hell of a lot easier to live with after that."

Bo and Jo partied late into the night after the no-hitter with Jack Quinn and his wife and several other friends. It was a memorable evening and broke up in time for breakfast.

"No matter what anybody says about us," Jo said, "we have always known how to live. What's life all about, if it isn't to have a good time?"

Nobody was having a better time than Bo and Jo. There was one minor complication. Belinsky desperately wanted to marry Jo and Jo was not divorced.

"He was insecure, really," Jo said. "He loved me and I loved him, but he was always afraid he would lose me. He worried about my divorce. I told him it didn't matter and that we loved each other and what difference did it make that we hadn't actually signed any papers together."

The bachelor playboy kept pressing Jo for her hand in marriage. He wanted her to get a Mexican divorce so they could be married immediately. Jo still wanted to get out of her previous marriage. They argued the point long into the night on several occasions in the late summer of 1968. When the season ended in Hawaii, Belinsky was offered a job pitching in Venezuela where he had been such a popular figure before making it to the major leagues. They were to leave for Venezuela in the late fall of 1968. But first there would be a stop.

In September of 1968 the Pittsburgh Pirates purchased the contract of Bo Belinsky. He was going back to the major leagues.

"Most guys take news like that with a party," said Bo. "I felt very depressed. I knew I would only be able to do well if I got a chance to pitch. It didn't seem like I would get a chance to pitch for the Pirates."

Pittsburgh was struggling along in the sixth place in 1968 under manager Larry Shepard. Shepard had been a long-time minor league manager in the Pittsburgh organization and had gotten a chance to manage the club after Harry Walker had been fired and interim manager Danny Murtaugh had turned down the full-time opportunity. Shepard was a low-key guy with all the usual minor league insecurities. He never quite seemed comfortable as the manager of a major league team. He had been considered a good judge of pitching but not much on hitters or outfielders. He once had a young man on the Columbus team named Don Bosch, an ulcer-ridden, gray-haired, twenty-five-year-old who stood about five-nine and weighed 165. Bosch was traded to the Mets and Shepard was asked his opinion of the young man.

"He's as good a fielder as Willie Mays," said Shepard.

Bosch came to the Mets spring training camp, blew the first fly ball hit to him, and blew hundreds more as one of the biggest flops in Mets history. Wes Westrum, never one to hide an opinion of a player, offered this capsule comment on his small outfielder.

"They told me they were sending me a center fielder, but instead they sent me a midget who can't catch a fly ball."

Shepard and Belinsky were oil and water. Belinsky didn't get to pitch very much. Shepard was not impressed with Belinsky's work in Hawaii or his no-hitter. He put him into a couple of games, Belinsky did poorly and he was forgotten. Then he was put on the Pittsburgh Pirates Columbus team. His short stay in the major leagues was over in three weeks.

"What the hell did they get me for?" asked Bo righteously. "I'm a starting pitcher and I didn't start one game. They were losing games and drawing flies. Maybe they thought I could sell a few tickets if I stood around the bullpen for a while. It was typical of baseball. They thought they could use me. What the hell did they care that I had to move all the way from Hawaii to get back to this? They bounce you around in baseball like you are a yo-yo. Nobody ever considers the fact that you are a person with feelings and have obligations. The hell with them. That's why I always looked out for myself. They never would look out for me."

Jo and Bo stayed around Pittsburgh for a few weeks after the season of 1968 ended. Then Bo decided he couldn't go on like this any longer.

"We have to get married," Bo announced. "Now. I can't wait another day."

"But, Bo, honey, I'm not divorced. I don't want you to go to jail for me or for me to go to jail."

"We'll get married in Venezuela."

"It wouldn't be legal."

"Then we'll get married in Mexico. That's always legal."

Bachelor Bo Belinsky was pressing in hard and Jo finally consented. She felt a little guilty about not being divorced after all these years, but she did love Bo. She would be his wife.

The next morning Janet Anderson was divorced from Robert Anderson by a Juarez, Mexico, justice of the peace. He signed the papers and Robert Belinsky and Janet Laws were then wed by the same man in a ceremony lasting thirty-four seconds.

"I was in love and I was married," said Bo. "It was unreal."

"We had been living together for some time anyway, so it didn't seem like such a big deal," said Jo.

Several months later, Robert Anderson was discovered by a private detective, served with divorce papers, did not contest the action, and Bo and Jo were married again legally in the United States.

"You know the first thing Bo did after we got married?" said Jo. "He threw my birth control pills down the toilet."

Belinsky loved Jo but was still unsure of her. He was jealous of every man walking down the street who looked at Jo. She was a gorgeous girl and most men walking down the street would look at her.

"Bo decided the only way he could hold me, the only way he would be sure of me was by having a baby. I didn't want to have a baby just then. I wanted to live a little, have fun, continue working, doing the things I wanted to do. Bo wouldn't hear of it. He wanted me to have a baby right away, right now."

Jo continued to sneak the birth control pills down when Bo wasn't looking.

"One day he found my birth control pills and went into a rage," Jo said. "He called me every name in the book. He said he didn't love me. He said as many cruel things as he could think of. He threw some of the pills out the window and flushed the rest of them down the toilet again. I don't think I have ever seen him as mad. And Bo can really get mad. So can I. That's part of our attraction for each other. We are always trying to see who can outshout whom. Bo usually wins."

The birth control pills disappeared forever and as so often happens in homes where there are no birth control pills, Jo Belinsky became pregnant. They spent a quiet, domestic winter in Venezuela with Bo pitching well again and living a simple life. Bo had been a star from his last appearance in Venezuela so he was treated marvelously. It didn't hurt to have Jo with him because the Latins pride themselves on knowing beauty, and Jo was certainly as beautiful a girl as had ever walked the streets of Caracas.

The winter league season ended and Jo and Bo returned to the small town of Whitaker, Pennsylvania, just outside of Pittsburgh.

One day the phone rang and it was Red Schoendienst, the manager of the St. Louis Cardinals.

"Bo, this is Red Schoendienst of the Cardinals."

"How are you, Red?"

"We have good reports on your pitching in Venezuela."

"Yeah, I did a good job down there, Red. What's on your mind?"

"Oh, I just wanted to tell you. The St. Louis Cardinals have purchased your contract and you will report to us for spring training in St. Petersburg. We need left-handed pitching. You'll have a good chance to make our club."

"Thanks, Red. I'll be there."

Belinsky had been purchased by Bing Devine, the general manager of the Cardinals, who had just resigned as general manager of the Mets to return to his home in St. Louis. Devine, who had gained a reputation as a master trader and a man who could salvage lost players, thought he had a find in Belinsky.

"He's still got a good arm," Devine said, "and our scouts say he can still pitch. We don't have any left-handers in the bullpen so he might be able to fit in there."

Belinsky wasn't able to fit into the St. Louis bullpen. He also wasn't able to fit in to the Cardinals family.

"I was smoking cigars then," said Jo, "and I was five months pregnant. I think that had as much to do with us not making that club as anything else."

On the day the Cardinals were to open spring training a big story appeared in the *St. Louis Globe-Democrat.* It told of the impending arrival of America's sweethearts, Bo and Jo, in the sedate scene of St. Petersburg. The story discussed Bo's future and indicated he would train with the Cardinals, on the roster of the Tulsa club, with a chance to make the big team. The headline captured the feel of the situation when it described the fact that Belinsky could make either club and read, "What Club? The Playboy Club."

"We had been going through this every place Bo played," said Jo. "It was good publicity for *Playboy* and it was a lot of fun. The other players always hated the attention we got but we didn't worry about that. We had been used to people being jealous of us."

The St. Louis writers quickly gravitated to Jo as she arrived in camp. They had all written about Bo before, but Jo was news. She was a mother-in-waiting, smoked big, black cigars, wore thick, dark sunglasses, put on big sunhats, and charmed the reporters out of their minds.

"I don't think any of this sat well with the other wives," Jo said. "I knew it was trouble when an interview appeared in the paper. Somebody asked me if I could cook. I said I could not. I said I couldn't even boil water. They asked me how we eat. I told them our houseboy cooked for us. I could see how that would go over with the wives of the struggling fifteen-thousand-dollar ballplayers. It probably wouldn't go over with the wives of the stars, either. Most ballplayers, even if they make a lot of money, are cheap. They are always worried about the whole thing ending. So they save and invest, instead of live. That's not our style. They like to keep the wives home with the kids, give them a mink, buy them a dishwasher, and swing on the road. They're all like that."

Things were getting a little touchy as Jo and Bo dominated the news in St. Petersburg. The rest of the Cardinals went about the business of getting ready for the season with little notice of Bo. He worked hard, got into shape, and was doing well in spring training games. Another team also trained quietly in St. Petersburg. The New York Mets, under the firm hand of manager Gil Hodges, were preparing calmly for the 1969 season. Six months later they would have the attention of all the baseball world.

"Late in March," Jo remembers, "the club had scheduled a boat trip for the wives of the players on Gussie Busch's yacht. I didn't want to go and I told Bo I wouldn't. It was getting near cutdown time. He said it was important that I went. I did go but I felt the icy stares all the way. Busch had invited the female press from St. Louis to interview the women. Instead of interviewing the wives of all the stars—Mrs. Bob Gibson, Mrs. Joe Torre, Mrs. Dal Maxvill, Mrs. Lou Brock—they interviewed me. This one little blonde reporter was all over me the whole trip. 'How do you make your eyes up?' 'Do you use different lipstick on different days?' 'Is that your real hair?' I really didn't want that much attention but what could I do?"

Things began going downhill for Belinsky as March drew to a close. He wasn't getting as much work as he had earlier and was now in a contest with a couple of younger pitchers for the final spot. The next day Jo was interviewed again by the *St. Petersburg Times.* It might have been the final crushing blow to Belinsky's chances with the Cardinals.

"Wherever we went we always hired a Cadillac. We liked to operate in style. This one day I'm driving downtown in St. Petersburg and this old lady just about runs me off the road. I was really steaming. The next day I'm at the park and I'm talking to one of the reporters. I told her about the incident. I kiddingly told her that people over fifty shouldn't be allowed to drive cars. In St. Petersburg almost everybody is over fifty. You can imagine how that went over. After it appeared in the paper we started getting hate mail from the old people. They called me all sorts of names and told me to drop dead. They said they hoped I was crippled and blind when I got old and crashed into a tree. They were beauties."

Two days later the Cardinals cut their squad. Belinsky was told he would not make the club and was being sent to Tulsa. Jo thinks it didn't have anything to do with his pitching.

"We didn't make the team because we weren't the typical baseball family. We didn't have the right image. We said the wrong things. If Bo was a star he could get away with it. If he wasn't, he had to kiss the right asses and say the right things to hang around. Bo isn't like that. It just wasn't worth it to him. We brought too much adverse publicity to the Cardinals. Bing Devine just didn't like us. He's an all-American square, beautiful wife, beautiful family, a Coke drinker, dammit, and he thought all his ballplayers should worship the game. What the hell for? It's a living like any other living. Does a coal miner worship the coal mine he works in? Bing is apple pie and the American flag. We're not. He wasn't a bad man, I'm not suggesting that, but he had different values. He had his way of doing things and we had ours. His way just happened to be the way he wanted it because he was the boss. So it was bye, bye, Bo."

Like Spec Richardson before him, Bing Devine paid Belinsky the supreme compliment. He sold him back to Hawaii. Not too many ballplayers ever wind up going back to the town they want from so many separate organizations such as the Los Angeles Angels, the Houston Astros, and the St. Louis Cardinals.

Bo and Jo returned to Hawaii, settled down in a beautiful cottage on the beach and together they watched Jo grow larger by the day. Bo Belinsky was on the threshold of becoming a father.

On the night of June 17, 1969, Jo was rushed to Queen's Hospital in Hawaii. Stevhanie Lehua Belinsky was born to Bo and Jo Belinsky. She weighed six pounds six ounces, had brown hair and green eyes, and looked an awful lot like her father.

Telegrams and gifts came by the dozens. Governor Burns and Senator Patsy Mink sent flowers. The next morning photographers came to the room to shoot pictures of Jo, Bo, and baby Stevie.

"We called her Stevhanie because we wanted her to have a nice name like Stevie when she grew up. We gave her the middle name of Lehua because it means flowers of the gods, and it was our way of saying thank you to Hawaii for all the good things that had happened to us there," said Jo.

Bo Belinsky, bon vivant, bachelor, high-liver, wild man, swinger, man about town when Hollywood was the town, was the father of a baby girl.

"It was really a scream," said Bo. "There I was getting up in the middle of the night giving Stevie a bottle and trying to pitch the next day. Now I knew what they had all been talking about through the years."

"Every day," said Al Michaels, "you would see Jo sitting in the stands with the baby. She was the perfect mother with the cute little outfit on the baby, her arms filled with a bag of diapers and nipples. There was Bo joining them after the game, riding home together, having a quiet dinner, and settling down to a simple married life. It certainly wasn't the picture of Bo Belinsky we all knew. I can't remember a baby having a greater impact on a man's life than that baby did on Bo's. He used to bore everybody silly talking about the baby. Imagine Bo Belinsky telling stories about changing diapers at three o'clock in the morning."

The Hawaii season ended and Bo, Jo, and Stevie set out for Santa Domingo for winter ball.

"This was the part I didn't like about Bo playing ball now that he was married," said Mrs. Anna Belinsky. "I just didn't believe it was right to drag a little baby all around the world. A baby needs a home."

When the winter season ended, Bo and Jo decided to return to Whitaker, Pennsylvania, where they had made some friends, and spend the rest of the winter there.

"I liked it there," said Bo. "It was different. A quiet little place, a shot-and-a-beer town outside Pittsburgh. I spent most of the day cooking cornish hen and crêpes suzette. Then we'd watch television, those silly afternoon game shows and make love. It was a ball."

Belinsky admitted he liked his new-found domestic life away from Hollywood, away from Vegas, away from all the sounds and sights of his youth.

"I am," said Belinsky, one day early in 1970, "too old for that other scene."

"Just about this time," said Jo, "we decided to give up this baseball life and get into something else. I was bored being a baseball wife and Bo wasn't going anywhere with his career. It was time to look around."

While Belinsky pondered what his future might be without a baseball in his hand or sweat socks on his feet, he received a call from Bob Howsam, the general manager of the Cincinnati Reds. St. Louis still owned Belinsky's contract. He had been technically on loan to Hawaii. Now they sold Belinsky's contract to the Cincinnati Reds for right-handed pitcher Dennis Ribant.

"Bo, we're happy to have you with us," said Howsam. "We think you have a chance to make this club. We have a fine club and we believe we have a chance to win the pennant. We'll see you in Tampa."

Belinsky had heard that song so many times before he almost burst into laughter. "I guess the only reason I didn't laugh," he said, "was because I wanted to believe it."

Belinsky went down to the local pool hall to celebrate. He ran a table and bought beers for everyone. Bo was going back to the big leagues again. He knew there was still hope for that golden ring. A lot of pitchers get lucky at thirty-three.

Down deep in his heart, Bo knew it wouldn't happen. He had kidded a lot of people for a lot of time. But there was one guy he never really could fool. That was the handsome, dark-haired, dark-eyed guy with the BB on his orange bathing trunks.

Some of those players would be a little shocked if they knew what the little ladies were doing back home when they were on the road.

—JO BELINSKY

The Last Hurrah

In the spring of 1970 Jo, Bo, and Stevie Belinsky headed south for the spring training camp of the Cincinnati Reds. Another team and another general manager were about to take a chance on Belinsky's left arm. He had pitched well again in Hawaii and the Reds thought there were a few more wins, a few more innings left in that old arm.

"I've been this route before," he said. "I know what they want. They need a few extra pitchers to throw batting practice in the spring. They won't give me a chance to pitch. What the hell difference would it make? I don't have any juice left in my arm anyway."

Belinsky arrived in Tampa, the spring training home of the Reds, and rented a beach house and a Cadillac. This would be the last waltz, but Bo would go out in style. It was his way.

"In 1969 with the Cardinals," said Jo, "I was pregnant and uncomfortable when I came to camp. This was different. Stevie was a baby and we were a little family and I took her to the park every day. It was boring but what else could I do? I wanted to be near Bo."

Belinsky was a fringe pitcher, a veteran trying to hang on and make the ball club. By the code of the road he and his wife should have stayed in the background waiting to be asked before they breathed or spoke.

"They have this caste system in baseball," said Jo. "The wives take on the importance of the husband. One or two wives run a club, call the others, tell them what to do, when to meet, when the picnics are scheduled, what to wear, who to talk to, what silly games to play. Wives of veterans don't get too close to wives of rookies. Stars aren't allowed to socialize with fringe players. On the Reds, Pete Rose was the team leader so Karolyn Rose was the heavy. She ran the show. She was the chief and all the rest of them were Indians. I got along great with her. But it was on equal terms. They befriended us but it wasn't the same with all the other wives. Mostly, they are a bunch of little, spoiled bitches. I didn't have to take any of their crap. I was a celebrity in my own right. Bo had been around and I had been around. We had our own scene. I couldn't stand sitting around playing bridge, gossiping about the other wives, drinking coffee all morning in the beach cottages. I knew right off that a lot of the players' wives didn't like me. I was a threat. I wasn't the cute little girl next door. They were damn jealous."

The pecking order among baseball wives has killed a lot of teams. While players cover up their jealousies for the good of the club, wives rarely bother. Jealousy and competition among wives has wiped out more baseball teams than broken legs or extramarital affairs.

Many people around the New York Mets felt the fame achieved by pretty, blonde Nancy Seaver, as the wife of Tom Terrific, did more to eliminate the Mets as a contender in 1970 after their Series win in 1969 than any other single factor.

"We had this engagement set up by comedian Phil Foster, at Caesar's Palace in Las Vegas," explained one Mets player. "They told us not to bring our wives. None of us did except Seaver. He brought Nancy and she hung around the show and the rehearsals every day. Imagine the problems we had explaining that to our wives when we got home."

Wives don't often get into hair-pulling episodes, but they do immerse themselves in petty gossip. Many players keep their wives away from other wives. Ballplayers are quick to blame their problems on other players, managers, and the press. Wives take the same route. When a pitcher loses a tough game on the second baseman's ninth-inning error, the team party the next day can be very strained.

Ron Hunt, a fine second baseman for the Montreal Expos, once summed up the situation of a major leaguer.

"A good ballplayer always wants to win," said Hunt, "but nobody takes care of you if you don't do the job. I was told early in my career to watch out for number one because nobody else will."

Wives think the same way. There is nothing as casual as a friendship between two wives of ballplayers.

"The first time we got traded," said the wife of a veteran player, "nobody called us up to say good-bye. I didn't understand it. Then I realized it. When you are traded, people forget you in an instant. All of a sudden they act as if you had a contagious disease. Being traded can be catching."

Unlike football, baseball players seem to welcome new players on their individual merits.

Pete Rose says he liked Belinsky from the first moment he met him in that Cincinnati camp.

"I went to bat for him. I told Sparky [Anderson] that he could still throw. I thought this screwball was a hell of a pitch and that he could help us. We were curious as hell about him. Everybody knew Bo by reputation, but he was a good guy. Cincinnati isn't Los Angeles. There were no Mamies around in Cincinnati. He couldn't have a night life if he wanted to. I'll say this for Bo. He made that club on merit. He worked hard in the spring and proved he could pitch. He was a team guy, too. He didn't sit around the bench hoping some other pitcher would break a leg. It isn't easy to transfer loyalty from one team to the next when you get traded, but Bo did it. I was just sorry he didn't stay around longer."

The Mets had won a miracle pennant in 1969. In the spring of 1970, they were going through the postpennant blues, counting their money, thinking about their new fame, fighting each other for the spotlight and the glory. In Tampa the Reds—led by the brilliant young catcher, Johnny Bench, and Rose, Bobby Tolan, Lee May, Tony Perez, and some fine young pitching prospects—were jelling into a team that would bust up the National League and the pennant race by late June.

The Reds broke camp in late March. Rookie manager Sparky Anderson, whose gray hair and lined face made him appear twice his age, took a team north that appeared to have the strongest offense in baseball. The only problem was pitching, especially the left-handed kind. Anderson thought he had solved that problem with the acquisition of Bo Belinsky.

"I could have helped that club," said Bo, "if they had let me pitch."

Belinsky was the tenth pitcher on the ten-man staff. A pitcher in that spot gets little work. Belinsky pitched a few innings and hung on. His chances for staying around all year didn't look that good. But he was not unhappy.

"I wanted to pitch more," Bo said, "but the Reds were a good bunch of guys. Pete Rose was one of the greatest guys I ever met in baseball."

Rose said the Reds made an effort to create team spirit. Rookies and stars roomed together and black and white players socialized. Very few instances of this are known in baseball.

"I have always thought a team is only as strong as its weakest player. If there is a lot of bitching and moaning going on around a club, it is hard to win. The last guy on the team may be needed to get that one hit, pitch that last out that can turn a game and turn a season. We were all there together, to win. That's what it's all about," said Rose.

Belinsky moved his family in to a garden apartment in the out- skirts of Cincinnati. Many of the other families lived nearby. It wasn't the most pleasant relationship possible for Jo.

"The guys would go on the road and the girls would get together for these boring bridge games. They'd call a picnic or some kind of outing. I didn't often go. I was bored with all this crap. I had to have fun, go out, live a little. I'm a jealous person. It galls me to be away from Bo. I know he's on the road, going out, having a drink, looking for a piece of strange. I'm not naïve. I've been around. I know what the hell is going on in the world. A lot of those wives would be shocked to learn what the hell was really going on while they stayed home. That's funny to think about because I think the guys would be shocked if they knew what the little ladies were doing back home while they were on the road. The guys think whatever they do is fine.

But if the girls search out a piece of strange, that's not allowed. Well, it works both ways and they ought to know about it."

Every so often, these clandestine affairs Jo referred to are actually occurring with other baseball players, especially in those two-team towns where a player always knows the schedule of the other team.

A Yankee ballplayer was married to a nyphomaniac. That was during World War II when there were three teams in New York. She had her choice of Dodger and Giant players while the Yankees were on the road. Another Yankee player swept in from his spring training camp in Florida one night to discover his wife comfortably nestled under the sheets with her boyfriend, this time not another ballplayer. Private detectives and photographers recorded that scene for posterity and the resultant divorce action was a piece of cake for the player.

Nymphomania seems to be a common ailment among wives of athletes. The girls are usually beauty queens, sensual, fussed-over most of their lives, suddenly married at eighteen, nineteen, or twenty, to the handsome stud high school hero. All of a sudden he's a professional baseball player and he's gone from home six months a year. Some players actually never take their wives and family with them to the town in which they play their entire careers.

The girls grow hungry for love and affection and their sex glands become operative with everybody and anybody. Loneliness can make strange bedgirls.

One famous American League ballplayer had to end his career prematurely when his wife's extramarital affairs became public knowledge in his hometown. He quit baseball, tried to make his marriage work but failed. A divorce resulted.

Another ballplayer got the message about his wife's desires in the old days of the "train leagues," as opposed to today's travel by air. His team pulled into town at 9 A.M. on an overnight train. While most wives waited in the train lobby or at home for their husbands, one catcher's wife leaped onto the train, forced her man back into a pullmen berth, and seduced him before he could get a change of venue. A late-leaving player walked by the berth, shook his head, and said simply, "Isn't love grand?"

Another loving wife once decided to surprise her mate when his team arrived in Baltimore after an overnight flight from California. She appeared at the hotel, talked the desk clerk out of room key, marched gingerly to her man's room and opened the door to surprise him. She got a little surprise, too. Her man was making it with some other girl.

"One thing I couldn't stand," said Jo, "was players on your own team trying to hustle you."

There was a young pitcher on the Reds, married, with a family, who lived in the same apartments with the Belinskys.

"We said good morning when we crossed in the halls. That was about the extent of our relationship. He got it into his mind that I was madly in love with him. One time, after Bo had been sent out to Indianapolis and I was still in Cincinnati with Stevie, the Reds had a party. I was lonely so I went. It was a real nice party until I had to go to the bathroom. This young pitcher follows me to the bathroom. His wife is sitting out there in the room and he's trying to grab me and kiss me against the bathroom door. He was drunk but that never is an excuse. I told him if he didn't get his hands off me I'd give him a shot right in his balls and go tell his wife. That cooled him off a little."

Johnny Bench, the handsome young bachelor catcher on the Reds and a killer with the girls, also had eyes for Jo.

"I danced with him at a party. He was cute but just a boy. When Bo heard about it he nearly went crazy," Jo said.

Most of the wives of players are sweet, innocent, small-town girls when they come to the big leagues with their husband. A girl like Jo, an actress, a Playmate, a girl who had entertained the troops in Vietnam, intrigued and puzzled them. They wondered about her. They wanted to get closer and they were afraid.

"At a party they would get a little braver and ask about Hollywood and some of the people we knew and what it was like to be in *Playboy*. A lot of them would ask about Bo's early career. They wanted to know about Mamie. I didn't care that they wanted to discuss Mamie. I told them Mamie was well before my time. Hell, Mamie was old enough to be my mother."

Belinsky had very little opportunity to pitch and by May, with the

Reds well ahead, stories began appearing in the Cincinnati papers that Bo might be sent out soon.

"That team really needed more pitching as it turned out. They had nothing but sore arms by the time the season ended and they got to the World Series," said Bo. "I think I lost out because the pitching coach didn't like me."

It is one of the strongest alibis a failing ballplayer can ever use. Belinsky used it as well as any. Few managers in baseball, if they are to last, would let personality interfere with their judgment as to a player's ability. But there are obvious choices to be made among fringe players. Belinsky was a fringe player. It was his misfortune in Cincinnati to come under the leadership of Larry Shepard. Shepard had been Belinsky's manager in Pittsburgh. Then he had lost his job and become a pitching coach under Anderson. While Anderson is a gregarious, warm, pleasant, understanding man, Shepard is a cool, aloof, intense individual. Few things are as embarrassing in baseball as a manager who loses his job and steps down to a coach's position. Some men can never adjust. Shepard, who worked all his life for that managerial spot, didn't accept the demotion without some bitterness.

"When I got the news that I was gone," said Belinsky, "I think Shepard laughed for the first time all season."

The Reds had just come back from a road trip when Anderson told Belinsky he was being sent to Indianapolis. It was a blow. Almost thirty-four years old and with a tired left arm, Belinsky knew he would never wear a big league uniform again.

"He was very depressed," said Jo. "He stayed out late and drank a lot. He came home and drank some more. He must have finished a bottle of vodka by himself. I had a few drinks with him. It got real late, maybe three, four o'clock in the morning. He was getting nastier and nastier as the hour got later. We started to argue. We were shouting at each other. The baby started crying in the next room. Neither of us seemed to care. We were just wild with anger. Now Bo reaches into a drawer and pulls out a gun. There had been some robberies around there and Bo decided to get a gun. Now he is holding the gun up in the air. He is calling me every name in the book.

"He grabs my hair and pulls me over to the mirror. He is shouting some terrible things at me and I'm shouting back at him. He's holding me with his right hand and he has that gun in his left hand. He says he is going to kill me. I told him he might as well go ahead. I told him he was crazy and I wouldn't live with him any more anyway. Now he puts the gun against my head. He pulls the trigger. I don't really know to this day whether or not he knew the gun was not loaded. He couldn't have really known anything. He was too drunk to know. I started shrieking. I thought I was dead. I looked for the blood. I was screaming and weeping uncontrollably. I just ran out of the house and out into the street. I didn't know what I was doing or where I was going."

Jo jumped into their car and drove off to get away from Bo. There was only one place to go. She drove to the home of Pete and Karolyn Rose. She woke them up and, carrying on hysterically, told them what had happened.

"We better call the cops," Rose said.

Rose picked up the phone, called the police, and identified himself as Pete Rose. He told them Bo was at home with a gun and asked them if they could please go over and take it away from him.

"I hadn't even thought about Stevie until them," said Jo. "I was too out of my mind with fear."

Three police cars responded to the call and pulled up in front of Belinsky's apartment. They walked to the door carefully, announced who they were, and with drawn guns were about to break down the door, when Bo opened it up. He was holding Stevie in his arms. She was crying hysterically.

"I think," said Jo, "Bo had pulled her out of bed and held her so the cops wouldn't shoot him when they walked through the door."

Belinsky had calmed down by now. He tried to soothe Stevie as the police questioned him. They asked for the gun. It was sitting atop a dresser.

"It's not loaded," said Bo. "I never load it. I have it around to scare anybody who might try to rob us. My wife knew that. We just got a little hot together. That's the way we are."

Belinsky and Stevie were taken to the police station, and Jo was waiting there with Pete Rose when they arrived. Jo took Stevie from him and they tried to stay calm.

"Now, Miss, you'll have to sign this complaint against your husband or we can't hold him. If you want to fill out the complaint, we'll lock him up for the night and he can go before the judge in the morning."

"Can I talk to him for a minute?"

"Sure, go ahead."

Jo and Bo walked off into a corner of the room and Bo said he was sorry. He blamed it all on the booze, convinced Jo he didn't mean it, admitted he was overly depressed and promised her it wouldn't happen again.

"I won't sign the complaint," Jo said.

"All right, lady, than we'll have to let him go."

Bo, Jo, and Stevhanie were allowed to leave. Bo went back to the apartment. Jo and Stevhanie went back with Pete Rose and spent the rest of the night with the Roses. It was safer all around that way.

"The next day we got back together again," said Jo. "Bo had sobered up and he was calmed down. What could I do? I loved the guy. He needed me."

Things stayed peaceful for Bo and Jo for a few more days. Then he left Cincinnati and reported to the Indianapolis ball club.

"I knew it was all over," said Bo. "The only reason I went was because I needed the money. Indianapolis was a big nothing. Just Trenton West. What the hell could I do in Indianapolis?"

He did very little. He pitched a few innings for the Indianapolis club, impressed nobody, had little heart for it, and was sent home on September 4, 1970. When he took off his uniform that final day, he knew it would be for the very last time. He had no regrets.

"I coulda been somebody," he says. "I really could have. I know I had the ability. I didn't have the motivation. I didn't want it bad enough. To be a star in the big leagues, you have to pay the price. I didn't want to pay it. There were too many other things to do. If you do them, and hell, everybody knows I did them, some day you have to pay the piper. I paid my debt. It was a gas. Where the hell else could a guy like me live in beach houses, meet the biggest people in the world, drive Cadillacs, and be wined and dined? I have no regrets. What the hell for? Who the hell cares if you feel sorry for yourself?"

In the fall of 1970, Belinsky decided to return to California. That was where he had his best shot.

"I was known out there. I was somebody. I figured something would come up. I didn't know what the hell I wanted to do. I figured I would land something. I had a lot of friends. I found out about that too. My friends sure did disappear when I was washed out of baseball. I was a good guy for them when my name was in the paper. All of a sudden I was nobody and they had some other young pitcher they liked. They're like broads. If you trust them, they'll cut your balls off and leave you in the street."

Jo, Stevie, and Bo settled into a motel apartment in Malibu. They had no money, no job, no opportunity, nothing to look forward to.

"Things were getting pretty tough," said Jo. "One of us had to go to work soon."

Jo made the decision. She took a job with *Playboy*.

"They had been after me for some time to work for them. I told them I wasn't interested as long as Bo was playing ball. I had to be with him. I had to be wherever Bo was going to be. That was the only way we would make it. We are so jealous of each other we have to be in each other's sight at all times. Now Bo was finished with baseball and I figured we would stay out here. I called *Playboy* and asked if the job offer still stood."

Playboy said it did. Jo was hired to handle their promotions in the Los Angeles area.

"It was a good job with good money. That's what we needed," Jo said. "Bo would stay home and take care of Stevie and I would go to work. I didn't mind it. I knew it would take Bo some time to get adjusted to being out of baseball. I was glad to get out of the house anyway. I just wasn't the housewifey type. Bo didn't mind staying home all day. He's lazy and he likes being a homebody. He thinks it's a ball to sip a vodka, watch daytime television, and fall asleep on the couch. Not me, I've got to be moving all the time. This setup looked like it actually would be good for us. Bo said he was happy staying home. At first, I believed it. Then I realized no man can be happy staying home all the time. Bo had to have a place to go, something to do with his time. So far he hadn't anything or anyone to turn to."

Bo said he was waiting for an offer. He had friends and he knew some of his friends would come through. He waited and waited. Nobody offered him part ownership of a baseball team or interest in a restaurant or the bartender's job at some plush eatery.

"A boutique. That's what I wanted," said Bo. "I have always liked clothes. That seemed the thing for me. I thought I could get a deal going and I could work up something. We had spoken to some friends in Cincinnati about that. I thought sure something like that would come through. That seemed like the thing to do for me. I knew I could do a hell of a job."

Jo worked daily and Bo stayed home with the baby. No friends called. Bo just sat home, smoked cigarettes, drank coffee, drank vodka, watched daytime television, played with the baby, and waited for Jo to come home.

"I spent most of the day talking to Jo on the phone at her office. I just couldn't stand being away from her, not for a minute."

By November of 1970, Bo and Jo were fighting regularly. They were picking on each other for small things. Jo would come home late from work and Bo would accuse her of stopping off somewhere with somebody. Bo would be drunk when Jo came home and that would lead to a fight. Belinsky, who had never drunk very much as a player, was now drinking more and more. It was helping him pass the time.

"We argued all the time," said Jo. "We argued about everything. It just didn't seem like we could make it together. When we were apart we missed each other like mad. When we were together we argued. It was a hell of an existence. I didn't know which way to turn. I loved him. I knew that. But I just couldn't see going on like this. He had to get something to do. That seemed to be the cause of much of our unhappiness."

One night Bo and Jo had gone out for dinner. They had been drinking a lot and were on their way home. They started arguing again. Bo accused Jo of making eyes at some guy in the bar. Jo heatedly denied it and told Bo he was driving her crazy with his insane jealousy. They shouted and screamed at each other.

"Bo was driving the car and he was looking at me instead of the road. There was a curve and all of a sudden I realized he wasn't going to make it. I could hear the wheels of the car screech. The car hopped off the road, jumped a curb, and crashed into a utility pole as Bo fought to control the wheel. Just before we hit I put my arm up in front of my face. It probably saved my face."

The car careened into the pole with a sickening crash. Bo's head went through the windshield glass and he was knocked unconscious. Jo's arm had saved her face, but her arm had been broken and two bones crushed in the crash.

"The car was a total wreck," she said. "We just lay there bleeding, waiting for help. A police car came along and called for an ambulance and a tow truck. Bo had been pinned against the window by the seat. The tow truck had to use a blow torch to free him. I was able to walk away from the car. When I got out of the car and looked at the damage I couldn't believe we were still alive. It was really incredible. The car had just folded up like an accordion."

Bo looked worse than Jo when they arrived at the hospital in Malibu, but Jo was actually more seriously hurt.

"My arm was severely damaged," she said. "The doctors examined me and told me they would probably have to amputate it. The bones were so badly crushed they didn't believe anything could save the arm. I begged them to try. They said they would take more X-rays and see what could be done. I don't know what it was but I seemed to respond well to the treatment. In a few days the doctors told me the bones were showing signs of actually knitting. They had taken a piece of bone out but they would somehow knit together and I would have full use of the arm, but it would be several months before it would be anything like normal."

The administrator of the Malibu hospital had just joined the hospital. He had recently arrived from Queen's Hospital in Honolulu. He had known Bo and Jo when Stevie was born there in the summer of 1969.

"He arranged to put us together in a private room in the hospital. This was supposed to be against hospital policy. Anyway we spent two weeks together in that hospital room. We were so glad to be alive and to be recovering that we didn't have a single fight. Of course, there weren't any reasons to fight. Neither of us was out of the other's sight."

When they recovered, Jo, Bo, and Stevie went up to Oregon to recuperate at the home of Jo's mother. Stevie would be taken care of and they could get some rest and attention. That worked out for about a week. Then came the next fight.

"My mother made a big Thanksgiving dinner," Jo said. "Everything seemed great. My mother really likes Bo. He can be awfully charming when he wants to be. I don't even remember what caused the fight. All I know is we started screaming at each other again and calling each other names. This time Bo said he didn't want to make up. He said it was all over. He packed up his stuff and he took off. I think he went back to Malibu and moved in with some friends."

Belinsky has always seemed happiest when he was around L.A. The phonies of Hollywood were his kind of people. He liked the idea of acting all the time. Hollywood was a good place for somebody who didn't work. Most of the people in Hollywood didn't work. He would fit right in. He stayed with friends, drank a lot, partied almost every night, ignored the realities of having a marriage or not having it, having a job or not having it. There always seemed to be a free meal someplace, a free bed, and a girl available. What else was there that Bo Belinsky really needed?

"He would call me every so often to see how I was doing," said Jo. "He didn't say anything about getting together. He just wanted to know what I was doing. I was happy, really, I was. I had my job, I kept busy, I had a baby-sitter for Stevie and I seemed to be getting along by myself. I really didn't have any definite plans one way or another about Bo. I just knew that we couldn't go on the way we had been going. There's only so much yelling and screaming anybody can take. I decided to just go along like this and see what happened."

Belinsky enjoyed his free life again and Jo kept busy on her job.

"By the spring of 1971 my arm was coming back to normal. I felt good again. I was so busy with my job that I really didn't have time to think about Bo. He would call a lot, we would talk, but I didn't have that same feeling. I started thinking about a divorce. I seemed to be getting Bo out of my system."

In May of 1971, Playboy was opening a new club in Denver. They needed someone to hire, train, develop Playboy Bunnies. They called Jo from Chicago and asked her if she would be interested in the job.

"The pay would be sensational and this was a management job. It wasn't just a job to look good for some client and sign autographs for dirty old men. This was organization and executive training. I would be involved in the hiring and training of the girls. I would also be managing the club when the general manager would be out. I would be doing something exciting that I had never thought of doing before. The whole idea fascinated me."

Jo told Playboy she needed some time to think about it. She didn't want to move out of L.A. to Denver without considering all the ramifications of the move.

"Bo was calling me a lot and if I just moved out that would really be the end of it," she said. "I really couldn't make up my mind if I wanted to do that. The guy had a mysterious hold on me. I didn't feel like making the move without telling him. I waited for him to call."

Bo called and Jo explained the details of the new deal. Bo said it sounded great. He encouraged her to take it.

"When you get settled up there maybe I'll come and take a look around. Maybe we can try it out up there, Jo, maybe we can make it again. Let me know where you'll be."

In late May, Jo Belinsky moved with Stevie to Denver. She found a pleasant apartment, got Stevie a nice baby-sitter and settled down in the clean, clear country of Colorado.

"It was a marvelous job," Jo said. "It was very exciting to get into the operation of a new Playboy club from the beginning. I was so busy I really didn't have time to think about Bo. I was really very happy in Denver."

Several weeks passed with no word from Bo. Then he called and said he would like to come up to Denver.

"I didn't know what to do about it," said Jo. "I guess I still loved him and every time he called there was some feeling that we could make it again if he could accept things as they were. I didn't care that he didn't have a job. I just didn't want him to be jealous of me, of my success, of the things I was doing and the people I was meeting. We had a great thing at one time and it wasn't based on the fact that he was a ballplayer or on the fact that I worked for *Playboy*. It was merely based on the fact that we cared for each other, we needed each other in a strange and desperate way. We had this incredible physical closeness when we were together. That's just the way our natures were. We fought hard and we loved hard. But Bo was the only one I had ever met who made that electricity come out of me. I knew it wouldn't be easy just forgetting him. I knew I had to try again and see if we could make a life together and make it work. It was the only thing I could do. You make some terrible decisions, you know, when you love somebody. You don't care how they treat you. You just know you love them and you have to be in the same room with them all the time."

Jo gave Bo another chance. She told him to join her in Denver.

It lasted about as long as all of their other patch-ups, just long enough to have another fight.

"It was beautiful for a few days," said Jo. "We made wild, passionate love and I believed we were going to get straightened out again. I felt that Bo had accepted the fact that he wasn't playing ball and he would soon get himself something to do. Hefner liked him and I thought maybe something could be worked up in the Playboy organization for him."

"Jo was a Bunny Mother," said Bo. "Would they make me a Bunny Daddy?"

Belinsky just couldn't see himself in the Playboy scene. He didn't know anybody in Denver (it was one of the few towns he hadn't ever played in) and he couldn't stay home alone all day with Stevie. The television reception in Denver, with the mountains blocking the picture, was lousy. That was as much a cause of their fighting as anything else.

"I tried to make it up there," says Bo, "but there was nothing for me, nothing. It was dullsville and I couldn't stand it. I'd stay home all day and by the time Jo came home, she was tired from her day's work and I was pissed off just staying home. We'd start out okay, put the baby to sleep, stay at home, and then start fighting. It didn't take me long to realize if Jo and I were going to make it, Denver would not be the place. I asked Jo to leave and go back to Malibu with me."

There was no reason for Jo to leave. The job was in Denver.

"Bo was insanely jealous of me now," said Jo. "He had nothing in his life and I had everything. It just wasn't the way things should be."

A few days after Belinsky came to Denver, he left. This time Jo decided it would be the end.

"I got a lawyer and decided to go ahead with a divorce. There was no more use in trying to make something work that obviously wasn't working. On June second I went into court in Denver and filed papers to divorce Bo."

The shock of an actual, legal divorce action was too much for Bo. He started drinking heavily again, called Jo angrily on the phone, threatened her with bodily harm, and said he would have her phone tapped, promised her she would not be allowed to go through with such a terrible deed.

"We couldn't get along and he knew it," said Jo, "but he was so jealous he couldn't conceive of giving me up altogether and having somebody else fall in love with me."

Belinsky was indecisive. He didn't want to go back together again with Jo, but he didn't want her to divorce him. In his strange way, he loved the girl desperately and passionately, more than he had ever loved anyone in his life. He knew she was good for him. He knew he had to try to change himself for her.

"I just didn't know how to change," he said.

While the divorce action lingered, Jo received another summons from Playboy. She had served so well as Bunny Mother in Denver that they wanted her to come to the Chicago office and head up their entire stable of Playmates.

"I would be involved in all the planning and promotion of the entire organization," Jo said. "It was a tremendous opportunity. I didn't think long about it. I had given up on saving my marriage. I decided to go to Chicago and build a life for myself out there."

Jo and Stevie left for Chicago in the summer of 1971. They moved into a Chicago apartment hotel and started a new life.

"Stevie was now two years old," said Jo. "For the first time I could

send her to nursery school. It was a lot cheaper than having somebody stay with her at home every day. She loved it, too, because it
gave her a chance to play with other children. We had moved so
much she never really got to know other children."

In some few weeks, Jo received a call from Trenton, New Jersey.
Bo's mother was on the wire. She was trying to save her son's
marriage.

"Bo needs you," said Mrs. Belinsky. "He knows the breakup is all
his fault but he doesn't want a divorce. He is begging you to wait.
He says he thinks he can change and be a good husband."

Mrs. Anna Belinsky is a sweet woman. Her motives were sincere,
but the complicated relationship of Jo and Bo Belinsky needed more
than the loving interest of a mother.

"I didn't call him and he didn't call me," said Jo. "This time I
thought it was all over."

Jo settled into her job in Chicago. She became deeply involved in
her assignment for Playboy. The American Civil Liberties Union
was planning a huge, Hollywood, star-studded benefit for November. Burt Lancaster was the chairman of the massive fund-raising
dinner and show. Other celebrities involved included Angie Dickin-
son, Zsa Zsa Gabor, Ryan O'Neal, Ralph Nader, and many, many
others. The ACLU had asked Hugh Hefner to provide some of his
Playmates as hostesses for the event. Jo was assigned by Playboy to
coordinate the activities of the Playmates and make all arrangements for their appearances. The event was to take place in Hollywood and Jo would fly to Los Angeles early in November to set
things up.

"My mother was in Los Angeles," said Jo, "and I called her and
asked her to meet me at the airport. It would be a chance to see her
again and spend some time with her before going on to the hotel.
She said she would."

At the time Jo was supposed to arrive, her mother suddenly discovered she would not be able to meet her. She called Jo and told
her she could not pick her up.

"Bo had called my mother in Los Angeles," Jo said, "and knew
I was coming out. He didn't know exactly when. He kept calling my
mother for information. My mother never gave him the exact arrival

I wish I had ten pitchers with Bo Belinsky's stuff and none with his head.

—GENE MAUCH

Bo Revisited

There is a joy about the late winter in Florida, the first real hot days, the sudden realization in a dozen towns around the state that baseball has come again. The old people appear out of nowhere again, pull their floppy hats down tight on their heads, sit motionless in the old wooden stands, almost unreal, like some recently revealed paintings, taking in the sun, reading a newspaper, looking up every so often to peak at some young hitter.

They are all over the state in a dozen different minor league parks. Today, early in March of 1972, they sit in the sun at Tinker Field on Tampa Avenue and Church Street in Orlando, Florida. A huge sign is painted high above the compact little park. It says, "Tinker Field, home of the Minnesota Twins."

Under the stands, in their clubhouse, away from the people, some forty young men in various states of undress, underwear torn, pants open, baseball shoes scruffy and torn, sweat running down their foreheads, towels pulled tight around their shoulders, walk in and out of a small room behind their clubhouse. They fix themselves huge sandwiches filled with cheese and ham and tomatoes, park

time. Now I had to decide if I wanted to see Bo again.
Stevie out with me because I would have to be in L.A.
I thought it wouldn't be right not to give Bo a chai
daughter. I decided to call him. He could drive me to
could talk for a few minutes and that would be it. I
anything more to happen out of it than that."

The plane landed smoothly in L.A. and Jo walked dc
Bo was coming up the ramp to meet the flight.

"I hadn't seen him for a while and he looked so diffi
didn't recognize him. He had let his hair grow long, hip
his face seemed different. He had been in L.A. for a w
he was suntanned again. Actually, he looked good b
different. Maybe he really was different."

Bo spotted Jo, moved quickly toward her, gave her a
lingering kiss, hugged Stevie, and presented his wife wit
bouquet of red roses and a giant bottle of perfume. He
animal in his hands for Stevie. He had thought of eve

"He drove me to the hotel and asked me for a date
I couldn't refuse, not after those beautiful flowers and
and the stuffed animal for Stevie. I looked at him, he s
and I knew then, dammit, that I was still in love with

themselves on a foot locker, swallow hard from containers of milk, laugh at the small jokes of their teammates.

In another small room, in the front of the clubhouse, a white-haired, fifty-four-year-old man, sitting in a swivel chair, a large uniform with number eighteen on his back, turns to greet a visitor. His name is William Joseph Rigney and he was the first major league manager of Bo Belinsky.

When informed it is not Tony Oliva's bad knee, or the struggle of Harmon Killebrew to remain young, or Jim Kaat's ailing arm that matters this day, Rigney laughs and his thin, lined face looks suddenly old, and weary. He is wearing dark glasses in the dreary clubhouse.

"Let's go out on the bench and talk," he says.

Rigney was born in Alameda, California, and broke into professional baseball in 1938 with Spokane. He was a tall, thin, spindly infielder of some limited skills. He could never hit much and his stamina was limited. He was aggressive and hardworking, a typical fringe player type, who made up in drive and determination what he lacked in the gifts of skills. In 1943 he entered the service. In 1946 he came back, made the New York Giants, played with them through 1953, was named manager in 1954 of their Minneapolis club, and was promoted to the Giants in 1956. In 1961 he was named the first manager of the Los Angeles Angels. In 1962 he was Belinsky's manager.

"Belinsky made a lot of mistakes," said Rigney. "His worst one was in not marrying that blonde. Mamie was smart, she was good for him. He was too dumb to know it, he was just so damn dumb, that guy. And a liar. Belinsky couldn't tell the truth if he wanted to. Remember the time he hit old Braven Dyer? I went down there and the first thing I asked both of them, Dean was the same way, was 'Which one of you will tell me the first lie?' The guy's lying on the ground out cold and they are telling me he attacked them. Did Bo tell you the story? Did he tell you he had a roll of quarters in his hand when he hit Dyer? A roll of quarters! Can you imagine that?"

Rigney leaned back on the bench at Tinker Field, away from the sounds of batting practice, away from the sun, away from those days in Los Angeles a lifetime ago.

"We drafted him at the winter meetings in 1961. We call out his name and some guy behind me, I don't even know to this day who it was, says, 'Bo will give Rigney a lot of white hairs.' Hell, I already was all white. I was all white when I was in the army. But Bo didn't help my ulcer, I'll tell you that. Bo could pitch but he had no desire. If he had his way he would stay home Monday, Tuesday, and Wednesday, and pitch on Thursday. That's the way he was. He liked pitching all right, I knew that, but he didn't like anything else about the game.

"He was night people and he dragged Dean along to pick up the check. He'd stay out until three, four o'clock in the morning every night and expect to pitch. It can't be done, I don't care who you are. Bo liked being a big shot. He had that big red Cadillac. He liked being ostentatious. I told him to trade it in, calm down a little, pay attention to baseball. He trades it in for a gold one. One time he was pitching and getting his jock knocked off. I go out to get him and he pleads for me to keep him in the game. I wasn't going to listen to any excuses but I wanted to hear what he had to say. Then he tells me he has a lot of friends in the crowd and if I take him out of the game now he will be very embarrassed. Bo was like that all the time. He worried about appearances, he worried about his image. He got to believing all those things they wrote about him there."

Bob Rodgers, Belinsky's catcher on the day Bo pitched his no-hitter and now a coach for Rigney with the Twins, walked by the bench.

"He's writing about Bo, Buck. Tell him a few things."

Rodgers laughed and Rigney just shook his head.

"I never thought Bo was all bad," Rigney said. "I just think he was in the wrong business. There was nothing wrong with his arm. Bo just wouldn't work. He thought all there was to pitching was showing up at the park five minutes before the game, grabbing the ball, and shutting somebody out. The worst thing that ever happened to him was that damn no-hitter. He got to thinking he was so good he didn't have to do anything else except go right to the Hall of Fame. Bo had ability, that's for sure. I think he had as much ability as Chance did, and Chance became a hell of a lot better pitcher. Bo had that good fast ball and that screwball. It was a hell of a pitch for him but Bo liked to finesse hitters. It was all great fun to him. He didn't want to bust them with a fast ball when he had them set up, he'd rather finesse them with a change. He'd love to see a hitter reach out for a pitch and look bad and pop up."

"We had some year out there that season. It was great fun. When you have a bad ball club and make it play better than it really should be able to play, it gives you satisfaction. That was a marvelous year. Belinsky and Chance had a lot to do with that year. I wish Bo had been able to continue. He wasn't a bad sort. He was a little nutty but Bo Belinsky was fun to be around. I wonder what would have happened to him if he had married Mamie; I wonder if it would have settled him down and made him pitch better. We'll never know, will we?"

Rigney got up from the bench, pulled his cap off his head and revealed a thin, balding top. He scratched his head, put his cap back on, and walked on out toward the field. Then he stopped for a moment, turned back toward the bench, and said, "Say hello for me the next time you see Bo."

It was the second week of March now and the exhibition games had begun. On the field at Yankee Stadium in Fort Lauderdale, Florida, the Montreal Expos threw baseballs back and forth in anticipation of their time for infield drill. The Yankees were finishingha up their drills and the Expos would soon run on to the dirt infield to loosen their arms and try their skills this bright sunshine-filled day.

"Gene's over with the B team," drawled Jimmy Bragan, a coach for the Expos. "He should be getting here right soon . . . Hea-yah he comes now."

Gene William Mauch, manager of the Montreal Expos, walked across the field to his bench. He is forty-six years old, a very handsome man with gray patches around the edges of his black hair. At seventeen years of age, he was signed by the Brooklyn Dodgers and assigned to Durham, North Carolina. At eighteen he was brought to Brooklyn by the Dodgers in 1944 at the lowest depth of their struggle to survive the rigors on their personnel of World War II.

He played for six major league teams in a career that covered some fifteen years. Like Rigney, he was a weak-hitting but pugnacious infielder. He was almost always described as "brash," a baseball term that seems to mean pushier than your limited ability would normally allow for. At twenty-seven, he was named the manager of the Atlanta Crackers in the Southern Association. He finished third but resigned the job at the end of the season because of "lack of maturity." Five years later he was hired to manage the Minneapolis club and has managed baseball teams for a living ever since. He resurrected the Philadelphia Phillies, after taking them over in 1960, missed the pennant by one game in 1964 after being ahead by ten, was fired in 1968, mostly because of the problems involving Richie Allen, was signed by Montreal as their first manager in 1969 and made them a competitive team inside of three years.

"Christ, you want to talk about Bo Belinsky," he said. "I've been trying to forget the guy for six years."

Mauch stares straight ahead when he talks, capable of carrying on an intelligent, well-ordered conversation at the same time as he observes his team in practice. His mind seems to be swallowing up bits and pieces of information, forcing them down into his head, working them over as a computer would, and coming out with digested and useful information.

"Bo was one of the most interesting guys I ever met in baseball. But for the very reasons that you are writing a book about him, the very reasons that a million people will read it, he couldn't be successful. He wouldn't pay the price. He had too many other things in his life. Bo had ability. He had a great arm, great stuff, and he knew how to pitch. He just didn't really understand what baseball was all about, the dedication, the work, the wanting to succeed, the sweating and the discomforts of playing the game. He wanted the fun and the glory. None of that comes without the pain. Bo didn't like the pain. I remember when we got him from the Angels. His reputation was well known. But I didn't have to be a Sam Spade when he joined us. He was a model citizen, no problems at all. He was in when he was supposed to be in, he did what I asked him, but he wouldn't push himself, he wouldn't give you that extra effort, that concentration. I knew we weren't going to change him when we got him. I've never tried to change any player.

"But I knew he had a healthy, strong arm. I had the feeling that he might have learned from his failures at Los Angeles and that he would suddenly develop into a good pitcher. He was young, twenty-eight, when we got him. We thought he just might decide to do it now. If he did I wanted him to be wearing my uniform, pitching for me, when he decided to use that ability he had. That's what makes you go with a guy like that. You think that any minute he will put it all together and then you will be able to make all the gambles worthwhile."

There was a pitched ball in batting practice. It struck Ron Hunt on the side of his leg. Hunt, who had set a record for being hit by pitches in 1971, never turned from the pitch.

"He even practices getting hit in batting practice," said Mauch. "Hunt has had to fight for everything he got. It came easy for Bo. Maybe that's why he didn't appreciate it. He pitched that no-hitter over there and he rode that for a long while. Hunt has a big day, goes four for four, the next day he's out early wanting to work on some things, wanting to do it again, not being satisfied. Bo was satisfied all the time, never really caring. You have to be smart to succeed in baseball. I don't mean only Phi Beta Kappas make it, but you have to learn things, to gain from your mistakes. From the first day I saw Bo to the last he never got any better."

Mauch said he liked Bo. He enjoyed listening to him.

"He would sit on the bench and tell our guys tales of Hollywood. I don't know what was true and what wasn't but everybody laughed. You need guys like that on a ball club. I didn'd mind having him around. He didn't cause me any trouble. I just wished he would have won more games for us."

The Yankees had finished their infield drill across the field and Ralph Houk, their manager, stood with one knee on the top step of the dugout ready to jump up as the umpires came on the field and exchange lineup cards with Mauch. One wondered then if Houk, a tough guy, former army major and war hero, a guy Mickey Mantle said he would have run through a brick wall for, could have done any better with Bo. Could any baseball manager have handled Bo? Could anybody have harnessed that strong arm and disciplined that free spirit?

Mauch looked across the field at Houk, saw the umpires were

coming onto the field and knew the game would soon begin. He held the lineup card in his right hand and his baseball cap in his left.

"Did you see Bo? What did he say about me? Does he hate me?"

"No. He just said you pitched him too much in relief and ruined his arm. He thinks you ended his career."

"That's funny," said Mauch. "I always thought I was trying to save it."

Mauch put the lineup card down on the bench. He put his cap back on his head. He saw that Houk was walking slowly to home plate with his jacket on against the slight chill of the Florida day. Mauch unbuttoned his jacket and threw it down on the bench. It was one of the little games he was good at. It was the way Vince Lombardi or Woody Hayes would have gone to home plate that day.

"I really enjoyed having Bo on the club," Mauch said. "I really did."

Mauch climbed up the steps of the dugout and headed for the home plate conference, the large number four in his uniform shirt being blown out a little by the breezes.

"You know," said Mauch over his shoulder as he left, "Bo would have been a lot better off in some other business."

One of the pleasantest towns in all Florida is Sarasota. It has much of the aura of wealth that is in Palm Beach without any of the stuffiness. St. Armand's Key is a delightful area of charming shops and boutiques. The Chicago White Sox train in Sarasota. They live in the Sarasota Motor Hotel and their players have the convenience of walking across the street to work in Payne Park.

There was more excitement around Payne Park this day than there had been for many seasons. The White Sox had made a major deal in the winter and had acquired the services of Bo Belinsky's friend, Gene Mauch's friend, and more importantly, Chuck Tanner's friend, Dick Allen.

Tanner was born in New Castle, Pennsylvania, in the western part of the state, long a hotbed for budding professional athletes. He had been a star athlete in baseball, basketball, and football and competed against other older members of Dick Allen's family. His career began in Evansville in 1946. He struggled for ten years before he made the major leagues with the Milwaukee Braves in 1955. He hit a homer on his first pitch in the major leagues, only the second player in history to accomplish that trick. He became Milwaukee's Rookie of the Year but hit only .247 as a part-time player for the Braves. In 1961 he joined the Los Angeles Angels and in 1962 he was a teammate of Bo Belinsky on the Angels. He started managing at Quad Cities in 1963 and managed in Hawaii in 1969. One of his pitchers was Belinsky. In 1971 he managed the White Sox to third place in the western division of the American League.

Tanner, square-jawed, gray-haired, rugged, with the masculine good looks of an eighteenth-century sea captain, sat at his desk under the stands at Payne Field late in March. There were papers all around and several lineup cards on the desk. He was on the phone when I walked in, but he smiled, shook hands, pushed his lineup card near me. I glanced at it and jotted down the names while he finished his conversation. Informed that I was not to be the thirtieth reporter that day to question him about Dick Allen, he leaned back in his chair and sighed.

"It's been a very rough day," he said.

Tanner studies a face as he addresses it. He has the most wonderful trait of making one believe the questions you ask, the conversation you bring, the thoughts you will offer are the most important topics he could possible run into this day. He talks rapidly, as if afraid that if there were a delay, you might leave his presence. In a town that had had bitter press relations when Eddie Stanky was the manager, the Chicago writers seemed totally enamored of Tanner and pleased at his open-faced style.

Belinsky's name was mentioned for the first time and Tanner said, without an instant's hesitation, "I love him."

He seemed moved when told that Belinsky spoke very highly of him and had said that his time with the Hawaii ball club, under Tanner, was absolutely the happiest time he had ever spent in baseball.

"Bo Belinsky was as fine an individual as I had ever met in baseball," Tanner said.

Nobody, not even Belinsky's own mother, had spoken that highly of him. It seemed doubtful if Tanner really meant these very kind words.

"Yes I do," he insisted. "Bo was a fine person with us. I didn't care about his reputation, I didn't care about what he had done before, or what he might do after. I judge a man on how he acts when he is on my ball club. Bo was perfect for us. Wait, I'll take that back. He once missed a bus. We were playing in Eugene, Oregon. Bo was eighteen minutes late. I called him into my office. 'Bo, you know the rules. I'll have to fine you.'

" 'Skip, I don't have any dough, I'm broke.'

" 'The rules are for everybody.'

" 'Can you wait until next payday to collect?'

"Bo knew that I had to fine him. I had to make sure everybody on the club knew it. You can't treat any player on the team differently when it comes to rules. I fined him and I think he paid it the next payday. I think it was only fifty dollars but it was the point we were making with him. He never was late for a bus again."

Tanner leaned back in his chair, stared up at the ceiling for an instant and said, "Bo must have prospered from that little lesson. He won the next nine games in a row and went back to the big leagues."

Tanner was there the night Belinsky pitched his no-hitter and he thought he was seeing the birth of a great pitcher.

"He was overwhelming that day. He could be that way when he was on. He was that way most of the time when he pitched for me in Hawaii. He seemed motivated. He had a wife and a baby and he wanted to do well. He worked hard, he did his running, he did everything a manager could want. He did the most important thing, he won."

The secret of Tanner's success seems to be his ability to relate well to all his players. He lets them get the glory. He is a partner with his players, not a competitor, for press attention, for the general manager's appreciation, for the owner's reward. Tanner seems to have found the secret of handling baseball players.

"I don't try to change them," he said. "I would no more think of changing Bo's style than I would think of changing his religion. A man must do what he must do. But he must be treated as a man and given responsibility. I have never found a player who would not respond to that kind of treatment. I don't care if they are controversial or not, they are all human beings."

Tanner said he never discussed Bo's past with him when he joined the Hawaii club.

"What did that matter? All I was interested in was seeing how well he would pitch. The rascal won a lot of games for me. Then he went back to the major leagues and got his pension back. I am very proud of any contribution I made to Bo's career. As far as I'm concerned he is a fine person, has a lovely wife and pretty baby."

A man who could say such nice things about Bo Belinsky would not have any trouble handling Allen or any other of the so-called problem players in baseball.

"I'd give Bo a job right now," Tanner said. "I wish I could help him out."

The manager of the Baltimore Orioles is a short, squat, bouncy man named Earl Weaver. He sits on the Orioles bench with his hat perched on the back of his head. He has emerged from a long, undistinguished career in baseball to become a celebrity with three pennants and a great deal of interest and excitement following him wherever he goes. Weaver is outspoken, reacts sharply to criticism, and finds managing a baseball team a joyous occupation. It is especially joyous for him since he had three straight winners. This spring he is worried. His team traded away Frank Robinson, considered by many the best money player in the game, and Weaver has been fencing all spring with sportswriters demanding to know if Baltimore will truly miss Frank Robinson.

Weaver started his professional baseball career in the St. Louis Cardinals organization in 1948 as a slick-fielding, no-hitting second baseman. He never made it to the major leagues though the Cardinals took him to their spring training camp for a look in 1952. In 1956 he managed for the first time at Knoxville. In 1959 he managed in the Baltimore organization at Aberdeen, South Dakota. One of his pitchers was Bo Belinsky. Weaver survived the summer with Bo, moved up through the Orioles organization, and was named the manager of the Baltimore team on July 11, 1968.

Weaver studied his lineup card. He laughed out loud when he was asked about Bo Belinsky.

"Ohh, Christ," he said, "he was a pistol. I had him in Aberdeen and he was just a kid, couldn't have been more than twenty, twenty-one years old, but he was the same as he was later on in the big leagues. Bo knew how to have a good time."

Weaver is short, not very good-looking, a pleasant, entertaining man, but not the kind of person who can command attention in a crowded room or force girls to turn their heads. He talked about Belinsky and it was clear that in a way, in some small way, he envied the life-style of Bo Belinsky. No one had ever accused Earl Weaver of turning the heads of a dozen Hollywood beauties.

"Bo had been around when I got him at Aberdeen. I tried to keep him in line but rules didn't mean anything to him. He thought the whole thing was a joke. He had a damn good arm. We had some arms on that club, Bo and Steve Dalkowski and I think Steve Barber was there, too. Bo lived in some flophouse, but at night you could see his dust whirling as he took off in his car for some swinging spot. Where the hell could someone go in Aberdeen, South Dakota? Bo found it! One day we were playing the Yankee club at Fargo and I think Bo had pitched a nine-inning game. Now it was over and I see him coming out of the ball park with Joe Pepitone of the Yankees. You never saw a wilder pair than Pepitone and Belinsky at that stage of their careers.

"Well, the two of them are really dressed for the kill and I see them hop into this car right in front of me. I knew that was going to be trouble, so I tried to warn them to take it easy. I told Bo that we had a curfew at midnight and he was expected back in his room by then and if he wasn't back he would be fined. I don't think he ever heard me or if he did, he didn't care. He was too young and too wild and too concerned with having a good time to worry about anything like that. I remember hearing the screech of those car wheels as they took off down the street, and I can still see the dust flying all over as they disappeared around the corner. I think I heard myself saying, 'Bo, you'll be fined if you don't make the curfew,' and I knew Bo didn't hear me and I realized there was no use in shouting. What the hell, Bo was going to be Bo and no man, no manager, no woman, nobody would ever stop him."

Weaver sat back on his team's bench, leaped from his seat now and yelled over to George Staller, who had once managed Bo. He had also fined Bo for breaking his hand in a fight.

"George had Bo in the minors," said Weaver. "Ask him about Bo."

Staller turned toward Weaver, made a face, and turned away. Staller was getting sick at the memory.

"Hell, you think Bo was bad. I had a guy on the club who was worse. He really was. He was really a madman. He went to some girl's house one time out there, banged on her door, and told her he wanted a blow job. She said she didn't like him," Weaver said, "and she wasn't giving no blow jobs to him. He mashed her face in. He wound up in jail and we had to leave for a road trip without him. At least, I never had to get Bo out of jail."

The game was about to begin and Earl Weaver started up the steps of his dugout with his lineup card.

"Bo wasn't no angel," said Weaver, "but I'll tell you this, he wasn't the worst guy I ever met in baseball, either."

The excitement of the spring builds gradually until the final days of March and the first days of April. Another baseball season was to begin and now the teams settled down for the serious days of training. It was the part of the season Bo Belinsky always hated. It was the anxious part of the year when managers would cut squads, players would disappear, some never to be seen again, and stars would begin planning their attacks on new records, new goals, and new wealth. On April 1, 1972, the pattern of normal life was interrupted by an outrageous attack on the order of things. The Major League Baseball Players Association had called the first strike in its history. Baseball would be shut down—like some damn coal mine or some shoe factory or some fertilizer plant—for two weeks while the players and owners negotiated for more pension money. April without a baseball game seemed an unreal event after all these years of tradition.

It snowed lightly on April 1 in Chicago. In the early afternoon, Bo Belinsky awoke from his bed in his fourth-floor apartment at the Montery Hotel and boiled some water for coffee. Jo was at work downtown at Playboy's plush new offices. Stevie was in nursery school. Bo pulled the shades and studied the wet streets.

"Damn," he said to no one and to everyone, "snow in April."

On that day, in that cold, dreary, gray, hotel apartment, with his wife at work and his child at play, the light falling snow would be the major source of excitement all afternoon for Bo Belinsky.

He who plays and runs away lives to play some other day.

—BO BELINSKY

Bo's Day Care Center

He had put in his time and his miles and now, in the early fall of 1971, Bo Belinsky, like some infant seeking warmth in the womb, had returned to the sounds of the ocean crashing against the sands at Malibu. It was almost ten years since he had first lit up the skies over Hollywood, crashed through the forbidden walls, and entered fully into the fantasies of this environment. It was the only place he felt really comfortable, the only place he could walk in bare feet, the only place he could still get a nod, a stare, a phone call that would break the boredom of the afternoon.

Belinsky sat in his bathing suit in his Malibu hotel apartment, dark glasses over his eyes, a glass of vodka at his side, his busty friend Helen hovering over him like a mother hen. His body was still firm and hard, ten years after the heights of his baseball career, his face older and more mature, but still handsome, his skin darker and more lined, but his appeal still physical and sensual. He thumbed through a couple of *Playboy* magazines on his coffee table, put them down, stared at the soap opera grinding into his conciousness, sipped from a cup of coffee, waved his hand at Helen for more service, had his cup refilled, leaned back on the couch and passed another hour of his life in repose.

He had left Jo in Denver and had come back to Malibu. There had been three meaningful things in his life, baseball, Mamie, and Jo. Two were irretrievable. The third seemed almost gone as well. He was consumed with thoughts of her incredible beauty, the warmth and joy he felt in her love, the anger and animosity he felt in those endless bitter arguments. He had come back from Denver, certain it was over, finally; free, ready to march to his own drummer again, to move with the wind, to set himself down here, there, and everywhere, not to think about his life tomorrow, but to suck up the pleasures of this very instant. He understood now, finally, they were not pleasures.

"I had come back from Denver convinced I was finished with Jo," he said. "It had been too much, the fighting, the screaming, the bad scene all around. I loved her but I couldn't live with her. What the hell good was it now? We were jealous of each other. We had to fight each other for our survival. Neither would give in. I had my scene and she had hers. We had to travel our separate roads. Bye, bye, sweetheart, let me know how you are doing. That's the only thing there was."

For a day, a week, a month, Bo was an instant hero again in Malibu. There were always guys, fat middle-aged men, losers, hangers-on, who would carry him for a free meal, a free bed, a sweater, a couple of gallons of gas, anything he needed for survival. His dependency on them was what they craved. They used him to promote themselves. It was no longer Autry and Ann-Margret and Winchell, but in Malibu, in some late night parties, Bo Belinsky still had some drawing power. The leeches would hang on to him, steal his pride, suck his blood, use him cruelly, rape him until he was dry. Then they would sail off. In a flash, another animal would appear from the jungle and the cycle would start again.

"There was always a broadie, every day, somewhere, somehow," Bo said. "They still seemed drawn to me. I wasn't even pressing it. They were just there, swarming around me like flies."

It was not Bo's style to come on strong. He was the personification of cool, that dark, handsome face, those slow, bedroom eyes, that slick talk, sometimes whiskey slick, that enveloped them. There would be a party and Bo would be on the fringes; and soon the fringes would grow into a circle and Bo would be in the center, giving enough to be entertaining, always holding back, always fearful of being exposed, never going one step past his bounds. It was Bob Rodgers, his catcher on the Angels, who had his own locker overrun so many times by the crowds around Belinsky, press, and hangers-on, who had leaned back in the Florida sun after it had all ended for Belinsky and said, "Bo couldn't make it cold-turkey with a broad, he just couldn't. You may not believe this, but Bo was a shy guy, insecure, a little afraid of girls."

Every once in a while a girl would come to him cold-turkey, throw herself at his feet, kiss his toes, beg his indulgence, and wind up his ever-loving slave. It is how he came to share Helen's largess.

"I was at a party on the beach one night, a long, late, lingering party," said Bo. "Much noise, much smoke, much drink. Now this girl, cool, not pushy, big tits, a little ancient, but a lot of smarts, is on me. There is a click-click-click and we are as one. It happens once in a while that way. I don't ask any questions and she doesn't ask me any. That always helps. We go home and soon we are setting up housekeeping together. Helen's a hooker by trade and works at night. She is home for coffee and service by day. It is what I need. We dig each other. She has been divorced, has kids someplace, can understand the complications and complexities of a man in trouble with his head. It is nice."

Belinsky set up housekeeping with Helen. She did the housework and the outside work. She paid the bills and soaked his feet. She asked nothing in return but a little love, a little affection, a little attention. Belinsky could always manage that. He could turn his head at a girl, focus those eyes, throw out that smile, and wipe away all doubts.

"I would call Jo once in a while," said Bo, "to find out how the baby was. She would be out and she would call back and Helen would answer. You could hear the electricity across the lines, but Jo understood. When I'm not there, I have to be somewhere."

"We weren't together and I knew Bo had to have his loving, so I couldn't be jealous. She was a hooker and she was making good money, and the funniest part of the whole business was the fact that Bo would send me some money every so often to help out with Stevie. I don't know if Bo ever told Helen that. It would be too much," Jo said.

The days passed slowly. Coffee, cigarettes, a couple of glasses of vodka would be lunch. There would be a party every so often, a long night of drinking, a few flashy young girls, all absorbed in this mysterious figure of Los Angeles past, a beach party, a ride up to the hills around Hollywood. There would be a special event every so often, a party planned for a new group that had never seen Bo's act.

One such party took place in a friend's huge, Hollywood Hills home, with endless bottles and assorted guests. Belinsky always was most comfortable with ballplayers, the people who understood best the pressures and the pains he had undergone.

"I had been friendly with a few of the Mets—Bobby Aspromonte, who had been my teammate at Houston, some of the others—and I invited a few of them out to one of our parties. I think I invited five or six. I hired a limousine to pick them up at the ball park. A dozen came. I didn't know half of them. That's the trouble with baseball teams. You can't just invite half of them to anything. It was a beautiful scene. They all had a hell of a time, especially this one pitcher, who got so drunk he fell off a balcony into some cactus trees in the courtyard. He didn't get hurt. He was too drunk to feel any pain. The party was good for them. The next day they beat the Dodgers. Then they asked me when the next party was going to happen."

Drinking and parties have always been as much a part of a ball-player's life as bats and balls. They are young, virile men with time on their hands.

"Most of the guys in baseball drink," Bo says. "Once in a while you meet an ice cream soda guy but it's rare. About all of them drink but only some of them get drunk."

Belinsky once had a roommate who could drink enormous amounts of whiskey and hold almost none of it.

"I was asleep one night and he comes in," said Bo. "He is usually pretty vicious when he's drunk so I hide my head under the covers as he stomps around the room. I peek over and I see him standing next to my bed. He's pissing on the floor. I'm a little mad and it stinks, but what the hell, it's not my hotel. Now he falls into bed and he's there maybe ten minutes. He jumps up again, bangs into the furniture, and pisses on the rug again. I didn't say a thing. Finally he gets back into bed with his clothes on and falls asleep. A couple of hours later I hear him get up, walk around the room, open a door, and start pissing. I thought he had finally made it into the bathroom. One thing bothered me. I didn't hear any water. Now I hear the door close and I look up. The son of a bitch had opened a closet door and pissed all over my clothes."

On those few occasions when he was sponsoring a party Belinsky was truly happy. He was with his own people, playing his own drama, hearing his own music, being entertaining and important, a person of substance and importance, an ego that was riding high. Then it would be back to the apartment of his hooker, back to the vodka and the coffee lunch, back to the crushed ego and the endless pursuit of tomorrow.

"It took me a year, maybe more, to realize I would not play ball again," said Bo. "I had quit but maybe I didn't mean it. I think I hoped somebody would come along and ask me again. I guess I dreamed about Tanner coming out to see me, to beg me to be his main man again, to at least work as his pitching coach or his director general or some damn thing. I know I wouldn't have taken it, I wasn't interested, I just wanted to be asked. I just wanted to turn him down. I just liked the idea of somebody caring."

Bo thought about his fifteen years in baseball and it was all gone like a puff of smoke, the laughs, the gigs he had played, the places and the people.

"No regrets," he said one day, "not a single one. Maybe the only thing I'm truly sorry about is hitting one guy in the face with a pitch. It was Jimmie Hall and he was with Minnesota and it was a damn accident. He never was the same again. A thing like that stays with you. I almost cost a guy his life."

Belinsky never had the killer instinct on the field. He was a lover, not a fighter. His mind even wiped away the bad people.

"I look back now and I can't even remember anybody I hated," he said. "I manage to get amnesia over those kind of guys."

The bad guys fade but the memory of the interesting ones stays, the stars, the public personalities, the folk figures.

"That was one thing," he said, "I got along with the big guys, really I did. They weren't jealous. And I always dug the black ball players. A lot of guys didn't. I'll get in the Hall of Fame because I gave up some big home runs to some big guys. I think of that now with a guy like Hank Aaron. He's driving on Babe Ruth's 714 and I gave him number 400. He came around the bases and I tipped my hat to him and he smiled. The next time I faced him I drilled him in the ribs. I tipped my hat to him again."

One sour star turned Belinsky off.

"I was in Jilly's one night in New York. Mickey Mantle was in there. He was really tucked in, very quiet, didn't want to be bothered by anybody so I made out like I didn't know him. He seemed secluded in himself, never smiling, never really happy. I remember one time he hit a homer off me, it went about two blocks. He never cracked a smile."

Belinsky faced all the big hitters, Harmon Killebrew, Frank Robinson, Willie Mays, Carl Yastrzemski, without many problems.

"They got me sometimes and I got them sometimes. Nobody really ate me up," he said.

"I guess the thing that bothered me most was the little hitters getting me. I remember how Hal Lanier used to kill me when he was with the Giants. He was a terrible hitter, maybe the worst I ever saw, but he owned me."

There are a half dozen guys Belinsky remembers fondly, Lew Burdette, Roger Craig, Tom Morgan, Steve Bilko, Bob Rodgers, a minor leage manager named Lou Fitzgerald, as the years passed. He has less than warm memories of a couple of other people.

"The one thing I hold against Bill Rigney is how he blackballed me out of the American League after the Dyer thing. People told me about that. He told people he just didn't want to have me around. If he didn't think I could pitch, well that's his opinion. But he sent me away without a chance. That was a bad rap."

Belinsky laughs now when he thinks of the success of two-time MVP Johnny Bench.

"When I was with Cincinnati he was a punky kid," he said. "He puts on that goody-goody image and he's trying to hustle every broad. He tried to hustle Jo and she wasn't the only one. He used to carry around a *Playboy* magazine with Jo's picture in it and let the centerfold hang out and and drag it around. Real kid shit. He was a smart ass. You watch. There's no way he'll be able to handle success."

Into the late fall of 1971, there were only dreams for Bo. He never much cared about tomorrow. Now, suddenly, Helen was no longer that much fun, Jo was so far away, Stevie never awakened him at night, the days were all one and the same. He reasoned that his salvation would come in Hawaii.

"I had heard they were going to build a new restaurant and club in the ball park in Hawaii. I thought maybe I could run it for Jack Quinn. I knew everybody, I would be the perfect man, I could bring people in and make a life for myself out there. I didn't push it. I didn't ask him. I thought he would call me when he needed me. That's always the way it's been. I never pushed myself on anybody. People who needed me always found me. I am never in the phone book but I leave clues behind me, I leave a trail that the bird dogs can follow."

Nobody ever followed Bo's trail better than Jo. She could smell him out at nine in the morning or six at night, anywhere his dancing shoes would take him.

"I loved him," Jo said. "It didn't matter that I wasn't living with him."

Jo would call from Chicago and the conversations would be an endless stream of double-talk, neither party giving an inch, neither side admitting that the only thing that mattered was being together, that they had to have that physical closeness, that violent love, that passion of two strong hearts if they were to survive. They would talk for twenty minutes about the weather.

"How is it out there?" Jo would ask.

"Nice. Real pleasant. How is it back there?" Bo would say.

"We had a trickle of snow yesterday. I guess winter is coming."

"It rained here yesterday, just a few drops. Cleared up right away."

It would go on like this and finally Jo would say she had to go back to work. She promised Bo she would call again soon.

Both of them seemed incapable of saying, simply, what was on their minds. Neither of them could concede the point and say, "I love you."

It was Thanksgiving now. The snow was falling heavily in Chicago. In Malibu, Helen was gone for a few days, back to Oregon visiting her children and her family. Jo and Stevie were in Chicago. Bo's parents were quietly alone in Trenton. There was no place for Bo to go. Holidays are ugly for lonely people. Suddenly, the party people had scattered, the daytime game shows on television were dreary, the coffee was wretched, and the cigarettes tasted as if they had been smoked long before they had gotten into Bo's pack.

The phone rang and Bo leaped to answer it.

"Is Helen there?"

"No, she's out fucking somebody."

Bo hung up. He knew it was time to move on, to seek a new fortune, a new scene, new sand, new water, new surf, new sounds. His lease had run out. He needed to breathe some fresh air again. He thought about Hawaii, about Mexico, about the Dominican and Venezuela, about playing ball in Japan, about touring Europe in a Mercedes, about dining with queens and princesses, about walking through the banks of Switzerland and the gaming tables of Monaco. He thought about a lot of things. True to his fashion, he did nothing. He waited and waited and waited.

Finally, the summons came.

The phone rang and Jo sounded deeply in anguish. Stevie was ill.

"She's coughing very badly," Jo told Bo, "and I called the doctor and he said she has to be watched. She's been up all night coughing and now she's spitting blood and she looks awful and she has a fever. Bo, I don't know what to do. What should I do?"

"Why don't you call the doctor again. He'll come over. He'll know what to do."

"Bo, I'm scared. I need you. Can you come to Chicago?"

He had heard the words and he didn't know if he wanted to hear them. What would it be like if he went back to Chicago and stayed with Jo? He felt that he wanted to be with her, but he had to know the terms. This just wasn't the time for a contract signing.

"Just a visit, Bo, just come out until Stevie is well again and I can go back to work. Just a visit, Bo."

"I'll call you tomorrow," he said.

He sat down on his couch and lit a cigarette. He poured himself a quick drink. He turned the volume of the television set up louder and did his thinking over the sounds of Johnny Carson. He stared up at the ceiling and looked down at the burnt-orange carpet. He walked into the kitchen and pulled some ice cubes out of the refrigerator. He looked at the counter of the sink and saw two, three, four bills for back rent sitting there unattended. He knew then it was time to split, he knew then it was the hour to call Helen in, pick up her trip ticket, and give her her honorable discharge. He called Jo back in Chicago.

"I'll get the first plane out in the morning," he said. "I'm a little short of bread, sweetheart, call the airlines and make a paid reservation for me, will you, like a doll. I'll pay you back as soon as I get my finances in order. I'll be making the first plane out."

Bo was a California man. He did not own an overcoat. His shaggy-haired mohair topcoat was not enough to fight off Chicago in late November. He stood outside O'Hare Airport and commandeered a cab. He carried a small bag. He didn't expect to stay more than a day or two. He was testing the water in Chicago. If it was to his liking there would still be time to smooth things out in Malibu before trying out the winter in the east. It had been many years since he had spent a November day east of the Mississippi. He remembered what he didn't like about it. The cab drove him toward town, down Lake Shore Drive, across the frozen tundra of Chicago, around the loop, and down to a residential hotel on a small street called Junior Terrace.

The Montery Hotel had been left over from another time, another place. The bellboy was bent over and feeble. The telephone operator was a white-haired grandmother. The desk clerk could not read without his glasses. The clerk insisted upon helping Bo up to Jo's room with his one small bag. He closed the door to the elevator. Bo hadn't seen such an elevator since he was twelve years old and visiting grandma regularly in the Bronx and banging precocious young maidens.

The hotel wasn't much to look at, but it was enough for Jo. She was supporting herself and her child and money wasn't that plentiful. She liked to spend what she had in more enjoyable ways than having a fancy apartment. She liked good clothes and jewelry. She liked to have her hair done and fill her room with flowers. Like Bo, she spent as fast as she made it.

Jo looked ravishing. She had been distraught by Stevie's illness, but she would not greet Bo without getting ready for him. He gave her a long, deep, physical kiss, and his whole body quivered. She held on to him hard and he wanted to make love. She said she had to leave in a few moments to go to the hospital. The doctor had put Stevie into an ambulance early that morning and rushed her to a hospital.

"He called a little while ago," Jo said. "She has pneumonia but he thinks she is going to be all right. He says she is responding well. I told him I would be there soon."

"I'll go with you. I want to see her."

"Oh, you don't have to go, Bo, you're probably tired from the trip."

"No, I'm fine. Let's go, before I start getting tired."

Jo picked up the phone and called the front desk.

"Could you please have a cab for me in five minutes?"

They rode out to the hospital, visited Stevie, who was recovering well, talked of everything except their own marriage, and went back to the hotel.

Stevie came home in a week and the doctor told Jo to keep her out of school for another couple of weeks until she fully recovered. Jo hired a baby-sitter who would come each day and care for Stevie until Jo could come home from work.

"I'll give the baby-sitter a few hours off a day," Bo said. "That way we can save some money."

Stevie was recovering well but she cried a great deal, especially in the mornings when Jo left for work. Bo tried to soothe her. It didn't do much good. Bo was a stranger.

"She didn't really know me," said Bo, "and she cried almost all the time she was around me. Then her mother would come home from work and she would just hang on to her dress. Jo couldn't even get away long enough to go to the bathroom. The kid was real clingy. She was old enough now, two and a half, to be able to leave her mother alone for a little while but she wouldn't do it.''

The miracle of children is their innate brilliance. Stevie had understood the situation better than Bo and Jo did. She knew the friction that was still lying under the surface. She knew that at any moment her father would leave, and she feared that her mother would go with him and she would be cast aside. It was built into the child's very being.

With Stevie recovered and Jo back to work, Bo grew bored and restless.

"I think I'll go back to California and get some things straightened out," Bo said.

"When will you be back?"

"When I get some things straightened out."

He flew off to the coast the next night. He had decided in his own mind that he wanted to be with Jo. He would not admit to her, or to himself, how much he needed to be with her. He was going through the withdrawal pains of the California scene and it was not easy. He had a final meeting with Helen and told her she wouldn't be going to Hawaii with him after all. He called some friends and announced he was going back east for a while. They asked him why. He said he had things to take care of. He did not tell them he was going back to Jo. He did not want them to think that he was weak, that he needed a woman, that he loved Jo and she loved him and the other "friends" were really nothing in his life. He did not want to tell them that he now realized nothing would ever become of him if he didn't make it with Jo. She loved him hard and a lot of men pass through this life and never experience that emotion. He knew then that he loved her hard, and he would somehow have to learn how to harness that physical love into some reasonable state of daily survival. He would have to be with her, to love her, to live with her, to survive, to allow her to work and prosper while he sorted things out in the quiet of a living room, in front of that television set, that vodka glass at his side, that coffee heating on the stove, that cigarette dangling from the corner of his mouth.

On the day before Christmas, Belinsky boarded a plane in Los Angeles for Chicago. He had two suitcases with him. It was all the worldly goods he owned. He had left some clothes behind in Malibu. Wherever he had been, wherever he had lived, he had always left some clothes behind. He couldn't stand good-byes. He hated the finality of the whole thing. He knew that if he left an old shirt, a torn pair of pants, a dirty pair of socks, that he had not really cut his ties. He knew that if he needed to go back to Trenton, back to Aberdeen, back to Caracas, back to Malibu, there would always be an old familiar shirt around to make him feel at home.

It was snowing heavily when Belinsky arrived in Chicago. He wore a spongy pair of California shoes when he walked into the street outside the airport to hail a cab. He thought about the sun at his Malibu pad and the new bathing suit he had just purchased and the party that he had just turned down only the night before. He thought about all that and he thought about Jo and Stevie. He knew now he wanted to make these two his life. He had had his summers and now he had to face up to the winters.

"I went back to Chicago because I wanted to be with Jo," he said. "I still didn't know what I wanted to do otherwise. I still figured something would come up. There had to be something for me in Chicago. It was a hell of a lot bigger place than Malibu."

Jo was moving up rapidly in the Playboy hierarchy. She was receiving more and more prestigious and responsible assignments. Some of them included travel. To save money, Bo volunteered to serve as Stevie's baby-sitter instead of hiring a woman.

"I liked it," he said, "it gave me something to do. I stayed home with Stevie, got to know her better, played with her, cooked her cereal, and took her out for walks. It wasn't a bad thing."

Alone most of the time, Stevie had learned to adjust to the absence of her mother at work. She learned to amuse herself for hours with the simplest toys. She became less clingy when Jo would show up and she was quickly developing another lasting relationship, this time with her father.

"There I was again," said Bo, "turning on some young broad."

Belinsky quickly settled into his new pattern of life. There would be a quick cup of coffee with Jo in the morning. Then he would look out the window and wait for the school bus to come along to take Stevie to nursery school. There would be affectionate embraces with

Jo, a quick but violent session of lovemaking if there were time, a fond farewell, another cup of coffee, another couple of glasses of vodka.

Some minutes after Jo left for her office downtown, the phone would ring and Jo would tell Bo that she had arrived safely at her office, that no men had accosted her on the street, that the office was as she had left it yesterday.

"Call me when you get back from lunch," he would say.

"Don't drink any more, sweetheart," she would say.

"Bring home another bottle."

Jo would go to lunch with some people from the Playboy organization, call as soon as she returned to her office and assure Bo she had not had more than one martini for lunch, had missed him deeply and would call again in an hour. At four or four-thirty she would call again and they would talk for another half an hour. Bo would be in his shorts, his feet up on the ends of the couch, the television set blaring away, his vodka glass half drained, the ash tray filled with two dozen crushed cigarettes.

"Hey, sweetheart, when will you be home?"

"I'll be leaving the office in fifteen minutes. Don't forget to look out the window for Stevie."

"I'll get her. I miss you, sweetheart. I love you."

"I love you, too, sweetheart. What would you like for dinner?"

"You."

They would laugh and Bo would hang up, turn the television channel to a new station and wait for the announcer to give the time. If Jo had not gotten out of her office soon enough, Bo would have to go on downstairs and pick up Stevie. He put on his pants, pulled on a sweater, got into a pair of slippers and headed down in the elevator. Stevie was deposited at the hotel door, they rode upstairs together and they would watch the children's programs, "Sesame Street," "Electric Company," "Zoom," until Jo would come through the door.

There would be the hustle of dinner, a bath for Stevie, some play time and then to bed for the child. Bo and Jo would relax on the couch, cover each other with kisses, and watch the late, late movie until one or the other of them would fall asleep in the couch.

"I was happy," Bo said, "I was with Jo and Stevie and I knew that something would come along, something always did. I didn't want to commit myself too soon and then not be available when the right thing showed up."

Every so often, a friend would call and invite them to dinner. It might be an old writer friend, or an old ballplayer friend—Dean Chance, Joe Pepitone, Wade Blasingame, somebody from Houston or Los Angeles or Philadelphia, somebody from summers past. The event would consume endless hours of preparation and incredible logistics in preparing Stevie for deposit at the baby-sitter's house or bringing the baby-sitter to them, or discussing the uniform of the night or wondering if they should have a drink one place and dine at another place. The decision would be made and Jo and Bo would be ready, she, a gorgeous, ravishing beauty, he, still handsome, with that dark face and long hair, the clothes still fitting perfectly, the cut right, the colors blending, the shoes shined, the outfit a perfect ensemble. Most of the time they would dine at a luxurious French restaurant called Chez Paul and it would be like the old days. They would walk in and a dozen people, waiters, maître d', friends, restaurant patrons would appear from nowhere to pay homage. Bo and Jo, on these nights, when care was taken and the effort was made, were still a striking couple, America's sweethearts, positive possibilities for turning a dozen heads in any restaurant they entered.

"Ahh, Bo, Jo, good evening," the maître d' would say.

"Pierre, my man, how goes it with you this night?"

"Fine, sir, fine. Do you wish the window table?"

"Yes, that would be splendid. How is the duck tonight?"

"Excellent. I recommend it highly."

'Fine. I'll probably have the *tournedos.*"

There would be laughter all around at Bo's little needle. They would be seated and as soon as they had reached their table the waiter would be upon them for a drink order. They would have a drink, order a search of the wine list, dine in magnificent splendor while enjoying the turning of heads throughout the room. Some people would turn to admire Jo's beauty. Others would turn to look at Bo, grow angry they did not recall the name that went with the familiar face, call the waiter over surreptitiously to inquire as to

identification and then explain to the women at the table just who
Bo Belinsky is. There would be smiles all around as if Bo's name
loosened some deeply seated libido in all around him.

The farewell at the restaurant would be made with much noise
and fanfare. Jo and Bo were celebrities and they were expected to
call attention to themselves, not in a boorish, obnoxious way, but
just loud enough to inform all the patrons that important people
dined here and they should be grateful when the maître d' seated
them with such speed.

On the way home, in the car, Bo would hold Jo tightly and like
young adolescents, they would giggle a lot and have a difficult time
keeping their hands off each other's bodies. They would pass
suggestive remarks as to how strongly they would love and hold
each other that night and the cabdriver would drive slowly with his
ear bent to the back seat. Bo would be chivalrous and open the cab
door for Jo, hold the hotel door open, allow her to enter the elevator
first, hold her hand as they walked through the hallway to their hotel
apartment.

The day would be remembered pleasantly for many days to come
and it would carry them through until the next person called, until
the next guest arrived, until there would be another reason to dress
up again, ride a cab downtown, dine in style, enjoy the luxury they
had known all these years despite a small bank account. There
always seemed to be somebody around to pay the bill.

In the late spring of 1972, Belinsky became a baseball fan for the
first time in his life. He went to a few games in Chicago, visited old
friends, watched games on television, practiced second-guessing
the managers.

On the tenth anniversary of his no-hitter, May 5, 1972, Bo was
interviewed by NBC. It brought him back into the sun for one quick
moment. Almost as soon as it happened, it passed. He returned to
the dreary hotel apartment, to his job as director of Stevie's Day
Care Center, to the cigarettes and the coffee and the glasses of
vodka.

"Bo's real depressed," said Jo, one day in June. "He thought sure
he would have something by now. He is too proud. He doesn't want
to go out and ask for it. He wants people to bring it to him, to beg

him to work for them. It doesn't work that way. Bo doesn't know that yet. He hasn't been out in the world enough to realize that. In baseball somebody would always come along to ask him to work for them. Nobody comes along outside of baseball to ask you to work for them. You have to ask them. I think he would do fine in a lot of things. Bo has a lot of personality. He could run a restaurant for somebody. He could open up a boutique. He could work in television. I think that's what he really wants. Bo is a great talker when he's turned on. When Joe Pepitone quit baseball to concentrate on his restaurant I thought Bo would go down and see him about a job. He wouldn't push him. He wants Joe to call him if he wants him. Joe is too busy to think about Bo. Bo has to learn that he has to go out and reach for it if he is going to get it. He has to reach for it. He doesn't want to reach. Bo wants it in his lap. It doesn't work that way. See, I'll tell you Bo's problem. Bo is afraid. Bo doesn't like the idea somebody might say no to him. People have been saying yes to Bo all of his life."

In early summer, no one had come along to say yes to Bo yet, and he sat in the hotel apartment one night talking about the days and nights that were slipping away.

"Something will break soon," he said. "I know that. I just have to hang on. You can't panic, see, you just have to stand off cool, waiting for that right move. You don't want to get into something that is bad for you. That's the trouble with half the world. They do things they don't want to do, they are working in one job and dreaming about another. I don't even know what the hell job to dream about. Maybe I'll be the commissioner of baseball or buy a ball club and hire Dean to manage it or maybe I'll become a ship's captain. Hell, maybe I'll just go back to pitching and win thirty or forty games and then they'll put my bust in the Hall of Fame. 'Come see Belinsky's bust' they will say. Wouldn't that be a gas?"

Wouldn't it?

His parents, his wife, his friend, Dean Chance, his baseball managers, and his teammates expected more from Bo. They are disappointed.

"He would have made more of himself," said Mrs. Anna Belinsky, "if they only had let him alone. They didn't really give him a chance, they moved him around, they told lies about him, they were always against him. He was outspoken. Baseball doesn't like people like that."

"Why did they have to make a relief pitcher out of him?" asks Ed Belinsky. "He didn't have that kind of arm. Why, if they left him alone as a starter he might have been a really great pitcher. He had the arm, I know he did, he really did."

"I think one of Bo's problems was money," said Dean Chance. "He never learned how to handle it. If you have money you are independent. Bo never had money so he was always at everybody else's mercy. Things got so bad once he took his money out of the baseball players' pension fund. I talked him into putting it back in. Nobody will need money in twenty years more than Bo Belinsky."

It is growing late and the silence of the apartment is oppressive as the visitor readies to leave and Belinsky asks him to stay again for one more drink. The thought enters the mind that Belinsky, tall and handsome and healthy, is an underachiever as he sits unemployed and unorganized in that dirty old hotel apartment. Yet, maybe, when the thoughts clear, he is really an overachiever, that he danced in the sun when others never saw it, that he compressed a lifetime into a few years, that anything that comes now is whipped cream on the pudding, a bonus to a life that few can ever reach.

"I have no regrets," Bo says, "not one, not even now, with nothing to turn to. I was there. I saw it and did it all. I heard music nobody else ever heard. I remember one time I was playing in Texas and the team bus stopped in Vera Cruz so we could eat. All the players got out to eat in one of those greasy spoons. I got out and heard some music. I followed it down the street and they were playing in front of a bar. I went in, had a few drinks, came out and started back for the team bus. Then I heard another group playing. I walked toward them. They were wild, beautiful, making wonderful sounds. I chased after them. Then another group and another and another. I was a kid then, how was I to know that was a hustle. All those joints had music on the street to entice you. I drank in each and every one of those bars. I listened to those buglers for hours.

"I woke up six days later. This big, buxom blonde was in bed with me and she is screaming in my tired ear, 'Belinsky, Belinsky'—only it came out Belinthsky, Belinthsky—'I am going to make you a great yanqui bullfighter. 'Right, sweetheart, now let's fuck.' It was the bugles that made me do it. I had lost my team to the music but I had found something so much nicer."

Belinsky got up from his chair and poured himself another drink. There was a huge smile on his face as he thought about the Mexican girl, the sounds of music, the days and nights in the sun and lights, from Los Angeles to Caracas, from Malibu to Miami.

"No regrets," said Bo. "Absolutely none. I wouldn't do a thing differently today, really I wouldn't. I couldn't if I wanted to. I've got to be me. That's what I am, that's who I am. I can't be anyone else and play by your rules. Look, I don't feel sorry for myself. I knew sooner or later I'd have to pay the piper. I knew it wouldn't last forever. I knew the costs would come due and I wouldn't have the cash for the bill. They can't shoot you if you don't pay. You just smile at them, stall them, and move on. I don't feel sorry for myself. I've been in the sun. You know who I feel sorry for? I feel sorry for those guys on my team, those guys on any team, those guys anywhere and everywhere who never heard that music."

Bo Belinsky threw back his head and laughed. He was the portrait of a happy man. What is a man, anyway, if he isn't the sum total of his memories?